Bloom's Modern Critical Interpretations

Bloom's Modern Critical Interpretations

Don DeLillo's
WHITE NOISE

Edited and with an introduction by
Harold Bloom
Sterling Professor of the Humanities
Yale University

CHELSEA HOUSE
PUBLISHERS
A Haights Cross Communications Company
Philadelphia

A Haights Cross Communications ◀▲ Company

Printed and bound in the United States of America

10 9 8 7 6 5 4 3 2 1

Library of Congress Cataloging-in-Publication Data

White Noise / Harold Bloom, editor ; Jesse Zuba contributing editor
    p. cm. -- (Modern critical interpretations)
Includes bibliographical references (p.) and index.
  ISBN 0-7910-7044-1
  1. Delillo, Don. White Noise. I. Bloom, Harold. II. Zuba, Jesse. III.
Series.
  PS 3554.E4425 W4838 2002
  813'.54--dc21
                            20020008254

Contributing editor: Jesse Zuba

Layout by EJB Publishing Services

Chelsea House Publishers
1974 Sproul Road, Suite 400
Broomall, PA 19008-0914

http://www.chelseahouse.com

Contents

Editor's Note

My Introduction traces the wavering line between comedy and apocalypse in Don DeLillo's *White Noise*.

Tom LeClair sees *White Noise* as DeLillo's tragi-comedy of fear, and categorizes its author as one of the "systems novelists": Pynchon, Gaddis, Coover, after which John Frow notes the odd design of an apocalyptic, domestic novel.

The book's complex associations between Hitler and Elvis Presley are noted by Paul Cantor, while Frank Lentricchia, dean of DeLillo critics, emphasizes first-person narration in *White Noise* and its relation to Romantic traditions, finding in Jack Gladney a diminished version of Leopold Bloom.

Leonard Wilcox uncovers in *White Noise* the closure of heroic narrative, after which Arnold Weinstein dares to find in DeLillo a contemporary Balzac or Zola.

A meditation upon lost icons of authority in *White Noise* is figured by Mark Conroy, while John N. Duvall centers upon television in the book's cosmos.

DeLillo's highly sophisticated consciousness of his aesthetic dilemma —to reflect our media culture without yielding to it—is Arthur Saltzman's subject, after which Paul Maltby concludes this volume by considering the author of *White Noise* as another Last Romantic, longing for transcendence and a language of vision.

Introduction

Don DeLillo's masterwork is *Underworld* (1997), which is long, uneven, and wonderful. *White Noise* (1985) would appear to be his most popular novel: the paperback in which I have just reread it is the thirty-first printing. I doubt that it will prove as permanent as *Underworld*, but revisiting clearly demonstrates that it is much more than a period piece. Critics frequently associate DeLillo with William Gaddis and Robert Coover, as with the formidable Thomas Pynchon. *Underworld* is something different, and may have more affinities with Philip Roth than with Pynchon. DeLillo, in *White Noise*, is a High Romantic in the age of virtual reality and related irrealisms. Frank Lentricchia, who has become DeLillo's canonical critic, is accurate in suggesting that Jack Gladney descends from Joyce's Poldy Bloom, and like Poldy, DeLillo's protagonist has a touch of the poet about him. One large difference is that Gladney is a first-person narrator; another is that Poldy has a benign immensity that Gladney cannot match. Though another cuckold, Poldy is a Romantic individualist, like Joyce himself. A century later, the amiable Gladney is trapped in a network of systems, another unit in the Age of Information.

DeLillo is a comedian of the spirit, haunted by omens of the end of our time. *White Noise* is very funny, and very disturbing: it is another of the American comic apocalypses that include Mark Twain's *The Mysterious Stranger*, Herman Melville's *The Confidence Man*, Nathaniel West's *Miss Lonelyhearts* and Pynchon's *The Crying of Lot 49*. That is a high order of company, and *White Noise* almost sustains it.

DeLillo is a master of deadpan outrageousness: Jack Gladney is chairman and professor of Hitler Studies at the College-on-the-Hill.

From *How to Read and Why*. ©2000 by Harold Bloom.

Though he is the American inventor of his discipline, Gladney has no affective reaction to Hitler: it appears to be a subject like any other these days, be it Eskimo Lesbian Studies or Post-Colonialism.

But all of *White Noise* is comic outrage; everything becomes funny, be it the fear of death, adultery, airborne toxic events, the struggles of the family romance, advanced supermarkets, or what you will. Simultaneously, everything becomes anxious, in a world where even the nuns only pretend to believe, and where the first three of Gladney's four wives each had some connection to the world of espionage.

Until *Underworld*, DeLillo's characters are curious blends of personalities and ideograms. Gladney is such a blend: we are persuaded by his love for Babette, his adulterous but well-meaning wife, and by his warm relations with his rather varied children. And yet he is as just as much Fear-of-Death as he is a husband and a father.

Where is DeLillo in *White Noise*? Close to the end of the book, he gives us a long paragraph of astonishing power and distinction, one of the most memorable passages in American writing of the later twentieth century:

> We go to the overpass all the time. Babette, Wilder and I. We take a thermos of iced tea, park the car, watch the setting sun. Clouds are no deterrent. Clouds intensify the drama, trap the shape of light. Heavy overcasts have little effect. Light bursts through, tracers and smoky arcs. Overcasts enhance the mood. We find little to say to each other. More cars arrive, parking in a line that extends down to the residential zone. People walk up the incline and onto the overpass, carrying fruit and nuts, cool drinks, mainly the middle-aged, the elderly, some with webbed beach chairs which they set out on the sidewalk, but younger couples also, arm in arm at the rail, looking west. The sky takes on content, feeling, an exalted narrative life. The bands of color reach so high, seem at times to separate into their constituent parts. There are turreted skies, light storms, softly falling streamers. It is hard to know how we should feel about this. Some people are scared by the sunsets, some determined to be elated, but most of us don't know how to feel, are ready to go either way. Rain is no deterrent. Rain brings on graded displays, wonderful running hues. More cars arrive, people come trudging up the incline. The spirit of these warm evenings is hard to describe. There is anticipation in the air but it is not the expectant

midsummer hum of a shirtsleeve crowd, a sandlot game, with coherent precedents, a history of secure response. The waiting is introverted, uneven, almost backward and shy, tending toward silence. What else do we feel? Certainly there is awe, it is all awe, it transcends previous categories of awe, but we don't know whether we are watching in wonder or dread, we don't know what we are watching or what it means, we don't know whether it is permanent, a level of experience to which we will gradually adjust, into which our uncertainty will eventually be absorbed, or just some atmospheric weirdness, soon to pass. The collapsible chairs are yanked open, the old people sit. What is there to say? The sunsets linger and so do we. The sky is under a spell, powerful and storied. Now and then a car actually crosses the overpass, moving slowly, deferentially. People keep coming up the incline, some in wheelchairs, twisted by disease, those who attend them bending low to push against the grade. I didn't know how many handicapped and helpless people there were in town until the warm nights brought crowds to the overpass. Cars speed beneath us, coming from the west, from out of the towering light, and we watch them as if for a sign, as if they carry on their painted surfaces some residue of the sunset, a barely detectable luster or film of telltale dust. No one plays a radio or speaks in a voice that is much above a whisper. Something golden falls, a softness delivered to the air. There are people walking dogs, there are kids on bikes, a man with a camera and long lens, waiting for his moment. It is not until some time after dark has fallen, the insects screaming in the heat, that we slowly begin to disperse, shyly, politely, car after car, restored to our separate and defensible selves.

It is a major American prose-poem, marked by the aura of the airborne toxic event, and yet balanced upon the edge of a transcendental revelation. DeLillo, who is so easily mistaken for a Post-Modernist End-Gamer, is rather clearly a visionary, a late Emersonian American Romantic, like the Wallace Stevens who turns blankly on the sand in *The Auroras of Autumn*. Light bursts through, and the sky, as in Stevens, takes on an exalted narrative life. Awe transcends fear, transcends the past of awe. Is it wonder or dread, an epiphany or mere, reductive pollution? What matters is that brightness falls from the air, before all the viewers return to their separate selves.

This is more than Transcendentalism in the last ditch, or Romanticism on the wane. Nothing is affirmed, not even illusion. We turn to DeLillo for woe and wonder alike, accurately persuaded of his high artistry, of something well beyond a study of the nostalgias.

TOM LeCLAIR

Closing the Loop: White Noise

"The American mystery deepens," says the native but disoriented narrator of *White Noise* (1985).[1] If DeLillo's three years of living and traveling outside the United States contributed to the scope and intricacy of *The Names*, its "complex systems, endless connections," this period of absence also resensitized him to the glut and blurt of this country, the waste and noise condensed in *White Noise*, which he began after his return in 1982.[2] Throughout his career DeLillo has alternated ways of exploring and creating that mystery he has said fiction should express, expanding his materials and methods to an undecidable spiral of intellectual complication or contracting his subjects and means to drill a test shaft into what he calls, in *Ratner's Star*, "the fear level ... the starkest tract of awareness."[3] *The Names*, with its wide range and subtlety, is the summation of DeLillo's work because it unites many of his essential themes and corresponds formally to the multiple collaborative systems we live among. *White Noise*, with its compression and ironic explicitness, is the ghostly double, the photographic negative, of *The Names*. It might be termed DeLillo's subtractive or retractive achievement, a deepening of the American and human mystery by means of a narrow and relentless focus on a seemingly ultimate subject—death. *White Noise* is about "closing the loop"—personal and mass dying, the "circle slowly closing" (241) of fear producing its object, and the closed-in structures man erects for

From *In the Loop: Don DeLillo and the Systems Novel.* © 1987 by the Board of Trustees of the University of Illinois.

safety. Furthermore, this novel is itself a tightly looped fiction and is a closing of a large loop in DeLillo's career: he returns not only to America, but also to some of the circumstances and methods of *Americana* and *End Zone*. Because of these returns and the explicitness of *White Noise*, DeLillo's systems orientation is once again evident, his connections with other systems novelists resoldered, and the coherence of his fiction clear. *White Noise* offers a fitting occasion to assess DeLillo's achievement as a whole, thus closing *In the Loop*.

The title of *White Noise* appears, quite appropriately, in *The Names*. The passage describes air travel, one of that novel's symbols of American-made alienation: "We take no sense impressions with us, no voices, none of the windy blast of aircraft on the tarmac, or the white noise of flight, or the hours waiting" (Na, 7). Like *The Names*, *White Noise* is narrated by a middle-aged father who seeks refuge from the largeness of things—the complexities of information and communication that surround him—in his marriage and children. He finds in family life "the one medium of sense knowledge in which an astonishment of heart is routinely contained" (117), and then, when family is lost to him as a source of safety, succumbs to a visceral obsession with violence; this obsession propels the second halves of the two novels' plots. The fear of death, which infects Owen Brademas and the cult in *The Names*, moves to the center of *White Noise*, driving its narrator/ protagonist, a composite of Brademas's anxieties and the cult's responses, into the double binds DeLillo knotted in *The Names*.

The subjects and techniques of *White Noise* are closer to a synthesis of *Americana* and *End Zone*, however, than to the multinational boundary crossings and Venn diagrams of *The Names*. *White Noise* has *Americana*'s small-town setting, its buzzing details of domestic life, an atmosphere polluted by electronic media, and DeLillo's early vision of America as a consumer nation symbolized by the supermarket, where David Bell finds the "white beyond white" of his father's advertising.[4] From *End Zone* DeLillo takes the collegiate setting, intellectual follies, and concern with large-scale ecological disaster. In recombining these earlier materials DeLillo restores a hard-edged explicitness to several methods that had been smoothed to subtlety in his more recent work. *White Noise* has in its action the literal circularity of *Americana*, and it has in its protagonist a character with the repetition compulsion of David Bell. These distinct and pervasive loopings are narrated in the ironic mode of *End Zone*, and *White Noise* also has that novel's sharp declination between "good company" and "madness."

While writing *White Noise*, DeLillo mocked what he called the "around-the-house-and-in-the-yard" school of American fiction, a realism about "marriages and separations and trips to Tanglewood" that gives its readers' reflected lives "a certain luster, a certain significance."[5] In "Waves and Radiation," the first of the three parts of *White Noise*, DeLillo represents with acute specificity the quotidian life of the Gladney family—Jack and Babette and their four children from various earlier marriages. Though tinged with some satire and foreboding, Part I establishes "around-the-house" expectations, the "good company" of *White Noise*. As in *End Zone*, which has a parallel structure of two balancing sets of chapters surrounding a center of irrational activity, "good company" abruptly shifts, in Part II, "The Airborne Toxic Event." *White Noise* becomes a disaster novel. While the Gladneys' safety is suddenly destroyed by the chemical spill that forces them to evacuate their home and town, the reader's expectations of the marital changes and vacations recorded in "around-the-house" realism are deconfirmed. In "The Airborne Toxic Event," DeLillo describes the chemical cloud, the process of evacuation, and several non-Gladney evacuees, but he also quickly subverts the conventions of disaster fiction. The cast of thousands and the long-running suspense of this subgenre are radically contracted in *White Noise*. In DeLillo's disaster, no one dies. The timing of the disaster within the novel is also skewed: preceded by twenty chapters, the 54 pages of Part II are followed by nineteen chapters as DeLillo quickly shifts from the event to his characters' response. Gladney, his family, and the town of Blacksmith look just as they did before this new kind of technological disaster, because its effects are invisible to the naked eye. Their response is to information—quantified measures of exposure, possible long-range consequences—rather than to entities, the scattered corpses or destroyed buildings of conventional disaster fiction. The disaster of *White Noise* is, ultimately, the new knowledge that seeps into the future from the imploded toxic event.

In Part III, "Dylarama," the reader understands that DeLillo is not only successively reversing two subgenres but is also, in the whole of *White Noise*, inverting yet another subgenre—the college novel—to illustrate for whom new knowledge is a threat. The book opens with Professor Jack Gladney, head of the Hitler Studies Department at College-on-the-Hill, describing the return of students in the autumn. It closes with summer recess an academic year later. Several of Gladney's colleagues have roles, and there is one classroom scene; but the political intrigues and intellectual adventures one expects from the college novel occur primarily within the confines of Gladney's home. His very contemporary family is wired to more sources of information than was a college student of Gladney's generation. While the university in *White Noise* is presented as trivialized by the nostalgic study of popular and youth culture, Gladney's children are making his family a center of learning. The irony of this inverted situation is that the professor and his teacher-wife attempt to resist knowledge and regress into nostalgia while their children, despite their fears, move forward and outward into the Age of Information, into awareness of large, complexly related systems. For the parents, this attitude toward knowledge is madness—as, for some readers, is DeLillo's inversion of the college novel, his making the Gladney children fearful prodigies. However, both the rapid shifts and reversals exist within a general verisimilitude, the grounding for DeLillo's mockery and exaggeration.

Although generically and rhetorically doubled, *White Noise*, when compared with *The Names* or even with *Americana*, is structurally and stylistically simple; it lacks their spatial forms, temporal dislocations, framed analogies, overlapping subtexts, and multiple voices. The physical action of *White Noise* is constricted and repetitive: Jack Gladney evades literal death by leaving Blacksmith and traveling to nearby Iron City in the novel's first half, and in the second half he returns to Iron City in quest of a drug that would let him evade his fear of death. Much of the intellectual action—Gladney's dialogues and meditations—is equally looping and reductive, marked by circular logic and sophistical argument. Like David Bell of *Americana*, who does not recognize that the auto test track at the end of the novel is a symbolic repetition of his job at the beginning, Gladney ends in Blacksmith where he began—with the reader unsure of how much the professor has learned from his spatial loops and compulsive repetitions. Other characters offer little assistance to the reader who attempts to gauge Gladney's development. Although *White Noise* displays some of the doubling also seen in *The Names* and *Americana*, the characters in Gladney's family, his acquaintances, and his friends exist primarily as sources of information or stimuli for Gladney, not as persons with plots and complex lives of their own.

DeLillo packs the text with disparate cultural signs and symptoms, but the simple chronological continuity with which Gladney orders his narrative has the effect of reducing it to a collection with apparently minimal connections, more an aggregate than a system. Although Gladney tells his tale primarily in the past tense, he seems to be recording both the trivia and trauma as they happen, not—like David Bell and James Axton—forming the materials from a later perspective. Gladney seldom recalls the past before the novel's events begin, and he plans the future only when forced to. "May the days be aimless. Let the seasons drift. Do not advance the action according to a plan" (98)—these are his desires before the disaster. Gladney allows gaps between episodes, sometimes suddenly shifts from description to dialogue or meditation, and composes in short chapters. Gary Harkness of *End Zone* used the same methods to create discontinuity within a basic chronological order. The only technique to intrude upon the novel's illusion of natural or unsophisticated recall is DeLillo's insertion of lists. Always composed of three items, usually the names of products, the lists do not always seem to be in Gladney's consciousness; rather, they are part of the circumambient noise in which he exists, a reminder of the author's presence, his knowledge of a larger context of communications. The lists are also a small analogue of the reductive organization of the text as a whole.

Gladney's sentences are like these lists: short, noun dominated, sometimes fragmentary, with few of the convolutions or Jamesian subordinations that show up in *The Names*. Often lexically and syntactically repetitive, Gladney's strings of declarations effect a primer style, an expression not of ignorance (for Gladney knows the language of the humanities) but of something like shock, a seeming inability to sort into contexts and hierarchies the information he receives and the thinking he does. Gladney's account of his life resembles the narration of a near-disaster that he hears at the Iron City airport, where a man "wearily" and "full of a gentle resignation" (90) describes the terror of preparing for a crash landing. When not neutrally—almost distractedly—recording, Gladney's voice does rise to complaint and, more frequently, to series of rhetorical questions for which he has few answers. A character who has to be forced to think and who resists the process, the self-limiting narrator of *White Noise* resembles Gary Harkness, who is as frozen by guilt as Gladney is by fear. But where the blank-faced narration of *End Zone* occasionally hinted that Harkness was playing a game, was intentionally unreliable, the survivor style of Gladney suggests a shrunken reliability. The reader perceives evasion, rather than power.

This structural and stylistic reductiveness creates a sense of "implosion," a word used several times in *White Noise*. The Gladneys' trash compactor is DeLillo's metaphor in the novel for the novel, for the characters' self-reducing double binds and the narrator's compression of the familiar and wasted. Searching for a wonder drug to relieve his fear of death, Gladney pokes through rubbish compacted into a "compressed bulk [that] sat there like an ironic modern sculpture, massive, squat, mocking":

> I jabbed at it with the butt end of a rake and then spread the material over the concrete floor. I picked through it item by item, mass by shapeless mass, wondering why I felt guilty, a violator of privacy, uncovering intimate and perhaps shameful secrets. It was hard not to be distracted by some of the things they'd chosen to submit to the Juggernaut appliance. But why did I feel like a household spy? Is garbage so private? Does it glow at the core with a personal heat, with signs of one's deepest nature, clues to

secret yearnings, humiliating flaws? What habits, fetishes, addictions, inclinations? What solitary acts, behavioral ruts? I found crayon drawings of a figure with full breasts and male genitals. There was a long piece of twine that contained a series of knots and loops. It seemed at first a random construction. Looking more closely I thought I detected a complex relationship between the size of the loops, the degree of the knots (single or double) and the intervals between knots with loops and freestanding knots. Some kind of occult geometry or symbolic festoon of obsessions. I found a banana skin with a tampon inside. Was this the dark underside of consumer consciousness? I came across a horrible clotted mass of hair, soap, car swabs, crushed roaches, flip-top rings, sterile pads smeared with pus and bacon fat, strands of frayed dental floss, fragments of ballpoint refills, toothpicks still displaying bits of impaled food. (258–59)

In its list-like style, discontinuities, and repetition, its jammed subgenres and intellectual foolishness, *White Noise* is—as one meaning of its title suggests—an "ironic modern sculpture," a novelistic heap of waste, the precise opposite of the living system and, as I said earlier, the formal negative of its systems-imitating precursor, *The Names*. This reversal is indicated by the design of the title page of *White Noise* and the first page of each part, where a roman numeral is printed in white on a black background. DeLillo uses this explicit negative to direct attention to the qualities of healthy living systems, which are symbolized in the book by that miniaturized organ, the brain: "Your brain," a colleague tells Gladney, "has a trillion neurons and every neuron has ten thousand little dendrites. The system of inter-communication is awe-inspiring. It's like a galaxy that you can hold in your hand, only more complex, more mysterious" (189).

Like the other systems novelists, DeLillo recycles American waste into art to warn against entropy, both thermodynamic and informational. *White Noise* has an apocalyptic toxic cloud striking from Pynchon's rocket-pocked heavens, a slow accumulation of garbage heaping up from Gaddis's commercial multimedia, and the self-destructive aberrations of victimization and power that Coover extends from individuals to states. The systems novelists' best works—*Gravity's Rainbow*, *JR*, *The Public Burning*—are, like *Ratner's Star*, the DeLillo novel most similar to them, massive disaster novels, industrial-strength "runaway" books. Though about a "runaway calamity" (130), *White Noise* is the compact, accessible model of their warnings, one more example of DeLillo's desire to be in the loop of general readers. Early in the novel DeLillo describes the trash compactor's "dreadful wrenching sound, full of eerie feeling" (33), qualities of *White Noise* that make it his most emotionally demonstrative book, an expression of his passionate concern with human survival, his rage at and pity for what humankind does to itself— reasons why, I believe, DeLillo was finally recognized with the American Book Award for this novel.

I have maintained throughout this study that DeLillo's expansive novels—*The Names*, *Ratner's Star*, and *Americana*—are his primary achievements. *White Noise*, on the other hand, is the best of his contractive books, those other novels that sharpen their bit to mine mystery. One of the few reviewers who did not praise *White Noise* complained that DeLillo, after eight books, "still seems like a writer making a debut."[6] I would construe this remark as a compliment, as evidence that DeLillo has retained a first novelist's receptivity, disturbing unpredictability, and enabling flexibility. If *White Noise* is a "first novel" about last things, it is also, at this stage of DeLillo's career, his last novel about his first things. It constitutes a closing of a loop, a deepening of the "American mystery."

In the "ironic modern sculpture" of *White Noise*, the central paradox is "the irony of human existence, that we are the highest form of life on earth and yet ineffably sad because we know what no other animal knows, that we must die" (99). This is the disastrous knowledge in the novel, arising from disaster and leading to it. Saturated with awareness of mortality and denials of that awareness, *White Noise* can be read as a dialogue with Ernest Becker's *The Denial of Death*, which is one of the few "influences" DeLillo will confirm.[7] Becker's book is an identifiable source for a long "looping Socratic walk" (282) and talk that Gladney has with the philosopher/magus of the book, Murray Jay Siskind. In *White Noise* and elsewhere, DeLillo seems to accept Becker's Existential and Rankian positions that the fear of death is the mainspring of human motivation and that man needs to belong to a system of ideas in which mystery exists. But DeLillo differs with Becker's conclusions that repression of the death fear is necessary to live and that "the problem of heroics is the central one of human life," for repression and heroic attempts to overcome death place Gladney in life-threatening situations.[8] Like Pynchon's rocket builders, Gaddis's empire builders, and Coover's high-wire performers, the Gladneys are victims of a self-inflicted double bind: fearing death and desiring transcendence, they engage in evasive artifices and mastering devices that turn back upon them, bringing them closer to the death they fear, even inspiring a longing for disaster, "supreme destruction, a night that swallows existence so completely," as Jack fantasizes, "that I am cured of my own lonely dying" (273).

To demonstrate the self-destructive loops of the Gladneys' sad foolishness, DeLillo employs a continuous ironic reversal, trapping and retrapping his characters in their contradictions. After giving Babette and Jack quite ordinary behavior that they hope will award them a sense of power over their death or protect them from awareness of it, DeLillo has their actions produce dangerous side effects and then the opposite of their intentions. As the Gladneys become increasingly obsessive, DeLillo also includes figures or situations that parody the Gladneys' actions and motives. Finally—and this is the achievement of *White Noise* that particularly needs to be illustrated—DeLillo presses beyond the ironic, extracting from his initially satiric materials a sense of wonderment or mystery, finding in the seeming rubbish of popular culture a kind of knowledge that would provide a more livable set of systemic expectations about life and death. The fundamental questions to which the novel moves forward and backward are: What is natural now? Has the nature of nature changed? If so, has our relation to nature changed? One result of these questions is Murray Jay Siskind's claim, like Ernest Becker's, that "It's natural to deny our nature" (296). If DeLillo begins with some of Becker's assumptions about the effects of mortal fear, the developing theme of nature in *White Noise* undermines the epistemological foundations of Becker's positions and offers the systems approach to mortality that Gregory Bateson presents in his summary book, *Mind and Nature*.[9] Impacted in situation and form, *White Noise* does come to have an intellectual expansiveness accompanying its emotionally enlarging ironies.

Suffering for years from the fear of death, Babette and Jack have settled on essentially three strategies for managing this fear: "mastering" death by expanding the physical self as an entity; evading awareness of their mortality by extending the physical self into protective communications systems; and sheltering the illusion-producing consciousness from awareness of its defensive mechanisms. While these strategies overlap, the novel's conceptual structure based upon them is circular. The simpler strategies manifest themselves at the beginning, then give way to more sophisticated methods, and then reassert themselves at the end when sophistication fails. Jack, at fifty-one, and Babette, in her mid-forties, believe size is power. He takes comfort from his imposing figure and reminds her that he enjoys the protection of her mass: "there was an honesty inherent in bulkiness" (7). If the Gladneys are physically large, their town of Blacksmith is small and safe, far from the violence of big cities. The village center is the supermarket, which provides the setting for numerous scenes in the novel and stands as a symbol of a physical magnitude that can help master death. For Jack, the purchase of goods confers safety: "in the mass and variety of our purchases, in the sheer plenitude those crowded bags suggested, the weight and size and number, the familiar package designs and vivid lettering, the giant sizes, the family bargain packs with Day-Glo sale stickers, in the sense of replenishment we felt, the sense of well-being, the security and contentment these products brought to some snug home in our souls—it seemed we had achieved a fullness of being that is not known to people who need less, expect less" (20). While the supermarket, like so much else in the novel, has an ironic underedge—the poisons in its products—and ultimately has a deeper meaning, initially it gives the Gladneys both a sense of physical expansiveness and what DeLillo elsewhere calls a "mass anesthesia," a means "by which the culture softens the texture of real danger."[10] From the consumption of supermarket perishables, the Gladney family ascends to the acquiring of durable goods at a giant shopping mall. When Jack is told that he appears to be "a big, harmless, aging, indistinct sort of guy" (83), he indulges himself and his family in a shopping spree. Using the quantitative terms that measure life force in the novel, Jack thinks of himself as huge: "I began to grow in value and self-regard. I filled myself out, found new aspects of myself, located a person I'd forgotten existed. Brightness settled around me" (84).

The ironic result of possessions occurs later: Jack's fear of dying is intensified, rather than relieved, by the objects he has collected over the years. When his things seem like weight he must shed, he rampages through his house, throwing objects away, trying to "say goodbye to himself" (294). Material growth requires money, but in *White Noise*, as in *Players*, money is no longer physical; to possess the simple force of things, Jack must have contact with a complex communication system. When he checks his bank balance by moving through a complicated set of electronic instructions, Jack says, "The system had blessed my life" (46). But since "the system was invisible," created by "the mainframe sitting in a locked room in some distant city" (46), Jack's material power depends on his vulnerable relation to something with few imaginable physical properties. Like the supermarket and the mall, the data bank both gives and takes away security; later, the computer readout of Jack's health history persuades him that his exposure to toxins has planted death within.

At the same time that the Gladneys' physical strategies gradually bring about ironic results, DeLillo includes figures or situations parodying physical mastery. The novel opens with a minutely detailed description of students returning to college. Their station wagons are stuffed with consumer products; their parents, confident in their power, look as though they have "massive insurance coverage" (3). At novel's end, though, panic strikes supermarket shoppers when the shelf locations of their insuring products are changed. The shopping mall is also a literally dangerous place: an aged brother and sister named Treadwell, disoriented by its "vastness and strangeness" (59), spend two days wandering there, and the old woman eventually dies from the shock. Even for the young, the power of the body can fail embarrassingly: Orest Mercator, filled with the best foods and carefully trained, aims to set a world record for days spent sitting with poisonous snakes, testing himself against death. He is bitten within the first two hours, doesn't die, and goes uncovered by the media.

While attempting to master death by ingesting the world, the Gladneys also try to protect the physical self from consciousness of its lonely finitude by projecting themselves outward into what they trust are protective and safe relationships: forming a marital alliance against mortality, making a family, participating in mass culture as well as mass transactions, creating a public identity. Like their consumerism, this social strategy leads to ironic traps and eventual absurdities. After four marriages each, Babette and Jack believe they have found partners with whom they can feel safe. For Jack, Babette is the opposite of his other wives, who all had ties to the intelligence community and enjoyed plotting. For Babette, Jack is solid, a stay against confusion. To show their concern for each other's happiness, DeLillo has them compete in giving pleasure: they argue over who should choose which pornography to read. They also compete in sadness, arguing about who wants to die first; each says to be without the partner would involve constant suffering. However, love, what Becker calls "the romantic project" (DoD, 167), is, for Jack, no match against death. He admits to himself that although Babette may want to die first, he certainly doesn't. They also say they tell each other everything, even their worst anxieties, but both in fact conceal their fear of death. Their mutual secret sets in motion possibly fatal consequences for both of them. Attempting to shelter and be sheltered from awareness in their alliance, the Gladneys bring closer to actuality what they most fear.

A similar ironic reversal characterizes their parenthood. Babette thinks of the children, gathered together from multiple marriages, as a protective charm: "nothing can happen to us as long as there are dependent children in the house. The kids are a guarantee of our relative longevity" (100). Therefore the Gladneys want to keep their children young, especially the last child, Wilder, who speaks very little, thus giving a secret pleasure to his parents. Although Jack argues with Murray Jay Siskind's theory that "the family process works toward sealing off the world," calling it a "heartless theory" (82), he and Babette attempt precisely this enforced ignorance. Ironically, the children are more willing to face threats to existence than are their parents. Steffie volunteers to be a victim in a simulated disaster. Denise pores over medical books to become familiar with toxins. Heinrich, at fourteen, knows science that shows how small are man's chances for survival. When the children's knowledge and questions penetrate their parents' closed environment, the kids become a threat—an inescapable threat, because Babette and Jack have scaled them into the nuclear structure.

The Gladney children are also the primary channel by which another danger—the electronic media, especially television—enters the parents' safe domesticity. In *Americana* television programming was a simplistic threat, a reductive conditioning agent that DeLillo associated with advertising. In *White Noise* television has more complex effects: conditioning and comforting, distorting and informing, even becoming, as I will discuss later, a source of mystery. As in Gaddis's *JR*, radio and television broadcasts frequently interrupt the conversations or narrative of *White Noise*, sometimes infiltrating the characters' consciousness without their awareness. At one level, the media offer Babette and Jack a soothing background noise, evidence beneath their conscious threshold that they are connected to a mass of other listeners. However, when Jack scrutinizes television, he concludes that it causes "fears and secret desires" (85)—despite the fact that most of the fragments to which Jack attends are bits of information, rather than seductive image-creations of the kind described in *Americana*. To reduce the "brain-sucking power" (16) of television, the Gladneys force their children to watch it with them every Friday evening. Irony occurs when disasters are shown, for television's power is increased, rather than reduced: "There were floods, earthquakes, mud slides, erupting volcanoes," says Jack; "We'd never before been so attentive to our duty, our Friday assembly.... Every disaster made us wish for more, for something bigger, grander, more sweeping" (64).

The effect of televised death is, like consumerism, anesthetizing. A seeming confrontation with reality is actually a means of evading one's own mortality, giving the viewer a false sense of power. Jack's fear of and desire for television's power lead him to think of the man who cuckolds him, "Mr. Gray," as a "staticky" (241) creature out of television, an unreal being who can be killed with a television character's impunity. This idea turns out to be half true. When Jack finally meets "Mr. Gray," he has little selfhood or memory; his consciousness and speech are filled with the fractured babble of the television he constantly watches. The contradictory effects of this most pervasive communications system are polarized by two parodic background characters—Heinrich's chess-by-mail partner, a convict who has killed five people after hearing voices speaking to him through television, and Jack's German teacher, who has recovered from deep depression by taking an interest in television meteorology. Ultimately both the positive effects and ironic countereffects of television are, like the polarities of the supermarket, recontextualized when DeLillo shifts attention from the content of television to the medium itself.

Unable to maintain family ignorance as a defense, Jack and Babette attempt to master death through professional study and charity, both of which draw a larger, protective crowd around them than their children can supply. Jack's position as founder and chairman of Hitler Studies confers authority and power. Attempting to grow into the role, he changes his name, adds weight, wears dark glasses, enjoys flourishing his black robe. He likes all things German, carries *Mein Kampf* as if it were an amulet, names his son Heinrich, and takes pleasure in owning a German weapon. He also takes secret German lessons. Sensing the "deathly power of the language," he says, "I wanted to speak it well, use it as a charm, a protective device" (31). In his well-attended lectures on the crowd psychology of the Nazis, he does for himself and his students what the Nazis achieved: "Crowds came to form a shield against their own dying. To become a crowd is to keep out death. To break off from the crowd is to risk death as an individual, to face dying alone" (73). As an expert in mass murder, Gladney possesses an intellectual power over death. Ironically, his expertise does not help him accept his own mortality and may well encourage him to attempt, late in the novel, to literally master death by killing "Mr. Gray." Babette's public role as reader to the blind and posture and diet instructor of the elderly gives her a power over others, like Jack's. The age of the students in her "crowd" keeps death in her consciousness, however, and their appetite for tabloid stories starts her on her quest for the ultimate evasion, the fear-relieving and brain-destroying drug Dylar. The crowds that first give Jack and Babette comfort, then prove dangerous, are finally one more source of uncertainty and mystery. DeLillo gathers into Blacksmith and the novel numerous background characters from various races and nations, with different languages and religions, mostly non-Western and exotic-seeming people whose presence questions the white American noise patterns and values within which the Gladneys would conceal themselves. In *White Noise*, the complex multinational world of *The Names* comes to small-town America.

In Part II, "The Airborne Toxic Event," the Gladneys' evasions have more directly harmful and more painfully ironic consequences. Divided into three untitled sections describing the evacuation from Blacksmith, the shelter outside town, and finally the further evacuation to Iron City, this Part not only repeats elements of Part I but also repeats itself, drawing tighter and tighter the loop of irony. Déjà vu, one of the symptoms of toxic exposure, is a principle of composition in Part II. The toxic cloud is first spotted by Heinrich. Though its danger is progressively confirmed by observation, the media, and police warnings, Jack and Babette attempt to deny its threat. Their attempt to protect their children from anxiety is revealed as a way of concealing fear from themselves—a doubly guilty action: delay brings increased physical danger to the children and it causes Jack to be exposed to the toxic cloud. The cloud itself cannot be denied, and when it appears overhead it is described, ironically, in terms that recall supermarket plenitude and media distraction: "Packed with chlorides, benzenes, phenols, hydrocarbons" (127), the cloud "resembled a national promotion for death, a multimillion-dollar campaign backed by radio spots, heavy print and billboard, TV saturation" (158). An amorphous, drifting, mysteriously killing mass, the "ATE" is the contemporary complement of Pynchon's pointed, swift, and explosive rockets. Like the rockets, the toxins were engineered to kill and thus give man control over the Earth; instead, they threaten their inventors and nature. DeLillo tips his hat to Pynchon with a radio advertisement that the Gladneys hear during the evacuation: "It's the rainbow hologram that gives this credit card a marketing intrigue" (122).

After demonstrating the ironic effects of unpreparedness in section 1, DeLillo increases the irony in section 2 by having Jack observe people who not only are prepared for disaster but seem to welcome it. Taken out of his safe place and moved to the shelter, the professor becomes the student; he is instructed in the facts of disaster and ways of living with or through it. Persuaded that "death has entered" (141), Jack finds himself filled with dread, needing some comfort, unable to believe in religion, tabloid faith, or the practical delusions Siskind suggests. At the end of section 2 he listens to Steffie's sleep-talk, "words that seemed to have a ritual meaning, part of a verbal spell or ecstatic chant" (155). Even after he realizes the words are "Toyota Celica," a product of consumer conditioning, he calls them a "moment of splendid transcendence"; her mantra allows him to feel "spiritually large" and to pass into a "silent and dreamless" (155) sleep. Jack's delusion and total relief from consciousness would seem to be an appropriate ending for the disaster section, but in section 3 DeLillo has the Gladneys ironically repeat the process of evacuation, this time with a trip to Iron City. Their flight is once again made unduly dangerous because of the Gladneys' denial and delay. When they reach Iron City, what they think will be an overnight stay turns into a nine-day siege among crowds that give none of the comfort Jack has lectured about. The final ironic indignity of Part II is that the disaster receives no television coverage.

In the first few chapters of Part III, "Dylarama," Babette and Jack, having returned to Blacksmith, attempt to drift along with old defenses. But new threats arise—Heinrich informs his family that radiation from electronic devices is more dangerous than airborne toxins—and Jack increasingly believes that his exposure is causing a large nebulous mass (corresponding to the cloud) to grow within. The possibilities for denying death begin to narrow, as does the range of the plot. Babette's importance in the novel, limited from the beginning by Jack's needs and his narration, diminishes as his thanatophobia becomes a symbolic mass, occupying more and more of himself and his story. Now he desperately seeks literal and extreme methods of evasion and mastery, with increasingly ironic and deadly consequences. He finds that Babette had secretly participated in experiments with Dylar, a drug meant to relieve the fear of death. Although Dylar has not worked for her, he plots to obtain a supply from her source, hoping that it will provide an automatic relief from mortal awareness. If Dylar is the ultimate evasion, predicted in *Americana* by a character who says, "Drugs are scheduled to supplant the media" (Am, 347), Jack's means are the ultimate mastery: killing. Already jealous of "Mr. Gray," the chemist to whom Babette has traded sexual favors for Dylar, Jack is also drawn to the expansion of self that Siskind says will occur during a murder. As Jack's actions become more desperate, they also become simpler, imploded. The novel circles back to its beginnings—to Jack's initial faith in ingesting products and growing in physical size; to entities and force replacing, as they do in *Great Jones Street*, participation in communication systems.

Before following out the consequences of Jack's violent quest for Dylar, I want to discuss the role of Murray Jay Siskind. This character appears in *Amazons*, a novel that was published in 1980 under the pseudonym Cleo Birdwell, the name of its protagonist/narrator.[11] *Amazons* is an entertainment about the first woman to play in the National Hockey League; DeLillo says he wrote the book with a collaborator. In it Murray Jay Siskind is a New York sportswriter who carries around a 900-page manuscript chronicling the Mafia takeover of the snowmobile industry. While Siskind is a comic figure in *Amazons*, in *White Noise* he has a much larger and more complex role. As a guest lecturer, he teaches courses on Elvis Presley and car-crash movies. His function is semiotic, "deciphering, rearranging, pulling off the layers of unspeakability" (38) in popular culture and, eventually, in Jack's life. Siskind's methods are to "root out content" and attend to the deep structures, "the codes and messages" (50), of all media. The title of Part I, "Waves and Radiation," is his phrase. Expressing his conclusions with confidence—"It's obvious" is his favorite phrase—Siskind is particularly convincing to Jack on "the nature of modern death": "It has a life independent of us. It is growing in prestige and dimension. It has a sweep it never had before" (150). Although he is important for DeLillo's purposes throughout the novel, Siskind most influences Jack in "Dylarama." There Siskind probes into his friend's repression of death, forcing Jack to recognize how his consciousness has protected itself from itself, the last and most sophisticated strategy of defense. Siskind's influence culminates during his last appearance in the novel when, as he and Jack take a "looping Socratic walk" (282) around Blacksmith, he points out Jack's failures at both evasion and mastery. He then suggests murder as a form of mastery.

Because of Jack's emotional state, Siskind is persuasive; but both Jack and the reader should remember Siskind's limitations, his errors, oddities, and games. He has been blatantly wrong in several of his analyses, including a conclusion about Babette, and unfair in the judgment of his landlord. He says he only speculates, but he also says that for him the best talk is persuasive. He admits a sexual attraction to Babette and admits as well that he covers up the qualities "that are most natural to him" (21) in order to be seductive. Although Siskind does offer Jack, as well as the reader, penetrating interpretations of the world, especially the meaning of its communications systems, Siskind's advice promotes a profoundly immoral act. Like the Gladneys, he compresses—implodes—the context of his thinking, ignoring the murder victim and Jack's role as husband and father, which would be endangered by his crime. A peripatetic Socrates, Siskind turns into Mephistopheles, a sneaky-looking, beard-wearing magus who infiltrates Gladney's consciousness, not by promising an advance in knowledge, as Faust's tempter did, but by claiming, "We know too much" (289). He suggests regression—"We want to reverse the flow of experience" (218)—tempting with ignorance and nostalgia. Siskind is also, in Michel Serres's systemic terms, the "parasite," the guest who exchanges talk for food and (simultaneously, in French) the agent of noise in a cybernetic system.[12]

The plot that Jack formulates in response to Siskind's temptation and disturbing "noise" has secrecy as a major appeal. Now that Jack cannot keep his impending death secret from his consciousness and his fear secret from his wife, he desires something private, a knowledge wholly his own. Such a secret would provide power, what Jack thinks is his "last defense against the ruin" (275) and what Ernest Becker calls "man's illusion par excellence, the denial of the bodily reality of his destiny" (DoD, 237–38). By killing his rival Jack will participate in the "secret precision" (291) of murder and will be able to consume a product created by "secret research" (192). Just after Siskind recommends murder to Jack, he quotes a letter from his bank about his "secret code": "Only your code allows you to enter the system" (295). But for DeLillo, here and in his other novels, secrets collapse a system in on itself, destroying necessary reciprocity and collaboration, denying man's place in multiple systems. The irony—perhaps the saving irony—of Jack's secret plotting is that he is no better a plotter than he has been a protector, no better a master than an evader. His murder plan seems based on the improbabilities of television crime, full of holes despite his constant, step-by-step rehearsal. He drives to Iron City in a stolen car, running red lights along the way. He plans to shoot "Mr. Gray" in the stomach and then put the gun in Gray's hand, implying a rather unusual suicide. While confronting and then shooting Gray, whose name is Willie Mink, Jack is mentally intoxicated. He understands "waves, rays, coherent beams" (308) and feels the air is "rich with extrasensory material" (309). Jack's intellectual expansion, his Murray-sight produced by adrenalin, ends when Mink shoots him. Using the metaphor of implosion, Jack says, "The world collapsed inward, all those vivid textures and connections buried in mounds of ordinary stuff.... The old human muddles and quirks were set flowing again" (313). Literally reminded of mortality, Jack forgets the Dylar and secrecy; he takes Mink to a hospital, saving his victim's life and, perhaps, his own tenuous humanity. The crazed Gray-Mink—who resembles Clare Quilty during the murder scene at the end of *Lolita*—is an exotic, colored double for Jack to recognize and accept. Like Jack, he has tried to master death by studying it, and to evade consciousness of death by ingesting products and media. Both Mink and Jack also come close to destroying themselves because of their obsessions.

If the novel appears at this point to drive toward a conventional hopeful ending, DeLillo springs several compacted reversals and ironies in its last few pages. Feeling spiritually "large and selfless" (314) after saving Mink's life, Jack discusses heaven with a German nun in the hospital. She undercuts any sentimental religious hope he may now have by saying that even she and her fellow nuns don't believe; they only pretend to for the sake of all those secularists, like Jack, who need belief not to disappear from the world. Immediately after denying Jack his nostalgia for literal transcendence, his vision of heaven as "fluffy cumulus" (317), DeLillo has Jack report in the last chapter what can be only termed a minor miracle, an event out of what Jack has earlier called "the tabloid future, with its mechanism of a hopeful twist to apocalyptic events" (146): Wilder rides his plastic tricycle across six lanes of busy traffic, beating death at odds it would take a computer to calculate. Perhaps Jack's achievement—a possible new relationship to death—is implied by his drawing no conclusions from Wilder's feat. He simply reports it as a fact of uncertain cause and effect, finding in it no evasion or mastery. This uncertain acceptance of the uncertain also marks the episode that follows Wilder's fide. Jack describes his and other Blacksmith residents' hushed viewing of brilliant sunsets, perhaps caused by toxins in the air: "Certainly there is awe, it is all awe, it transcends previous categories of awe, but we don't know what we are watching or what it means, we don't know whether it is permanent, a level of experience to which we will gradually adjust, into which our uncertainty will eventually be absorbed, or just some atmospheric weirdness, soon to pass" (324–25). As the "fluffy cumulus" would make a good religious finale, these naturally or unnaturally "turreted skies" would provide a conventional humanistic ending for *White Noise*. But DeLillo chooses to conclude with a scene in the supermarket, where Jack and elderly shoppers disoriented by the new locations of products "try to work their way through confusion" (326). What the shoppers "see or think they see ... doesn't matter," Jack says, because the checkout "terminals are equipped with holographic scanners, which decode the binary secret of every item, infallibly. This is the language of waves and radiation, or how the dead speak to the living" (326). In the adjacent tabloid racks, he concludes, is "everything we need that is not food or love ... the cures for cancer, the remedies for obesity. The cults of the famous and the dead" (326). In this last paragraph DeLillo passes to the reader the uncertainty that Jack has found dangerous throughout the novel. Here Jack may be speaking literally, which would suggest continuing delusion; or ironically, which might imply a reductive reversal of his earlier delusions; or figuratively, which could be a final achievement, the register of doubleness and uncertainty, resistance to the "binary" simplification he mentions. At the end of *White Noise* the American mystery does deepen, as white space follows Jack's final enigmatic words.

The ambiguities of DeLillo's final chapter send the reader back into the novel to consider the crucial question implicit in the book's packed ironies and explicit in many of DeLillo's references to the concept of nature: What is "the nature and being of real things" (243)? The theme of the natural in *White Noise* is both pervasive and piecemeal, stroked into the texture of the book in such a way as to defy categorization, a jumble of perceptions, queries, assertions, and speculations like the mixture in the trash compactor that provides "signs of one's deepest nature" (259). The nature of inorganic matter or processes is discussed by numerous characters, ranging from Siskind, who comments on the "heat death of the universe" (10), to Heinrich, who possesses specialized knowledge of submolecular matter, to others who meditate on such common subjects as rain and sunsets. The Gladney family gets information about plants and animals from "CABLE NATURE" (231). Characters are particularly interested in laboratory animals and "sharks, whales, dolphins, [and] great apes" (189), animals that blur the distinction with humans. If, asks Heinrich, "animals commit incest ... how unnatural can it be?" (34). The nature of various human groups is a subject for frequent analysis. A colleague of Jack's says, "Self-pity is something that children are very good at, which must mean it is natural and important" (216). Of his fellow Blacksmith residents, Jack states, "It is the nature and pleasure of townspeople to distrust the city" (85). Babette believes that men have a capacity for "insane and violent jealousy. Homicidal rage" and, further, "When people are good at something, it's only natural that they look for a chance to do this thing" (225). Man's physical nature is most thoroughly treated in Heinrich and Jack's several colloquies on the brain. As for "undisclosed natural causes," Jack says, "We all know what that means"

(99). Characters define the nature of love, sex, and shopping; they discuss human products from "the nature of the box camera" (30) to the "natural language of the culture" (9). "Technology," says Siskind, "is lust removed from nature" (285). Finally, the nature of individuals is described and judged: Jack says that "it was my nature to shelter loved ones from the truth" (8), that Steffie looks "natural" in her role as victim, and that Wilder is "selfish in a totally unbounded and natural way" (209).

Because of these multiple categories of the natural, the general response of Jack Gladney (and, I believe, of the reader) is uncertainty about some single natural order. "The deeper we delve into the nature of things," Gladney concludes, "the looser our structure may seem to become" (82). This "looseness," what the systems theorist would call "openness" or "equifinality," is an intellectual disaster for Babette and Jack. This dangerous uncertainty is caused not only by *what* they have come to learn, but also *how*. In the inversion of the college novel, they are instructed by their children and receive often fragmented information from the communication loops that penetrate their ignorance. The knowledge that Heinrich and others impose on Jack and Babette is often specialized, taken out of its scientific context and expressed in its own nomenclature. This new information frequently requires the Gladneys to deny the obvious, accept the improbable, and believe in the invisible. The "waves and radiation" are beyond the capability of "natural" perception: knowledge of them cannot be had without the aid of technological extensions of the nervous system. Because of the Gladneys' schooling and expectations, this new world they inhabit seems remarkably strange. Babette believes, "The world is more complicated for adults than it is for children. We didn't grow up with all these shifting facts and attitudes" (171). She and Jack remember the three kinds of rock but are unprepared for the systems-ranging science that Heinrich seems to find natural. Jack's career is based on a nineteenth-century notion of history, the anachronism of charisma and mass movements, the irrational in terms of personal or social—rather than molecular—forces. What he calls the gradual "seepage" of poison and death into the present is alien to him because he has "evolved an entire system" (12) around the charismatic figure of Hitler. Babette's expectations are even more simplistic: she tells Jack, "I think everything is correctible. Given the right attitude and proper effort, a person can change a harmful condition by reducing it to its simplest parts" (191). Accompanying the obvious irony here is the negative effect of her analytic method. The splitting of reality into smaller and smaller parts has produced both the "finger-grained" (35) physical danger that Jack remarks and the atomized information that resists a structure, a whole.

The emotional consequences of the Gladneys' uncertainty are

nostalgia; guilt: "Man's guilt in history and in the tides of his own blood has been complicated by technology, the daily seeping falsehearted death" (22); and fear: "Every advance is worse than the one before because it makes me more scared" (161), says Babette. Like their responses to death, the Gladneys' responses to uncertainty about nature have the ambivalent force of taboo—attraction and repulsion. When they try to understand why they and their children enjoy watching disasters, Jack's colleague explains the attraction as normal, "natural.... Because we're suffering from brain fade. We need an occasional catastrophe to break up the incessant bombardment of information" (66). If this answer only increases their uncertainty, Murray Jay Siskind's paradox—"It's natural to deny our nature" (297)—is the ultimate statement of the circularity within which the Gladneys feel trapped. They are unable to know what they want, and unable to not know what they don't want.

The best systems treatment of the Gladneys' problems is Gregory Bateson's *Mind and Nature*, a book about what man can (and, particularly, cannot) know about living systems. Bateson succinctly diagnoses the kind of response the Gladneys have to their contemporaneity: "a breach in the apparent coherence of our mental logical process would seem to be a sort of death" (M&N, 140). The Gladneys' strategies for evading uncertainty overlap with their defenses against mortality—closed spatial, psychological, and social systems. The destructive consequences of their intellectual implosion are DeLillo's photo-negative methods for pointing to his systems-based conception of nature, mind, and mortality. Because nature, whether strictly defined as living systems or more widely defined as the world in its totality, is a complex of multiple, overlapping systems, many of which are open, reciprocal, and equifinal, the coherence of either/or logic, a major basis for delusions about certainty, should not, suggests DeLillo, be expected to apply to the simultaneous, both/and nature of phenomena. "My life," says Babette, "is either/or" (53). When the Gladneys attempt to impose expectations inherited from closed systems of entities on the open world of communications, what Bateson calls "the tight coherence of the logical brain" is "shown to be not so coherent" (M&N, 140). Unable to adapt to incoherence, the Gladneys verge toward the self-destructiveness and delusion that Bateson predicts for the "victims" of uncertainty: "In order to escape the million metaphoric deaths depicted in a universe of *circles* of causation, we are eager to deny the simple reality of ordinary dying and to build fantasies of an afterworld and even of reincarnation" (M&N, 140).

What the Gladneys refuse to accept and what forms the basis for DeLillo's understanding of systemic fact and value is the loop: the simultaneity of living and dying, the inherent reciprocity of circular causality that makes certainty impossible. Their refusal is rooted in mechanistic science, that extension of common-sense empiricism which defines the world as a collection of entities, a heap of things like the Gladneys' compacted trash, rather than as a system of energy and information. The way Jack expresses his question about fundamental reality—"the nature and being of real *things*" (my italics)—illustrates his epistemological error, which also leads to either/or categorizing, because "things" are separate and separable. Siskind tells the Gladneys that in Tibet death "is the end of attachment to things" (38). For DeLillo the detachment from "things" is not exotic transcendence but looping good sense, recognition of the systemic nature of nature.

Adaptation to uncertainty is a common theme in contemporary fiction. DeLillo gives it a "hopeful twist" in *White Noise* by demonstrating the benefits of systems-influenced uncertainty. If, as the Gladneys feel, the nature of the contemporary world is "strange," does not this fact, recognized and accepted, reduce the feared strangeness of death and even offer possibilities of hope? Put another way: If we are uncertain about life, wouldn't our uncertainty about death be natural and less feared? Discussing modern death in language that applies as well to modern science, Siskind sums up the Gladneys' dual fear: "The more we learn, the more it grows. Is this some law of physics? Every advance in knowledge and technique is matched by a new kind of death, a new strain. Death adapts, like a viral agent. Is it a law of nature?" (150). Later he leads Jack astray, drawing the conclusion that "fear is unnatural" (289). The alternative to Siskind's ultimately murderous conclusion is articulated by the elusive neuroscientist Winnie Richards. "I have a spacey theory about human fear," she tells Jack. "If death can be seen as less strange and unreferenced, your sense of self in relation to death will diminish, and so will your fear" (229). Jack asks, "What do I do to make death less strange?" He answers his own question with clichés about risking his life, thus missing the less dangerous and more intellectually promising alternative of admitting life's strangeness, its refusal to be consumed by human appetite or human needs for coherence, the human-invented "law of parsimony." Like the biologist Zapalac in *End Zone*, Richards advances a systems-like position that could, if accepted, make contemporary death "an experience that flows naturally from life" (100), as Jack says of death for Genghis Khan.

Also flowing from this pervasive strangeness or mystery might be a sense of hope, or at least the possibility that human existence could be open rather than closed. Jack and Babette have chosen, in a phrase used to describe their family, to "seal off" death and the dead. They choose to believe that death is the end of human identity. People around them believe in quite literal continuation, even in the apparently ridiculous tabloid versions of reincarnation and extraterrestrial salvation. While the senior citizens' appetite for "the cults of the famous and the dead" may well be a reversion to "superstition," a word repeated throughout *White Noise*, the elderly characters' belief could also be, as Jack implies in the shelter, the result of adjustment to the new natural world shot through with scientific implausibility. Their tabloids constitute a literalized bastardization of incomprehensible possibility, their "acceptance and trust ... the end of skepticism" (27). Skepticism of the reductionist, mechanistic kind would be rid of all belief, but DeLillo suggests in *White Noise* that he shares Michael Polanyi's (as well as Gregory Bateson's) position that "in attributing truth to any methodology we make a nonrational commitment; in effect, we perform an act of faith ... [that] arises from a network of unconscious bits of information taken in from the environment," what Polanyi calls "tacit knowing."[13] Mechanism believes the world is closed; systems theory assumes it's open and accepts uncertainty. The German nun tells Jack that she and her small band are keeping faith alive, but in fact contemporary science—not "fools, idiots, those who hear voices, those who speak in tongues" (319)—is the primary source and reminder of the necessity of faith. Many aspects of contemporary life that the Gladneys use to evade or master death and uncertainty could also be tacit means of man's adjusting to the inherent existence of faith and mystery in his experience. One working title of the novel was "The American Book of the Dead." Both the Tibetan and Egyptian Books of the Dead, as well as the Mexican Day of the Dead, are alluded to in *White Noise*. These sacred books, Siskind explains to Jack, prepare us for death. While the experiences of the supermarket, television, or scientific knowledge do not prepare contemporary man in the specific and literal ways, as the Books of the Dead or the tabloids do, these everyday events can offer a communal experience of the invisible, a sense of mysteriousness that implies that neither life nor death has been settled, closed. Perhaps lack of conclusiveness means lack of conclusion.

Murray Jay Siskind is the tutor in mystery. DeLillo hedges Siskind's influence in several ways—by making him hyperbolic and occasionally wrong in his statements, by giving him an immoral influence—but I believe DeLillo means the reader to take seriously Siskind's analysis of essentially religious experience in secular forms. By immersing himself "in American magic and dread" (19), Siskind arrives at conclusions shared by Gregory Bateson. "The conventional view is that religion evolved out of magic," but, says Bateson, "I think it was the other way around—that magic is a sort of degenerate religion," a superficial but powerful way to answer the religious need "to affirm membership in what we may call the *ecological tautology*, the eternal verities of life and environment" (M&N, 232). It's in Siskind's realm, the supermarket, that the tabloids, which DeLillo states are "closest to the spirit of the book," are found.[14] These tabloids, DeLillo says, "ask profoundly important questions about death, the afterlife, God, worlds and space, yet they exist in an almost Pop Art atmosphere," an atmosphere that Siskind helps decode. In his family Jack experiences "magic," "secondary levels of life ... extrasensory flashes and floating nuances of being" (34), the "debris of invisible matter" (64); however, he is slow to find a similar mysteriousness outside the home. To Siskind, the supermarket is packed not with the physical goods that the Gladneys consume, but with communications, messages: "This place recharges us spiritually, it prepares us, it's a gateway or pathway. Look how bright. It's full of psychic data.... Everything is concealed in symbolism, hidden by veils of mystery and layers of cultural material. But it is psychic data, absolutely. The doors slide open, they close unbidden. Energy waves, incident radiation. All the letters and numbers are here, all the colors of the spectrum, all the voices and sounds, all the code words and ceremonial phrases" (37–38). He finds the same plenitude in television: it "offers incredible amounts of psychic data. It opens ancient memories of world birth, it welcomes us into the grid, the network of little buzzing dots that make up the picture pattern.... The medium practically overflows with sacred formulas if we can remember how to respond innocently and get past our irritation, weariness and disgust" (51). Even technology has a similar, perhaps ironic mysteriousness: "New devices, new techniques every day. Lasers, masers, ultrasound. Give yourself up to it," Siskind tells Jack. "Believe in it. They'll insert you in a gleaming tube, irradiate your body with the basic stuff of the universe. Light, energy, dreams. God's own goodness" (285).

Two episodes, closing Parts I and III, suggest that Jack begins to learn to see as Siskind and, I believe, DeLillo do. When Jack views Babette on television, he wonders if she is "dead, missing, disembodied? Was this her spirit, her secret self, some two-dimensional facsimile released by the power of technology, set free to glide through wavebands, through energy levels, pausing to say good-bye to us from the fluorescent screen?" (104). He says, "I began to think Murray might be on to something. Waves and radiation" and confesses that "strangeness gripped me" (104). The last episode occurs at the supermarket and ends the novel. The confusion of the elderly in the aisles doesn't matter, Jack says, because the "holographic scanners" are in place, decoding "the language of waves and radiation, or how the dead speak to the living" (326). I have said that this ending was uncertain, and it remains so. However, considered as the culmination of the theme of nature and mystery, Jack's final words imply that he may be ready to accept the uncertain activity below the surface of our perceptions, activity that may—and only may—mean that the world of the living and the world of the dead are not wholly separate, closed off.

While satirizing how contemporary man uses and is used by his objects, his things, DeLillo also shows how a new perception of what is now natural—systems among systems, communications, inherent uncertainty, mysteriousness—can accommodate man to his condition as knower and even squeeze a modicum of hope from the junk into which a reductionist way of knowing has historically converted natural complexity. This is the looping accomplishment of *White Noise*. Morris Berman, in his study of science since the Renaissance, asserts that the effect of systems thinking is a "reenchantment of the world," a sense of participation in systemic mysteriousness. Understated and uncertain, the ending of *White Noise* implies this possibility, this futurity—if not for Jack Gladney, then for the reader who knows more than he. Although *White Noise* seems most similar, among systems novels, to the collected noise of Gaddis's *JR*, I believe that DeLillo's is ultimately a larger-minded work, going beyond Gaddis's massive pessimism to ally itself with the more radically open system of Pynchon's *Gravity's Rainbow*, in which the voices of the dead—the long-extinct organisms that become petroleum, the recently dead humans who speak from the Other Side—are not wholly drowned out by the roar of the killing rockets.

The ambiguities of DeLillo's title and the pattern of reference composed around it summarize the doubleness of the novel. First, the phrase is itself a synesthetic paradox. In general scientific usage, "white noise" is aperiodic sound with frequencies of random amplitude and random interval—a term for chaos. In music, however, "white noise" is the sound produced by all audible sound-wave frequencies sounding together—a term for complex, simultaneous ordering that represents the "both/and" nature of systems (and irony). "Panasonic," a word that appears by itself as a paragraph on page 241, was another working title of the novel, one that indicates DeLillo's concern with recording the wide range of sound, ordered and uncertain, positive and negative.

The pattern DeLillo builds around noise parallels the thematic developments I've been discussing. The characters in *White Noise* consume sounds as they consume supermarket products. The sounds of home appliances, such as the "mangling din" (34) of the trash compactor, and the chatter of children give Jack comfort. In the supermarket he is "awash in noise. The toneless systems, the jangle and skid of carts, the loudspeaker and coffee-making machines, the cries of children. And over it all, or under it all, a dull and unlocatable roar, as of some form of swarming life just outside the range of human apprehension" (36). At the mall there is a similar "human buzz of some vivid and happy transaction" (84). The voices of radio and television, like the noise of stores, tell Jack he's not alone, allowing him to evade the feared silence of the cemetery he visits. For Jack, a sense of mastery comes from the private sounds of lovemaking, his voice lecturing, the chants of Nazi crowds, his voice as a weapon in Willie Mink's room, the explosion of the gun. The speculative dialogues he holds with Siskind initially distract his consciousness from mortality. But like the Gladneys' behavior in the novel, sounds have ironic effects and reversals. These are the alarms, commercial messages, confusing information, the "aural torment" (241) of cuckoldry, anxiety while pronouncing German, the news of secret plots, spoken ideas with deadly consequences, shrieks of madness from the asylum, and the noise of primal terror from airplane passengers who think they are about to crash: "terrible and inarticulate sounds, mainly cattle noises, an urgent and force-fed lowing" (92). With this negative evidence in mind, Babette wonders, "What if death is nothing but sound? ... You hear it forever. Sound all around. How awful" (198). The opposite extreme is the tabloid hope that "some voice or noise would crack across the sky and we would be lifted out of death" (234) by UFOs.

While expressing polarities, the sound motif, like the novel as a whole, comes to signify a wide-ranging awareness of systemic mystery, a new knowing and non-knowing. In evolution, Anthony Wilden reminds us, noise is an intrusion "converted into an essential part of the system so as to maintain the relationship between system and environment"; the "efficient system" will "seek to maintain stability by ACCEPTING noise, by incorporating it as information, and moving to a new level of organization (evolving)."[15] In the human organism, as conceptualized by Michel Serres, noise is the constant internal background against which the organism transforms "disorder into potential organization" with language, thus creating what Serres describes as a loop: "negentropy goes back upstream," and the flow of time is bent.[16] In more everyday terms, Heinrich reminds his father of human perceptual limits: "Just because you don't hear a sound doesn't mean it's not out there ... they [sounds] exist in the air, in waves. Maybe they never stop. High, high, high-pitched. Coming down from somewhere" (23). What we experience as silence may be communication. What we hear as static may have meaning. Listening to Wilder cry for nearly seven straight hours, Jack thinks that "inside this wailing noise" might be "some reckless wonder of intelligibility" (78). An early sentence comparing traffic noise to the murmur "of dead souls babbling at the edge of a dream" (4) seems like a throwaway simile until, near the novel's end, Jack hears the sizzle of his freezer as "wintering souls" (258) and, listening to women talk, says, "All sound, all souls" (273). In *White Noise* DeLillo collects the familiar sounds of American culture and universal fear; he then both turns them up, exaggerating their foolishness for ironic effect, and turns them down, finding in the lower frequencies a whisper of possibility, of uncertainty beyond our present range of knowledge. DeLillo's is the noise of disaster and the noise of mystery. Which shall we hear, which shall we make—in the loop?

Though crammed with communications from every medium, *White Noise* has few of the explicitly metafictional or metalinguistic elements that characterize *The Names* and most other DeLillo novels. However, its several references to literature indicate the essential nature of *White Noise* and the methodological coherence of DeLillo's fiction from *Americana* onward. Jack Gladney, for all his intellectual limitations, is offended by conventional, perhaps popular and sentimental irony: "How literary," he thinks, "peevishly. Streets thick with the details of impulsive life as the hero ponders the latest phase in his dying" (281). But Gladney also sympathizes with a former wife who "reviewed fiction for the CIA, mainly long serious novels with coded structures. The work left her tired and irritable, rarely able to enjoy food, sex or conversation" (213). DeLillo's "implosive" strategy in *White Noise*, his soliciting of conventional, "good company" expectations which he mashes into "madness," is the middle ground between popular "literary" and high literacy. But, as usual, DeLillo interrogates himself, as well as the genres he works between and among. The aesthetic efficacy of "implosion" is metaphorically questioned by Dylar, "a wonderful little system" (188) engineered to relieve fear. Winnie Richards describes the Dylar capsule in terms that could refer to the novel: "It self-destructs. It implodes minutely of its own massive gravitation.... Once the plastic membrane is reduced to microscopic particles, it passes harmlessly out of the body in the time-honored way" (188).

Is fiction a drug? Does it merely relieve our mortal fear by allowing us to evade ourselves for a time, giving us a sense of mastery over the textual world and the text itself? DeLillo allows these implications to surface, but his methods preclude evasion or mastery for the reader. DeLillo takes the reader into complicity with Gladney and his "around-the-house" desire for evasive safety, then confutes that desire with the disaster, a massive cloud exploding outward from its small container. In so doing, DeLillo achieves the effect that his novelist Brand in *Americana* wants and describes in terms of ingestion: to "detonate in the gut of America like a fiery bacterial bombshell" (Am, 110). The double loop of *White Noise*—Jack Gladney's repeating his pre-disaster foolishness in his search for Dylar—makes obvious the delusive mastery of plotting, both real and fictional. DeLillo's assumption about the function of fiction seems to be stated by a background character who works for "Advanced Disaster Management": "The more we rehearse disaster, the safer we'll be from the real thing" (205). Fiction as simulation of disaster or madness—this conception of fiction's work is consistent across DeLillo's novels, all of which illustrate how self-destruction can arise out of the genres, forms, codes, ideas, and systems that readers and characters may initially think are "good company." While revealing the danger of various conventions, ideologies, and closed systems, DeLillo also reconstructs, by the end of each novel, mystery, even possibility. His looping method does not substitute one closed system for another.

DeLillo's double-binding or looping strategy is not only consistent in his books but also congruent with their subjects—the multiple communications loops of contemporary life in all its manifestations from the personal to the social, the physical body to the body politic, the ecological to the technological. DeLillo's constant concern is postindustrial America in a multinational world: how different aspects of our postmodern condition unite in great knowledge and great danger. Because his perspective is that of the systems thinker, who examines value in terms of survival, DeLillo offers through his fiction a wide-ranging, original, profound, and (when his novels are read together) synthetic commentary on the destructive and reconstructive circumstances of contemporaneity. *White Noise*, though compacted in form, represents the breadth and depth of DeLillo's concern. It plays together the frequencies of his previous books: the body of *Players*, the brain of *The Names*, the family life of *Americana*, the mass media of *Great Jones Street*, the political violence of *Running Dog*, the ecological disaster of *End Zone*, and the cultural knot of knowledge and mystery that *Ratner's Star* ties.

White Noise also more explicitly reveals DeLillo's reasons for the consistency of his looping materials and methods, not just in this novel, but in his earlier work as well. DeLillo wants to elicit the interest of those general readers who are soaked in or shot through with our culture of entertainment, the media that we consume and that consume us. One of DeLillo's motives is, I believe, voiced by Jack Gladney when he says, "I feel sad for people and the queer part we play in our own disasters" (126). Heinrich's discussion of knowledge supplies another motive for this author who believes our disasters are often caused by false models and impossible intellectual expectations: "What good is knowledge," Heinrich asks his father, "if it just floats in the air? It goes from computer to computer. It changes and grows every second of every day. But nobody actually knows anything" (148–49). DeLillo's knowledge, except perhaps in *Ratner's Star*, does not go "from computer to computer," from learned author to specialist reader, but is stroked into accessible and entertaining narratives that dramatize (in phrases from *The Names*) "the latest research" on "how minds work" in and on personal and cultural life. Though he is as knowledgeable about systems as are Gaddis and Pynchon, DeLillo is, in his orientation to the reader, more similar to Coover, who works his knowledge into the texture of his fictions in order to achieve affect, a reciprocity between text and reader.

Cohering in subject, perspective, method, and effect, DeLillo's novels form a fictional system, a dynamic whole modeling the qualities of living systems: circularity, reciprocity, openness, complexity, formal relationships, flexibility, and equifinality. My purposes have been to examine how the parts of this whole relate to one another, to show how the individual novels are themselves looping wholes, and to evaluate the significance and success of each, hoping to give the gnomon of DeLillo's work an informed and thorough attention so far lacking in academic criticism and, understandably, in the reviews. Two reviews of *White Noise*—one negative, one positive—summarize the current critical opinion about DeLillo that *In the Loop* is meant to revise and supplement. Reviewing *White Noise* in the *Washington Post*, Jonathan Yardley calls DeLillo a "writer of stupendous talents" and *White Noise* "arguably DeLillo's best novel," but Yardley proceeds to voice familiar complaints: DeLillo is derivative, a "pamphleteer" who retails "the shopworn campus ideology of the '60s and '70s," including an attack on "the numbing and corrupting influences of technology."[17] DeLillo's plot is a "catalogue," its major event a "deus ex machina," and its ending "contrived." None of his characters "acquires any genuine humanity" because, according to Yardley, DeLillo is "interested in ideas and institutions ... but not in people." Though a "gifted writer," DeLillo engages in "too much chatter, too much of which is merely brittle." His novels are, to Yardley, "empty" at the core because the author does not speak "from the heart."

At the other critical pole is John Aldridge, who opened his review of *White Noise* in the *Chicago Tribune* with the following quote: "Don DeLillo belongs, along with Thomas Pynchon and William Gaddis, to a select group of writers working in the uncharted outer spaces of the American novel and producing what is clearly the most adventurous and original fiction in recent times. In fact, with this his eighth novel, DeLillo has won the right not only to be ranked with Pynchon and Gaddis but recognized as having surpassed them in brilliance, versatility and breadth of imagination."[18] Both the plot and characters have, for Aldridge, "the exact look and feel of contemporary reality." It's in DeLillo's "fierce satirical exaggeration" of this reality that Aldridge locates his value, but DeLillo's "bravely disturbing novels" have unfortunately earned him "vast unpopularity."

What close scrutiny of *White Noise* reveals—and I think the same is true for all of DeLillo's books—are a subtlety of craft and complexity of vision that neither the negative Yardley nor the positive Aldridge recognizes. Much of this study has been occupied with illustrating that Yardley's critiques simply do not fit DeLillo's deceptive and elusive work. I've also been concerned to show that the kind of praise that Aldridge voices doesn't very precisely correspond to DeLillo's achievement. DeLillo's looping novels are, indeed, "bravely disturbing," but he is not merely a "fierce" critic of contemporary life and technology, as *White Noise* manifests. "Vast unpopularity" with either the general or specialist reader also need not be DeLillo's reward if the reader—any reader—will follow with some care the loops that DeLillo traces. What cannot be imposed on any reader is appreciation of a sensibility. Often detached and rather defensively ironic in his early work and in the two short, third-person novels, *Players* and *Running Dog*, DeLillo has in his last two books allowed himself greater emotional range, combining his wit with compassion for contemporary man's self-destructive tropisms. What can be recognized by reviewers and academics, and what this study ultimately points toward, is the crucial, encompassing question to which DeLillo's sensibility responds and which his fiction, along with the works of other systems novelists and systems theorists, asks: Do our thinking and behavior and fictions correspond to all that we do know, and can know, about living systems and how they survive? If we will match our actions with our knowledge, as DeLillo does in his novels, contemporary and post-contemporary humankind could survive, head off personal and global self-destruction, prevent a final closing in the loop.

NOTES

1. Don DeLillo, *White Noise* (New York: Viking, 1985) 60; further references will be parenthetical.
2. Don DeLillo, *The Names* (New York: Knopf, 1982) 313; further references will be parenthetical (Na).
3. Don DeLillo, *Ratner's Star* (New York: Knopf, 1976) 4.
4. Don DeLillo, *Americana* (New York: Pocket, 1973) 198; further references will be parenthetical (Am).
5. Robert R. Harris, "A Talk with Don DeLillo," *New York Times Book Review*, 10 Oct. 1982: 26.
6. R. Z. Sheppard, in *Time*, 21 Jan. 1985: 71.
7. In a letter to me, dated 8 Nov. 1985.
8. Ernest Becker, *The Denial of Death* (New York: Free Press, 1973) 7; further references will be parenthetical (DoD).

9. Gregory Bateson, *Mind and Nature* (New York: Bantam, 1980); further references will be parenthetical (M&N).

10. Don DeLillo, "American Blood," *Rolling Stone*, 8 Dec. 1983: 27.

11. Cleo Birdwell, *Amazons* (New York: Holt, Rinehart and Winston, 1980).

12. Michel Serres, *The Parasite*, trans. Lawrence R. Schehr (Baltimore: Johns Hopkins Univ. Press, 1982).

13. Morris Berman, *The Reenchantment of the World* (New York: Bantam, 1984) 128–29.

14. Caryn James, "I Never Set Out to Write an Apocalyptic Novel," *New York Times Book Review*, 13 Jan. 1985: 31.

15. Anthony Wilden, *System and Structure*, 2nd ed. (London: Tavistock, 1980) 400, 410.

16. Michel Serres, "The Origin of Language: Biology, Information Theory, and Thermodynamics" in *Hermes: Literature, Science, Philosophy*, ed. Josue V. Harari and David F. Bell (Baltimore: Johns Hopkins Univ. Press, 1982) 81.

17. Jonathan Yardley in *Washington Post Book World*, 13 Jan. 1985: 3, 10; all quotes in this paragraph are from this review.

18. John Aldridge in *Chicago Tribune*, 13 Jan. 1985: 31–32; the remaining quotes in this paragraph are from Aldridge's review.

JOHN FROW

The Last Things Before the Last: *Notes on* White Noise

T he edges of the earth trembled in a darkish haze, Upon it lay
the sun, going down like a ship in a burning sea. Another
postmodern sunset, rich in romantic imagery. Why try to
describe it? It's enough to say that everything in our field of vision
seemed to exist in order to gather the light of this event.
—Don DeLillo, *White Noise*

Götterdämmerung. Why try to describe it? It's been written already, by
Conrad, among others. Postmodern writing always comes after, the
postmodern sunset is another sunset, an event within a series, never an
originating moment but mass-produced as much by the cosmological system
as by the system of writing. But the word postmodern here means more than
this: this passage from *White Noise* refers back to an earlier one about the
effects of an industrial (or postindustrial) disaster:

> Ever since the airborne toxic event, the sunsets had become
> almost unbearably beautiful. Not that there was a measurable
> connection. If the special character of Nyodene Derivative
> (added to the everyday drift of effluents, pollutants, contaminants
> and deliriants) had caused this aesthetic leap from already

From *The South Atlantic Quarterly* 89, no. 2 (Spring 1990): 413-429. © 1990 by Duke University
Press.

> brilliant sunsets to broad towering ruddled visionary skyscapes,
> tinged with dread, no one had been able to prove it.

The conditional clause structure and the repeated negation convey a pessimistic sense of undecidability, but it seems clear that industrial poison is a crucial component of the postmodern aesthetic, "rich in romantic imagery"—and vice versa. We could as well say "another poisonous sunset," or speak of an "airborne *aesthetic* event." It is not that the postmodern marks the return of aestheticism, a nonironic deployment of the full romantic cliché, but rather that it is the site of conjunction of the beautiful and the toxic, of Turner's *Fire at Sea* (1835), his "broad towering ruddled visionary skyscapes" and our postindustrial waste. This is thus, in Lyotard's sense, an aesthetic of the sublime: "With the sublime, the question of death enters the aesthetic question." It involves *terror* (the skyscapes are "tinged with dread") and ineffability, "the unpresentable in presentation itself." Why try to describe it? The twist here is that the sense of the inadequacy of representation comes not because of the transcendental or uncanny nature of the object but because of the multiplicity of prior representations. Priority of writing, priority of television, priority of the chain of metaphors in which the object is constructed. "We stood there watching a surge of florid light, like a heart pumping in a documentary on color TV."

Nor is there a lack of irony so much as a kind of self-effacement before the power of the stories which have gone before. The DeLillo passage I quoted at the beginning continues: "Not that this was one of the stronger sunsets. There had been more dynamic colors, a deeper sense of narrative sweep." Far from declining, the great nineteenth-century narratives continue to infuse the world with meaning, with a meaningfulness so total that the only possible response is ambivalence. The skies of this belated world are "under a spell, powerful and storied." They take on

> content, feeling, an exalted narrative life. The bands of color
> reach so high, seem at times to separate into their constituent
> parts. There are turreted skies, light storms, softly falling
> streamers. It is hard to know how we should feel about this. Some
> people are scared by the sunsets, some determined to be elated,
> but most of us don't know how to feel, are ready to go either way.

Malign and beautiful, interpretable not so much to infinity as within an endless loop between two contradictory poles, this labile postmodern object causes "awe, it is all awe, it transcends previous categories of awe, but we don't know whether we are watching in wonder or dread." Singular but recurrent, an event (a change, a deviation, a production of newness) within the serial reproduction of sameness, it announces (but how typically *modernist* a gesture) nothing but its own gesture of annunciation: "There was nothing to do but wait for the next sunset, when the sky would ring like bronze."

> In a town there are houses, plants in bay windows. People notice dying better. The dead have faces, automobiles. If you don't know a name, you know a street name, a dog's name. "He drove an orange Mazda." You know a couple of useless things about a person that become major facts of identification and cosmic placement when he dies suddenly, after a short illness, in his own bed, with a comforter and matching pillows, on a rainy Wednesday afternoon, feverish, a little congested in the sinuses and chest, thinking about his dry cleaning.

White Noise is obsessed with one of the classical aims of the realist novel: the construction of typicality. What this used to mean was a continuous process of extrapolation from the particular to the general, a process rooted in the existence of broad social taxonomies, general structures of human and historical destiny. Social typicality precedes the literary type—which is to say that the type is laid down in the social world; it is prior to and has a different kind of reality from secondary representations of it. First there is life, and then there is art. In *White Noise*, however, it's the other way round: social taxonomies are a function not of historical necessity but of style. Consider this description of the parents of Jack Gladney's students:

> The conscientious suntans. The well-made faces and wry looks. They feel a sense of renewal, of communal recognition. The women crisp and alert, in diet trim, knowing people's names. Their husbands content to measure out the time, distant but ungrudging, accomplished in parenthood, something about them suggesting massive insurance coverage.

This type is not a naive given, an embodied universality, but a self-conscious enactment; the middle-class parents know the ideality they are supposed to represent, and are deliberately living up to it. But this means that the type loses its purity, since it can always be imitated, feigned; or rather that there is no longer a difference in kind between the social category and the life-style which brings it into everyday being: the type ceaselessly imitates itself—through the ritual assembly of station wagons, for example, which "tells the parents they are a collection of the like-minded and the spiritually akin, a people, a nation."

It is thus no longer possible to distinguish meaningfully between a generality embedded in life and a generality embedded in representations of life. The communal recognition that constitutes the social class is part of a more diffuse system of recognitions conveyed through an infinitely detailed network of mediations. When Jack tries to characterize the convicted murderer his son Heinrich plays chess with, he draws on a range of mass-cultural information, like those psychological "profiles" that construct, above all for television, a taxonomy of criminal types: "Did he care for his weapons obsessively? Did he have an arsenal stacked in his shabby little room off a six-story concrete car park?" A computer operator "had a skinny neck and jug-handle ears to go with his starved skull—the innocent prewar look of a rural murderer." Those who would be affected by the airborne toxic event would be "people who live in mobile homes out in the scrubby parts of the county, where the fish hatcheries are." The type of the bigot, embodied in Murray Siskind's landlord, is "very good with all those little tools and fixtures that people in cities never know the names of," and tends to drive a panel truck "with an extension ladder on the roof and some kind of plastic charm dangling from the rearview mirror." The whole of this world is covered by a fine grid of typifications, so detailed and precise that it preempts and contains contingency.

If the type is susceptible to minute description, then the traditional novelistic tension between detail and generality falls away, and Lukács's account of typicality becomes unworkable. For Lukács, typicality is best embodied in the category of particularity (*Besonderheit*), which stands midway between philosophical generality (*Allgemeinheit*) and descriptive detail, or singularity (*Einzelheit*); in a postmodern economy of mediations, however, where representations of generality suffuse every pore of the world, the opposition between the general and the singular collapses as they merge into a single, undialectical unity. The *petit fait vrai* of the realist novel, the meaningless detail whose sole function is to establish a realism effect, is no longer meaningless. Reconstructing the scene of his wife's adultery, Jack mentions objects like "the fire-retardant carpet" and "the rental car keys on the dresser"; the definite article here marks these—as it does in much of Auden's poetry—not as concrete particulars but as generic indicators; they are not pieces of detail broken off from the contingent real but fragments of a mundane typicality.

The complexity and intricacy of the type—whether it is a character, a scene, or a landscape—is made possible by the constant repetition of its features: it is reproduced as a sort of amalgam of television and experience, the two now theoretically inseparable. At its simplest, this inseparability gives us something like the image of the grandparents who "share the Trimline phone, beamish old folks in hand-knit sweaters on fixed incomes." This is of course a joke about typicality, or rather about its construction in Hollywood movies and television advertising. A somewhat more complex play with typification is this:

> A woman in a yellow slicker held up traffic to let some children cross. I pictured her in a soup commercial taking off her oil-skin hat as she entered the cheerful kitchen where her husband stood over a pot of smoky lobster bisque, a smallish man with six weeks to live.

This description depends on the reader's recognition of the particular soup commercial, or at least the genre of commercials, that is being parodied by role reversal, and by the substitution of the traffic warden's yellow raincoat for the traditional and stereotyped fisherman's yellow raincoat—a substitution of the urban and feminine for the premodern world of masculine work. But part of the effect of this passage, as of that quoted at the beginning of this section, lies in its stylistic trick of pinning down the type (welcoming spouse at hearth) to an absurdly particular detail. What most of these typifications have in common, however, is their source in a chain of prior representations. Jack's dying, for example, is projected through a characterology taken from the movies, as in Murray's line to him that people "will depend on you to be brave. What people look for in a dying friend is a stubborn kind of gravel-voiced nobility, a refusal to give in, with moments of indomitable humor." "The cliché is a simulacrum, an ideal form that shapes and constrains both life and death.

Let us say that this new mode of typicality has two features: it is constructed in representations which are then lived as real; and it is so detailed that it is not opposed to the particular. The name usually given to it in the genre of postmodernity is the simulacrum. Here are some notes:

(1) Early in *White Noise* Jack and Murray visit the most photographed barn in America. They pass five signs advertising it before reaching the site, and when they arrive there find forty cars and a tour bus in the car park, and a number of people taking pictures. Murray delivers a commentary: "No one sees the barn," he says. "Once you've seen the signs about the barn, it becomes impossible to see the barn.... We're not here to capture an image, we're here to maintain one. Every photograph reinforces the aura.... We've agreed to be part of a collective perception. This literally colors our vision.

A religious experience in a way, like all tourism.... They are taking pictures of taking pictures.... What was the barn like before it was photographed? ... What did it look like, how was it different from other barns, how was it similar to other barns? We can't answer these questions because we've read the signs, seen the people snapping the Pictures. We can't get outside the aura. We're part of the aura. We're here, we're now." To this should be added another comment: "Murray says it's possible to be homesick for a place even when you are there."

(2) At the center of Walter Benjamin's argument about the mechanical reproduction of representations was the thesis that it would have the effect— the liberatory effect—of destroying the quasi-religious aura surrounding the work of art. It is clear that the opposite has happened: that the commodification of culture has worked to preserve the myth of origins and of authenticity.

(3) In the main street of DeLillo's Iron City is "a tall old Moorish movie theater, now remarkably a mosque"; it is flanked by "blank structures called the Terminal Building, the Packer Building, the Commerce Building. How close this was to a classic photography of regret."

(4) The evacuation of Jack and his family is conducted by an organization called SIMUVAC, which is "short for simulated evacuation. A new state program they're still battling for funds for." When Jack points out to one of its employees that this is not a simulated but a real evacuation, he replies: "We thought we could use it as a model"; it gives them "a chance to use the real event in order to rehearse the simulation."

(5) For Plato, the simulacrum is the copy of a copy. Violating an ethics of imitation, its untruth is defined by its distance from the original and by its exposure of the scandal that an imitation can in its turn function as a reality to be copied (and so on endlessly).

The most influential contemporary account of the simulacrum and the chain of simulations is that of Baudrillard. His is a melancholy vision of the emptying out of meaning (that is, of originals, of stable referents) from a world which is henceforth made up of closed and self-referring systems of semiotic exchange. In a state of what he calls hyperreality the real becomes indefinitely reproducible, an effect, merely, of the codes which continue to generate it. From the very beginning Baudrillard has been hostile to the scandalous opacity of systems of mediation. His is a historical vision: there was a referent; it has been lost; and this loss, as in Plato, is the equivalent of a moral fall.

By contrast, the account that Deleuze gives of the simulacrum in *Différence et répétition*, while retaining the formal structure of the Platonic model, cuts it off from its ties to a lost original, and cuts it off, too, from all its Baudrillardian melancholy. The world we inhabit is one in which identity is simulated in the play of difference and repetition, but this simulation carries no sense of loss. Instead, freeing ourselves of the Platonic ontology means denying the priority of an original over the copy, of a model over the image. It means glorifying the reign of simulacra, and affirming that any original is itself already a copy, divided in its very origin. According to Deleuze, the simulacrum "is that system in which the different is related to the different through difference itself."

(6) The most horrifying fact about the evacuation is that it isn't even reported on network television. "Does this thing happen so often that nobody cares anymore?" asks one man. "Do they think this is just television?"

(7) The smoke from the chemical spill is initially called a "feathery plume," then a "black billowing cloud," and finally an "airborne toxic event." Steffie and Denise, Jack's daughters, keep experiencing the symptoms described in the bulletin preceding the current one. One of these symptoms is *déjà vu*, and Jack wonders, "Is it possible to have a false perception of an illusion? Is there a true *déjà vu* and a false *déjà vu*?" Later his wife Babette has a *déjà vu* experience of *déjà vu*.

(8) "The phone rang and I picked it up. A woman's voice delivered a high-performance hello. It said it was computer-generated, part of a marketing survey aimed at determining current levels of consumer desire. It said it would ask a series of questions, pausing after each to give me a chance to reply." Steffie, answering its questions, reads the label on her sweater: "virgin acrylic."

(9) Peter Wollen writes that in "an age marked by an ever-increasing and ever-accelerating proliferation of signs, of all types, the immediate environment becomes itself increasingly dominated by signs, rather than natural objects or events. The realm of signs becomes not simply a 'second nature' but a primary 'reality.' (The quotes around 'reality' mark the effacement of the traditional distinction between reality and representation in a world dominated by representations.)"

(10) Lighted by helicopters, the airborne toxic event moves like an operatic death ship across the landscape: "In its tremendous size, its dark and bulky menace, its escorting aircraft, the cloud resembled a national promotion for death, a multimillion-dollar campaign backed by radio spots, heavy print and billboard, TV saturation."

The world of *White Noise* is a world of primary representations which neither precede nor follow the real but are themselves real—although it is true that they always have the *appearance* both of preceding another reality (as a model to be followed) and of following it (as copy). But this appearance must itself be taken seriously.

Consider these two passages about an adult looking at sleeping children: "I looked for a blanket to adjust, a toy to remove from a child's warm grasp, feeling I'd wandered into a TV moment." And "[t]hese sleeping children were like figures in an ad for the Rosicrucians, drawing a powerful beam of light from somewhere off the page." Both moments are mediated by another moment, a memory or a metaphor which shapes them, endows them with a certain structure; this structure is a part of their reality. It is quite possible to distinguish one reality (the sleeping children) from another (the TV moment, the ad for the Rosicrucians), just as we can in principle distinguish literal from metaphorical language; it is possible for the novel to be ironical about the gap between these two realities. But this distinguishing and this irony are insecure. Real moments and TV moments interpenetrate each other—and it is, in any case, another (novelistic) representation which offers us this reality and this distinction. The world is so saturated with representations that it becomes increasingly difficult to separate primary actions from imitations of actions.

Indeed, it seems that it is only within the realm of representation that it is possible to postulate a realm of primary actions which would be quite distinct from representation. During the evacuation Jack notices groups of refugees:

> Out in the open, keeping their children near, carrying what they could, they seemed to be part of some ancient destiny, connected in doom and pain to a whole history of people trekking across wasted landscapes. There was an epic quality about them that made me wonder for the first time at the scope of our predicament.

What he is seeing is of course a movie; and it is precisely because it is cinematic, because of its "epic quality," that the scene is real and serious to him. "Epic" here perhaps means something like "naive," lacking self-consciousness, and above all lacking any awareness of the cinematic nature of the experience. This paradox is even clearer in the case of Jack's fantasy about the death of Attila the Hun: "I want to believe he lay in his tent, wrapped in animal skins, as in some internationally financed movie epic, and said brave cruel things to his aides and retainers." The image is again of a heroic lack of self-consciousness, a naive immediacy to life and death:

No weakening of the spirit. No sense of the irony of human existence…. He accepted death as an experience that flows naturally from life, a wild ride through the forest, as would befit someone known as the Scourge of God. This is how it ended for him, with his attendants cutting off their hair and disfiguring their own faces in barbarian tribute, as the camera pulls back out of the tent and pans across the night sky of the fifth century A.D., clear and uncontaminated, bright-banded with shimmering worlds.

It is only in the movies, only through cultural mediation, that a vision of nonmediation is possible—and therefore absurd.

The central mediating agency in this world is television; indeed, for "most people there are only two places in the world. Where they live and their TV set. If a thing happens on television, we have every right to find it fascinating, whatever it is." The major statement is a speech made by Murray. He tells his students that

> they're already too old to figure importantly in the making of society. Minute by minute they're beginning to diverge from each other. "Even as we sit here," I tell them, "you are spinning out from the core, becoming less recognizable as a group, less targetable by advertisers and mass-producers of culture. Kids are a true universal. But you're well beyond that, already beginning to drift, to feel estranged from the products you consume. Who are they designed for? What is your place in the marketing scheme? Once you're out of school, it is only a matter of time before you experience the vast loneliness and dissatisfaction of consumers who have lost their group identity."

The assumptions are astounding: we know that human worth can't be measured in terms of our relation to consumption—to money and commodities—and that the order of things transcends "the marketing scheme." But all that Murray is doing is stating the central, the deadly serious principles of a capitalist society. This is really how it is, the marketing scheme really does work, for most purposes, in a capitalist society, as the scheme of things; the whole social organization is geared to this equation. The propositions are monstrous, but only because we find it so hard to believe in the true and central awfulness of capitalism.

Television comes into this because of its crucial role in marketing—and this is to say that its importance lies not in the sheer quantity of representations that it generates, nor even in their content as messages, but in the fact that they are always directly linked to commodity production and the generation of profits, and that in order to serve these ends they work as an integral part of a system for the shaping and reshaping of human identity. Murray's students are thus "beginning to feel they ought to turn against the medium, exactly as an earlier generation turned against their parents and their country." When he tells them that "they have to learn to look as children again. Root out content. Find codes and messages," they reply that television "is just another name for junk mail."

But cultural criticism—the moralistic critique of the mass media that has been the stock in trade of liberal journalism—is of course not an option, certainly not for this novel, which is much more interested, in its own ironic but unconditional way, in, for example, Murray's quasi-mystical experience of television. It is, he says, "a primal force in the American home. Sealed-off, self-contained, self-referring." Television

> offers incredible amounts of psychic data. It opens ancient memories of world birth, it welcomes us into the grid, the network of little buzzing dots that make up the picture pattern. There is light, there is sound. I ask my students, "What more do you want?" Look at the wealth of data concealed in the grid, in the bright packaging, the jingles, the slice-of-life commercials, the products hurtling out of darkness, the coded messages and endless repetitions, like chants, like mantras. "*Coke is it, Coke is it, Coke is it.*" The medium practically overflows with sacred formulas if we can remember how to respond innocently and get past our irritation, weariness and disgust.

A whole aesthetic is elaborated here, although unfortunately it's made up of the dregs of other aesthetic systems. Murray has the quixotic ability to disregard the banal surface of television and, with all the innocence of a formalist semiotician, to discover a cornucopia of aesthetic information in its organization. The key term here is "data," a meaningless word which suggests that the relevant level at which to decode the television message is that of the physical structure of light on the screen—but in fact the word has the effect of conflating this level with other levels of information. Gestalt and perceptual psychology mingle with genre theory and a mysticism of the proper name in Murray's postcritical celebration of the medium. For his students, however, television is "worse than junk mail. Television is the death throes of human consciousness, according to them. They're ashamed of their television past. They want to talk about movies." Murray is a postmodernist. His students, wishing to return to the high modernism of cinema, are postpostmodernist.

> The smoke alarm went off in the hallway upstairs, either to let us know the battery had just died or because the house was on fire. We finished our lunch in silence.

When the jug-eared computer operator taps into Jack's data profile (his history—but what history? "Where was it located exactly? Some state or federal agency, some insurance company or credit firm or medical clearinghouse?") he finds that "[w]e have a situation": "It's what we call a massive data-base tally." This tally doesn't actually mean anything except that Jack is "the sum total of [his] data." Like so many signifying structures in *White Noise* it offers a profound interpretability but withdraws any precise meaning, or is at best deeply ambivalent. It's nothing but data, raw and unreadable. And what constitutes data is of course not something given, as the word suggests, but a set of constructs, figures whose significance lies not in their inherent structure but in the decision that has been taken to frame them in a certain way. The word embodies all the pathos of an impoverished and institutionalized empiricism. Its faultiness is caught in a joke about the search for contamination in the girls' school; the search is carried out by men in Mylex suits, but "because Mylex is itself a suspect material, the results tended to be ambiguous."

Whereas the sign causes unease, a sense that there is more to be known, the proper name is the site of a magical plenitude. Proper names tend to come in cadenced triads: "The Airport Marriott, the Downtown Travelodge, the Sheraton Inn and Conference Center." "Dacron, Orlon, Lycra Spandex." "Krylon, Rust-Oleum, Red Devil." They appear mysteriously in the midst of the mundane world of novelistic narrative, detached, functionless, unmotivated. At the end of a paragraph on Babette's fear of death, "the emptiness, the sense of cosmic darkness," occurs the single line: "MasterCard, Visa, American Express." The sonorous, Miltonic names lack all epic content, and they are intruded into the text without any marker of a speaking source. In a later episode the sleeping Steffie, speaking in "a language not quite of this world," utters two words

> that seemed to have a ritual meaning, part of a verbal spell or ecstatic chant.
> *Toyota Celica.*

> A long moment passed before I realized this was the name
> of an automobile. The truth only amazed me more. The
> utterance was beautiful and mysterious, gold-shot with looming
> wonder. It was like the name of an ancient power in the sky,
> tablet-carved in cuneiform.

Here there is a definite source for the utterance, but in another sense Steffie
is not this source: the words are spoken through her, by her unconscious but
also, as Jack recognizes, by the unconscious of her culture. Yet for all their
commercial banality (the same that echoes gloriously through a phrase
caught on the radio: "It's the rainbow hologram that gives this credit card a
marketing intrigue"), the names remain charged with an opaque significance,
so that Jack remarks: "Whatever its source, the utterance struck me with the
impact of a moment of splendid transcendence."

The question of the source of enunciation of these proper names
remains an interesting one, as there seems to be a definite progression in the
novel from an apparently impersonal enunciation to more localized points of
origin. In a description of the supermarket, "full of elderly people who look
lost among the hedgerows," the words "Dristan Ultra, Dristan Ultra" occur
on a separate line but are enclosed within inverted commas, which indicates
a diegetic source—probably a public address system in the supermarket. The
words have the same sort of status as the voices emanating from the
television and the radio that punctuate the life of the house. At other times a
psychological source seems to be indicated—when the words "leaded,
unleaded, super unleaded" intrude into Jack and Babette's desperate
lovemaking; or when the spelled out acronyms "Random Access Memory,
Acquired Immune Deficiency Syndrome, Mutual Assured Destruction" cross
the text as Jack is crossing the slum districts of Iron City. At other times there
seem to be verbal associations flowing between the proper names and their
textual context: "I watched light climb into the rounded summits of high-
altitude clouds. Clorets, Velamints, Freedent." The movement is not just the
phonetic one from clouds (perhaps "cloud turrets") to Clorets but is also a
circuit between the novel's imagery of sunsets and the poetry of advertising.
Another example: Jack experiences "aural torment" as he imagines Babette
making love to the mysterious Mr. Gray:

> ... Then gloom moved in around the gray-sheeted bed, a circle
> slowly closing.
>   Panasonic.

Like the syllables of the Proustian name, the last word is multiply motivated.
"Pana-" is the circle slowly closing, "sonic" is Jack's aural torment, and there

are overdetermined traces of "panoramic" and, of course, television. But as with the name in Proust, the point is the excess of the poetic signifier over its component parts, its transcendental character, its plenitude. The poetic word comes from elsewhere, and if it seems to be spoken by a character (like the woman passing on the street who says "a decongestant, an antihistamine, a cough suppressant, a pain reliever"), this is nevertheless only a proximate source, a relay. The proper name is its own absolute origin.

At lunchtime Wilder sits surrounded by "open cartons, crumpled tinfoil, shiny bags of potato chips, bowls of pasty substances covered with plastic wrap, flip-top rings and twist ties, individually wrapped slices of orange cheese." Meals in this house lack the monumental solidity of the meals in *Buddenbrooks* or even in the James Bond novels; they are depthless, physically insubstantial. At times the staple junk food is opposed to the "real" (but never achieved) lunch of yogurt and wheat germ, but the truth of the matter is that eating has entirely to do with surfaces. Even chewing gum is described in terms of its wrappings.

The supermarket is the privileged place for a phenomenology of surfaces. Murray is a devotee of generic brands, and he takes their "flavorless packaging" to be the sign of a new austerity, a new "spiritual consensus." The packaging on supermarket goods, he says, "is the last avant-garde. Bold new forms. The power to shock." But even unprocessed and unpackaged foods take on the *form* of packaging: "There were six kinds of apples, there were exotic melons in several pastels. Everything seemed to be in season, sprayed, burnished, bright." And later: "The fruit was gleaming and wet, hard-edged. There was a self-conscious quality about it. It looked carefully observed, like four-color fruit in a guide to photography. We veered right at the plastic jugs of spring water." The kitchen, too, is a place of containers and packagings— the freezer, for example, where "a strange crackling sound came off the plastic food wrap, the snug covering for half eaten things, the Ziploc sacks of liver and ribs, all gleaming with sleety crystals."

But the force of this is not a sentimental regret for a lost world of depths, a nostalgic opposition of surface to substance. There is a depth to be found in this world (this house, this novel), but it is not a fullness of being; rather, it's the other end of the packaging process, a sort of final interiority of the wrapping. Jack comes across it when he searches through the trash bag of the compactor:

> An oozing cube of semi-mangled cans, clothes hangers, animal bones and other refuse. The bottles were broken, the cartons flat. Product colors were undiminished in brightness and intensity.

Fats, juices and heavy sludges seeped through layers of pressed vegetable matter. I felt like an archaeologist about to sift through a finding of tool fragments and assorted cave trash.

This is the heart of domesticity:

> I found a banana skin with a tampon inside. Was this the dark underside of consumer consciousness? I came across a horrible clotted mass of hair, soap, ear swabs, crushed roaches, flip-top rings, sterile pads smeared with pus and bacon fat, strands of frayed dental floss, fragments of ballpoint refills, toothpicks still displaying bits of impaled food. There was a pair of shredded undershorts with lipstick markings, perhaps a memento of the Grayview Motel.

The list is of an accretion of wastes that have come full circle from the supermarket but which still retain the formal structure (and even the "undiminished colors") of the presentation of surfaces. At the heart of this inside is nothing more than a compacted mass of outsides.

White Noise is a domestic novel, continuously concerned with the secret life of the house—with the closet doors that open by themselves, with the chirping of the radiator, with the sounds of the sink and the washing machine and the compactor, with the jeans tumbling in the dryer. The narrator writes of the "numerous and deep" levels of data in the kitchen, and speaks of the kitchen and the bedroom as "the major chambers around here, the power haunts, the sources." But the center of the life of the house is the voice of the television. This is what it says:

> Let's sit half-lotus and think about our spines.
> . . . .
> If it breaks easily into pieces, it is called shale. When wet, it smells like clay.
> . . . .
> Until Florida surgeons attached an artificial flipper.
> . . . .
> (In a British voice): There are forms of vertigo that do not include spinning.
> . . . .
> And other trends that could dramatically impact your portfolio.
> . . . .

This creature has developed a complicated stomach in keeping with its leafy diet.

. . . .

Now we will put the little feelers on the butterfly.

. . . .

Meanwhile here is a quick and attractive lemon garnish suitable for any sea food.

. . . .

Now watch this. Joanie is trying to snap Ralph's patella with a *bushido* stun kick. She makes contact, he crumples, she runs.

. . . .

They're not booing—they're saying, "Bruce, Bruce."

Television is about everything. It is about the ordinary, the banal, information for living our lives. It is rarely the voice of apocalypse.

PAUL A. CANTOR

"Adolf, We Hardly Knew You"

after the plastic surgery, the
guitar lessons, the war, hitler
learns he can sing. high atop his
pink palace, he wonders why he didn't
think of this before. his fans are
better, his outfits brighter, and the
drugs are the best he's ever had. people
love him. he still can't act, but hell,
now he gets paid for walking funny.[1]
                                    —Keith Alley

ADOLF HITLER is no laughing matter. In a world where truth is now
generally thought to be relative, Hitler often seems to stand as the lone
remaining absolute: the incarnation of absolute evil. Even the most broad-
minded tolerance for cultural diversity seems to stop short of embracing
Nazi culture as a legitimate human possibility. Hitler has become an
argument stopper: "You say all value is subjective: Does that mean we have
no objective grounds for condemning what Hitler did at Auschwitz and
Buchenwald?" in short, people who can agree on nothing else will join
together in rejecting Hitler and all he stood for. To defend or admire Hitler

---

From *New Essays on White Noise*. © 1991 by Cambridge University Press.

is to risk removing oneself from the acceptable range of rational discourse and branding oneself as a dangerous extremist or an outright kook.

Don DeLillo is a disturbing writer, and nothing shows more clearly how disturbing he can be than his unconventional treatment of Hitler in *White Noise*. The novel centers on Jack Gladney, a professor who specializes in Hitler studies at a small college. What is so striking about the way Hitler is presented in the novel is its overall blandness. In Gladney's world, Hitler appears to be just another subject of academic discourse, arousing no special passions. Speaking of Hitler, Gladney says at one point: "It's not a question of good and evil" (63). In *White Noise*, Hitler does not seem to evoke the moral indignation and even metaphysical horror that have become our standard cultural response to the *Führer*. In fact, the whole idea of Hitler studies quickly becomes comic in DeLillo's portrayal, especially when he links it to the study of another twentieth-century giant, Elvis Presley.

Whatever one may ultimately conclude about DeLillo's treatment of Hitler, it is surprising that critics have generally not viewed it as at least a problem to begin with. Many discussions of *White Noise* do not so much as mention Hitler; most touch on the subject only in passing, seldom even noting the oddness of what DeLillo does with Hitler in the novel. The only critic I have found who chooses to make an issue of Hitler in *White Noise* is Bruce Bawer. In a generally negative assessment of the novelist's career, he writes: "Perhaps the most disturbing aspect of *White Noise* is Jack's fascination with Hitler."[2] Bawer is troubled by the way Hitler is in effect assimilated to the mainstream of Western culture in *White Noise*:

> DeLillo's offense, to my mind, is that he refuses to make distinctions. To him, as to Jack Gladney, the question of Hitler is simply "not a question of good and evil." Nor, it is clear, do moral distinctions enter into his appraisal of any human act. (41)

Bawer is obviously being hasty here in identifying DeLillo with one of his characters, and assuming that just because Hitler is not a moral issue for Jack Gladney, he is not one for his author. Nevertheless, Bawer is right to raise Hitler as an issue in discussing *White Noise*. The bland acceptance of DeLillo's treatment of Hitler in academic circles seems to mirror the very phenomenon *White Noise* portrays: a scholarly world so open-minded that it can now accommodate any subject without evidently blinking an eye. Bawer is also right to note that DeLillo's interest in Hitler is not confined to *White Noise*. Among his earlier works, *End Zone* contains a character named Hauptfuhrer, and *Great Jones Street* contains a rock group which assumes the name of Hitler's father, Schicklgruber. DeLillo's most extensive treatment of

Hitler occurs in *Running Dog*, a novel which deals with the search for a supposedly pornographic film of the *Führer* in his last days in his Berlin bunker. Clearly DeLillo is fascinated with the phenomenon of Hitler, and presumably believes that to understand the twentieth century, we must somehow come to terms with Hitler and Nazism. If we want to appreciate DeLillo's achievement fully, especially in *White Noise*, we must accordingly examine his portrayal of Hitler.

2

Before rushing like Bawer to condemn DeLillo for moral indifference to Nazism, we ought to recognize that *White Noise* is not itself an example of Hitler studies, but rather a novel which portrays a professor involved in Hitler studies. DeLillo may be trying to characterize the contemporary world by showing that such a phenomenon as Hitler studies has become possible in it. In fact, DeLillo could find no better example of the flattening-out of contemporary existence than the routinization of Hitler's charisma at the College-on-the-Hill. Like all of DeLillo's work, *White Noise* portrays postmodern America. Faced with an ideology of freedom and self-development, and swamped by an overabundance of material resources, DeLillo's Americans are set adrift in a sea of possibilities, which, being equally available, become equally valuable, or, what is the same thing, equally valueless.

In particular, this situation results in the distinctively postmodern attitude toward history as a kind of museum, or, better yet, a supermarket of human possibilities, where people are free to shop around for their values and identities. Modernism defined itself in opposition to previous history, rejecting movements such as Romanticism and Victorianism in the name of the new truths it claimed to have discovered. Modernism conceived of itself as coming at the end of history in the sense of its culmination, the privileged moment when traditional myths were shattered and the truth finally emerged once and for all. The modernist skyscraper, for example, starkly proclaims its truthfulness, scorning all previous architecture for failing to understand the principle that form follows function. As the heir to the modernist heritage, postmodernism finds itself forced to live in the posthistorical moment. No longer thinking of itself as advancing beyond previous movements or eras to some kind of authentic and definitive truth, postmodernism adopts a new—one might say more tolerant—attitude toward history. History loses its linear thrust into the present and beyond, becoming instead a repository of equally available styles and ideas. Consider the typical postmodern building, with an Egyptian pyramid here, a Roman arch there, and a Renaissance portico somewhere else. This is the flattening out of history: removing the privilege from any particular historical moment and hence equalizing all historical possibilities.

DeLillo portrays this process most tellingly in the wide repertory of imagined sexual roles available to Jack and his wife, Babette. Looking for the stimulation of pornography, this postmodern couple can take their pick from everything history has to offer:

> I said, "Pick your century. Do you want to read about Etruscan slave girls, Georgian rakes? I think we have some literature on flagellation brothels. What about the Middle Ages? We have incubi and succubi. Nuns galore." (29)

The problem with this pornographic cornucopia is that it overwhelms Jack and Babette, draining the eroticism from their existence. From the way they endlessly talk about and analyze their love life, it is clear that they have become too self-conscious about sex. With all the imaginative possibilities open to him, Jack is finally reduced to the basest level of erotic stimulation:

> I decided on the twentieth century. I ... went down the hall to [my son's] room to find a trashy magazine Babette might read from, the type that features letters from readers detailing their sexual experiences. This struck me as one of the few things the modern imagination has contributed to the history of erotic practices. There is a double fantasy at work in such letters. People write down imagined episodes and then see them published in a national magazine. Which is the greater stimulation? (30)

For DeLillo the twentieth century has characteristically added to the history of erotic practices not a new form of sexual act, but a new form of *recording* sexual acts. The self-reflexive and mediated quality of this erotic pleasure is what makes it postmodern. What stimulates people is reading their own fantasies printed by the national media.

Jack's statement, "I decided on the twentieth century," is particularly revealing. Postmodern man is so obsessed with his autonomy that he refuses to accept even his historical moment as a matter of fate. Rather it must become a matter of free choice, like one's job or one's hairstyle. Because the whole range of history seems to be open to Jack, he can claim not to have been born into the twentieth century but to have chosen it. The price one pays for this complete freedom in adopting one's role in life, however, is that it becomes merely a role. In *White Noise* the autonomous self becomes the inauthentic self As this episode shows, the sexual identities of Jack and Babette dissolve into a sea of erotic possibilities. To gain the freedom they crave, they must transpose sex onto an imaginary plane, where their supposedly most private experience turns out to be mediated by the fantasies of others. Thus one of the central symbols in *White Noise* is the twentieth-century supermarket, as explained by Jack's colleague, Murray Jay Siskind:

> "Unpackaged meat, fresh bread," he went on. "Exotic fruits, rare cheeses. Products from twenty countries. It's like being at some crossroads of the ancient world, a Persian bazaar or boom town on the Tigris." (169)

Here is the postmodern situation in capsule: Everything, no matter how exotic or rare, is equally available, from all over the world, and indeed seemingly from all eras of history. Everything is neatly arranged, everything is labeled, and, presumably, everything has a price.

It is while strolling up and down the aisles of the vast supermarket of academic possibilities that Jack Gladney comes upon an item marked *Hitler* and thus discovers his life's work:

> I invented Hitler studies in North America in March of 1968. It was a cold bright day with intermittent winds out of the east. When I suggested to the chancellor that we might build a whole department around Hitler's life and work, he was quick to see the possibilities. It was an immediate and electrifying success. (4)

However German its subject, Gladney's department of Hitler studies is a characteristically *American* phenomenon. DeLillo stresses the initial arbitrariness of Gladney's choice of Hitler as the basis for his academic career, no matter how obsessive he may later become about the topic. To underline the inauthenticity of Gladney's commitment to Hitler studies, DeLillo points out that Jack does not even know German and thus must fake his way through his career as a Hitler expert (31). Like a good businessman, Gladney comes up with the idea of Hitler studies as a clever gimmick at a specific moment in time, when no one else sees the potential in the enterprise. He merchandises the idea like a commercial product. His success has less to do with the intrinsic quality of the idea than with its novelty. Jack finds an open niche in the academic marketplace and exploits it to the fullest.

Once a horrifying phenomenon like Hitler can be represented, it can be stripped of its aura and turned into a commodity. DeLillo shows this process concretely in *Running Dog*, where the putative film of Hitler becomes a hot item, sought after and bid for by a wide range of business interests. Gladney becomes the envy of his colleagues such as Siskind because of the skill with which he develops his Hitler line:

> You've established a wonderful thing here with Hitler. You created it, you nurtured it, you made it your own. Nobody on the faculty of any college or university in this part of the country can so much as utter the word Hitler without a nod in your direction.... He is now your Hitler, Gladney's Hitler.... The college is internationally known as a result of Hitler studies.... You've evolved an entire system around this figure.... I marvel at the effort. It was masterful, shrewd and stunningly preemptive. (11–12)

Jack's appropriation of Hitler follows familiar patterns of capitalist enterprise, including product promotion and consolidation of a territory. Hitler would seem to symbolize all the irrational and dangerous forces that have destabilized modern life, but for Gladney he provides the solid foundation of a successful career. When one of Gladney's former wives asks politely, "How is Hitler?" he replies: "Fine, solid, dependable" (89). This surprising transformation of the once willful tyrant into someone reliable is the result of the increasing familiarity and reproducibility of his image in the marketplace. Through the power of the media, representations of Hitler have proliferated and permeated every corner of twentieth-century-life:

> "He was on again last night."
> "He's always on. We couldn't have television without him." (63)

Television brings Hitler into our homes and hence domesticates him, assimilating him into the mainstream of modern life.

Beyond the attenuation of the horror of Hitler that results from his achieving a kind of celebrity status in the media, DeLillo focuses on what happens to the *Führer* when the academic world gets its dessicated and dessicating hands on him. Along with intermediate Calculus and Introductory French, Hitler enters the course catalogue in the form of the only class Chairman Gladney teaches:

> Advanced Nazism, three hours a week, restricted to qualified seniors, a course of study designed to cultivate historical perspective, theoretical rigor and mature insight into the continuing mass appeal of fascist tyranny, with special emphasis on parades, rallies and uniforms, three credits, written reports. (25)

As always the brilliant parodist, DeLillo captures perfectly the style of college catalogues, which can turn the most exciting subject into something prosaic and banal. Absorbed into the academic world, what many consider to be the most frightening reality of twentieth-century life contracts in scope ("three hours a week, restricted to qualified seniors") and becomes a matter of routine ("three credits, written reports"). The sober course description actually contains a bombshell when it speaks of the *continuing* mass appeal of fascist tyranny, suggesting that the phenomenon of Hitler has not been successfully suppressed and contained. But buried as it is in a course catalogue, this revelation loses all its force, soon to become the subject of term papers rather than of public alarm.

The culmination of the marketing of the *Führer* in *White Noise* is the academic equivalent of a trade show, the Hitler conference Gladney organizes:

> Three days of lectures, workshops and panels. Hitler scholars from seventeen states and nine foreign countries. Actual Germans would be in attendance. (33)

DeLillo is aware of how all-pervasive the ethos of capitalism has become in America. Even academic language is infected by the hucksterism of the advertising world. The advance billing of the conference only underlines the absurdity of trying to capture the enormity of the phenomenon of Hitler within the confines of "three days of lectures, workshops and panels." The international makeup of the conference reflects the characteristic cosmopolitanism of the postmodern world, in which the distinctive meaning of Hitler as a national phenomenon—it was after all *National* Socialism—threatens to dissolve. On the face of it, the idea of coming to a random small town in the United States in order to study Hitler seems ridiculous. Only the promise of "actual Germans" in attendance seems to offer any hope of authenticity in the conference.

But the conference proves to be a meaningless affair, failing to confront the seriousness of Hitler in any way. Like most academic conferences, it turns out to be largely a diversion for the participants, a kind of vacation:

> About ninety Hitler scholars would spend the three days of the conference attending lectures, appearing on panels, going to movies. They would wander the campus with their names lettered in gothic type on laminated tags pinned to their lapels. They would exchange Hitler gossip, spread the usual sensational rumors about the last days in the *führerbunker*. (273–4)

Hitler has become all too familiar to these scholars, reduced to the level of a mere subject of gossip. DeLillo's satire is right on target. The name tags with the gothic lettering are the perfect touch of academic kitsch in the scene. The cosmopolitan cast of characters only serves to highlight how national differences have been flattened out in the postmodern world: "It was interesting to see how closely they resembled each other despite the wide diversity of national and regional backgrounds" (274). Although Gladney feels even more inauthentic than usual in the presence of the "actual Germans," it turns out that they are no more capable than he of responding to the Nazi phenomenon with any depth: "They told Hitler jokes and played pinochle" (274).

The density of satiric detail in passages such as this suggests, contrary to Bawer, that DeLillo is distanced from the attitude of his characters toward Hitler. For DeLillo the academic treatment of Hitler becomes emblematic of a larger cultural problem. Any attempt to articulate the horror of a phenomenon like Hitler must inevitably fall short of the mark, and, what is worse, risks draining the horror by assimilating it into familiar categories. Given their distinctive habits, academics are in fact the least capable of coming to terms with Hitler and Nazism. Scholars hate to deal with or even acknowledge the unique; they always want to lump phenomena together under categories, to find continuity where others see discontinuity, in short, to place phenomena in "traditions." By setting *White Noise* within the academic world, DeLillo may have taken us close to the bloodless heart of postmodernism. What I have been calling the distinctively postmodern attitude toward history is, *mutatis mutandis*, a characteristically scholarly attitude: that all periods of history are equally valuable and worthy of study. It is a curious fact that postmodernism as a cultural phenomenon has coincided with the era in which the university has come to play an increasingly dominant role in cultural life, as a patron, an arbiter of taste, and an interpreter of meaning to the general public. Far from wholly identifying with professors like Jack Gladney, DeLillo may be using *White Noise* to suggest how the academic world, with its inability to deal with phenomena like Hitler authentically, has contributed to what might be called the postmodernization of contemporary life.

3

One could thus defuse the criticism of Bawer with the argument that the idea of Hitler studies in *White Noise* is only DeLillo's measure of the power of the alliance of the media and the academy in the postmodern world to trivialize even the most significant of historical phenomena. But this approach runs the risk of trivializing *White Noise*, making it tame and thus draining it of its power to disturb. DeLillo may play Hitler for laughs in *White Noise*, but he takes him seriously as well. Hitler is so potent a reality that even all the forces of the postmodern world cannot wholly drain him of his frightening aura. That, in fact, is why Gladney becomes obsessed with Hitler. In a world "full of abandoned meanings" (184), Gladney is searching for someone who can restore significance and value to his life, and the powerful image of Hitler offers fullness to his emptiness. As Siskind explains to Jack:

> "Helpless and fearful people are drawn to magical figures, mythic figures, epic men who intimidate and darkly loom."
> "You're talking about Hitler, I take it."
> "Some people are larger than life. Hitler is larger than death. You thought he would protect you.... 'Submerge me,' you said. 'Absorb my fear.' On one level you wanted to conceal yourself in Hitler and his works. On another level you wanted to use him to grow in significance and strength." (287)

DeLillo is not a participant in the Hitler phenomenon, but its pathologist. In Jack's comic—because halfhearted, academic, and postmodern—way, he repeats the tragedy of Weimar Germany. DeLillo understands the psychological appeal of totalitarianism. When people lose their traditional bearings in life, especially religious guidance, they are wide open to the power of anyone who appears to have the conviction and self-assurance to lead them and thus restore meaning to their lives. DeLillo has a chilling sense that in the twentieth century only the criminals have the courage of their convictions. That is why one of the characters in *Running Dog* admires the Mafia:

> "Who are the only ones who believe in what they're doing? The only ones who aren't constantly adjusting, constantly wavering—this way, that way...."
> "The families," she said.
> "They're serious. They're totally committed. The only ones. They see clearly, *bullseye*, straight ahead. They know what they belong to. They don't question the premise."[3]

Uninfected by modern or postmodern doubts, the Mafiosi are still capable of genuine commitment and hence can recapture something of "Renaissance glory" (218). Like Thomas Mann in his analysis of fascism in his story "Mario and the Magician," DeLillo grasps the power of the man with a single-minded will in a world of individuals who have lost the ability to will.

It is significant that DeLillo refers to the Mafia in *Running Dog* as "the families." One of the keys to its power is its organization into families, a structure that is absent in the diffuse, anarchic, postmodern family at the center of *White Noise*. DeLillo is aware of the component of group psychology in the psychology of fascism. When people seek meaning in a totalitarian leader, they are seeking communal meaning, a restoration of their sense of belonging to a meaningful group. Gladney's course centers on the group psychology of fascism:

> Every semester I [showed] propaganda films, scenes shot at party congresses, outtakes from mystical epics featuring parades of gymnasts and mountaineers.... Crowd scenes predominated. Ranks of thousands of flagbearers arrayed before columns of frozen light, a hundred and thirty anti-aircraft searchlights aimed straight up—a scene that revealed a geometric longing, the formal notation of some powerful mass desire. (25–6)

The Nazis understood the importance of myth and ritual in building up a will to community and a communal will. They reveal the other side of the media in the twentieth century. DeLillo shows how media representations may dissipate the force of a phenomenon like Hitler, but he also suggests how Hitler himself was able to use the media to build his power. This passage dwells on Nazism as a theatrical force. The key to the Nazis' political success was their ability to stage their meetings, especially for the film cameras.

This passage also suggests why Gladney speaks of the *continuing* mass appeal of fascist tyranny. DeLillo suggests that the spiritual void that made Hitler's rise to power possible is still with us, perhaps exacerbated by the forces at work in postmodern culture. What we learn about Nazism in the course of *White Noise* casts the seemingly innocent opening of the novel in a sinister light. In a scene familiar to all college teachers, DeLillo pictures the mass arrival of parents dropping off their children at school at the beginning of the fall semester:

> This assembly of station wagons, as much as anything they might do in the course of the year, more than formal liturgies or laws, tells the parents they are a collection of the like-minded and the spiritually akin, a people, a nation. (3–4)

With tongue in cheek, DeLillo suggests how attenuated America has become as a community, how little holds it together as a nation. Americans are no longer united by a common religion ("liturgies") or even by political forces ("laws"). All they have to unite them is a common culture, reflected in this communal rite-of-passage, but this common culture is itself highly attenuated, less a matter of values and beliefs than of what are usually called "lifestyles":

> The parents stand sun-dazed near their automobiles, seeing images of themselves in every direction. The conscientious suntans.... They feel a sense of renewal, of communal recognition. The women crisp and alert, in diet trim. (3)

These people do have something in common, but it is something superficial, a look, the image of sun-tanned athleticism cultivated in soft drink commercials.

In *White Noise*, DeLillo views community as something that has become deeply problematic. The problem is clearest in the Gladney family, which can find little in common except watching television. Family solidarity is threatened in the contemporary world because it rests on a form of myth, a kind of error undermined by all the forces for enlightenment at work today. Gladney argues with Siskind over the claim that "the family is the cradle of the world's misinformation":

> I tell Murray that ignorance and confusion can't possibly be the driving forces behind family solidarity... He asks me why the strongest family units exist in the least developed societies.... Magic and superstition become entrenched as the powerful orthodoxy of the clan. The family is strongest where objective reality is most likely to be misinterpreted. (81–2)

Here is the dilemma *White Noise* poses: One can have community, but only if it is rooted in myth or error; if one wants truth and rationality, one will have to pay for it in the form of widespread anomie and rootlessness.

It is thus the atavistic character of Nazism that DeLillo sees as responsible for its hold over masses of people. Though fully willing and able to exploit the technological resources of the modern media, Nazism is in some sense a turn against modernity, tapping into the primitive strata of the psyches of its followers. Precisely because Nazism is irrational, because it rejects the Enlightenment, it fills a need in a modern society that has lost its cohesiveness as rational inquiry undermines the mythic basis of communal solidarity. Gladney sees a quasi-religious dimension to Hitler's power and mystique: He "spoke to people ... as if the language came from some vastness beyond the world and he was simply the medium of revelation" (72). Ultimately Gladney traces Hitler's hypnotic, erotic power over crowds to the fact that he filled a religious need in them:

> Many of those crowds were assembled in the name of death.... They were there to see pyres and flaming wheels, thousands of flags dipped in salute, thousands of uniformed mourners.... Crowds came to form a shield against their own dying.... To break off from the crowd is to risk death as an individual, to face dying alone. (73)

In this view, Nazism is the modern substitute for religion, using theatrical techniques to re-create and recapture the power of ancient ritual to give people a sense of participating in something larger than their individual selves and thus overcoming their fear of death.

Right after this lecture, in one of the most disturbing moments in *White Noise*, Jack reveals that he and his colleague Murray have been participating in the very phenomenon they have been analyzing: mesmerizing an audience ("We all had an aura to maintain"). Jack's lecture on crowd psychology has itself produced a crowd: "People gathered round, students and staff, and in the wild din of half heard remarks and orbiting voices I realized we were now a crowd" (74).[4] Here is DeLillo's concrete evidence of the continuing mass appeal of fascist tyranny: Even a lecture about Hitler can have something of the effect of an actual speech of Hitler. However troubling they may be, DeLillo is concerned with showing parallels between German fascism and contemporary American culture. To be sure, at first sight the connection DeLillo establishes seems to be ridiculous: He pairs Hitler with Elvis Presley. The Hitler lecture I have been discussing is actually a dialogue between Gladney and Siskind, in which—each promoting his academic specialty—they offer parallels between the German dictator and the American rock star, chiefly focusing on their devotion to their respective mothers and their devotion to death.[5] As plausible as some of these parallels sound, even Gladney has his doubts about allowing his subject Hitler "to be associated with an infinitely lesser figure, a fellow who sat in La-Z-Boy chairs and shot out TVs" (73–4).

Still, DeLillo may be on to something. No matter how weird his fiction may become, reality has repeatedly found ways to outdo his imagination, as the Bhopal disaster exceeded the airborne toxic event in *White Noise*. In another case of life imitating art, the American music business has produced a would-be rock star named Elvis Hitler. The title track of his 1988 album with Restless Records is called "Berlin to Memphis." The record company promoted the album with a sticker saying, "The Twentieth Century's Two Greatest Overnight Sensations in One Band. It's Hell with a Pompadour."[6] Although this album could hardly be described as a success, overnight or otherwise, it does offer confirmation of DeLillo's point that somehow the mass appeal of the dictator and the rock star are alike. Both touch similar chords in their audiences, both are in fact performers in the age of mass media, both fill a void in the everyday lives of common people, both appeal to primitive emotions, both fascinate crowds by the image, and reality, of violence.[7]

DeLillo explores the rock star side of this equation in *Great Jones Street*, whose hero, Bucky Wunderlick, understands the way he appeals to the darkest fantasies of his public. Bucky's popularity rests on his ability to embody and express the primitive urges of his fans:

> Fame requires every kind of excess.... I mean danger, the edge of every void, the circumstances of one man imparting an erotic terror to the dreams of the republic.... Even if half-mad he is absorbed into the public's total madness.[8]

Although critics and interviewers try to humanize Wunderlick's music, he insists on his potential for brute violence: "What I'd like to do really is I'd like to injure people with my sound. Maybe actually kill some of them" (105). In *Great Jones Street*, DeLillo develops the intimate connection between the rock star and death (see especially p. 231). It is not just a matter of death as the ultimate marketing tool in moving a star's records off the shelves, a fact of the business epitomized when one wag remarked at the time of Elvis's demise: "Good career move." The death of the rock star becomes part of his legend, usually the crowning part. Like the beloved of a Renaissance sonneteer, only in death can the rock star pass into a world of pure imagination and hence truly become a myth.

Elvis has certainly become an American icon since his death, his image impressed on everything from lamps to bourbon bottles. His presence in American culture today is no doubt more pervasive than if he were still alive. As DeLillo is well aware, Elvis dominates supermarket tabloids as much as any living superstar, whether with rumors of his survival in some strange form or the sort of psychic prediction parodied in *White Noise*: "The ghost of Elvis Presley will be seen taking lonely walks at dawn around Graceland, his musical mansion" (145). Clearly Elvis has come to fill some kind of psychological and spiritual need in the American people, becoming in effect canonized and the object of quasi-religious worship, complete with pilgrimages to Graceland. The fact that, as DeLillo notes, Elvis is conventionally referred to as "the King" (64) suggests what his function in American culture is. In the midst of the postmodern flattening of distinctions, people need to look up to something, and their media celebrities become a debased version of an aristocracy they can worship.[9] The American Elvis cult is a postmodern simulacrum of the German Hitler cult. In the midst of a genuine economic and political crisis, the Germans turned to Hitler for their salvation. Not faced with problems of this magnitude, but still experiencing a spiritual void, Americans turn not to an actual political leader but to a purely artificial image of greatness, the celebrity. The *Führer* is dead, long live the King.

4

What are we to make of the initially bizarre but ultimately significant parallels between Hitler and Elvis in *White Noise*? My first thought was to invoke Marx's famous formula:

> Hegel remarks somewhere that all facts and personages of great importance in world history occur, as it were, twice. He forgot to add: the first time as tragedy, the second as farce.[10]

It seems at first plausible to regard Elvis as the farcical equivalent of the tragedy Hitler brought on Germany. DeLillo could be commenting on the differences between the first half of the twentieth century and the second. A serious eruption of mythic irrationalism and systematic violence in the authentic realm of politics is parodied by a mere representation of it in the life of a media celebrity, whose heroic deeds are confined to roles on the screen and who therefore exists largely as a mere image. Elvis's relation to Hitler would thus be another powerful emblem of the swerve to postmodernism in our era.

Or perhaps DeLillo is commenting on the difference between Europe and America. As the offshoot of Europe, America does seem destined to imitate its origin, often in diminished forms. In conceiving the relation of another former colony to its parent, Salman Rushdie parodies Marx's phrasing: "Europe repeats itself, in India, as farce."[11] In *The Satanic Verses*, Rushdie explores the relation between premodern authenticity (religion based on revelation) and postmodern inauthenticity (films about religious revelation). At one point his characters begin to live out a parody of the story of *Othello*:

What follows is tragedy. —Or, at the least the echo of tragedy, the full-blooded original being unavailable to modern men and women, so it's said. —A burlesque for our degraded, imitative times, in which clowns re-enact what was first done by heroes and by kings.[12]

It is tempting to use this passage to characterize what happens in *White Noise* as well. Jack Gladney achieves a kind of superficial depth in his life by a process of *imitatio Adolphi*. Rejecting shallow American conventions, he seeks authenticity by giving his son the German name of Heinrich Gerhardt Gladney:

> I wanted to do something German. I felt a gesture was called for.... I thought it was forceful and impressive.... I wanted to shield him, make him unafraid. People were naming their children Kim, Kelly and Tracy.... There's something about German names, the German language, German *things*. I don't know what it is exactly. It's just there. In the middle of it all is Hitler, of course. (63)

If Jack sounds somewhat unsure of what the real value of German things is, we should remember that he is praising the German language as an outsider. At this point he still does not know how to speak it. When he finally addresses the Hitler conference in German, he is forced to reject what is distinctive about the magical language and seek out its common ground with ordinary English:

> I talked mainly about Hitler's mother, brother and dog. His dog's name was Wolf. The word is the same in English and German. Most of the words I used in my address were the same or nearly the same in both languages. I'd spent days with the dictionary, compiling lists of such words. I made many references to Wolf,... a few to shoes and socks, a few to jazz, beer and baseball. of course there was Hitler himself I spoke the name often, hoping it would overpower my insecure sentence structure. (274)

In the end, Jack's attempt to become German stays on the merely verbal level; he cannot work himself into the deep structure of the language; he can never really become German; he is merely a postmodern simulacrum of a German.

But by comparing Hitler and Elvis is DeLillo really pointing to the notion of an authentic Nazi Germany versus an inauthentic postmodern

America? The difficulty with this interpretation of *White Noise* is that Nazism in the novel is presented as itself imitative and hence inauthentic:

> I told Murray that Albert Speer wanted to build structures that would decay gloriously, impressively, like Roman ruins.... He knew that Hitler would be in favor of anything that might astonish posterity. He did a drawing of a Reich structure that was to be built of special materials, allowing it to crumble romantically—a drawing of fallen walls, half columns furled in wisteria. (257–8)

We see here that the Nazis were themselves imitating a model of earlier greatness, namely, ancient Rome (a pattern even clearer in the Italian brand of fascism). Evoking the Romantic image of the ruin, Speer reveals the aesthetic side of Nazism, which turns out to be a *derivative* aesthetic. Speer's architectural proposal sounds curiously postmodern, along the lines of what is now called deconstructivism in architecture. DeLillo suggests how much of Nazism was a hollow facade: just for show.

I have been talking about Nazism as some kind of primeval phenomenon, an eruption of authentic barbarism in the twentieth century, which becomes inauthentic only in contemporary media representations. But, in fact, with all his emphasis on Nazi rallies, parades, and films, DeLillo suggests that Nazism is itself a simulacrum of greatness and nobility, more the product of Leni Riefenstahl's camera than the heroic deeds of Nietzschean *Übermenschen*.

DeLillo develops this view of Hitler and Nazism more fully in his earlier novel, *Running Dog*. Dealing as it does with the search for a supposedly pornographic film of Hitler—"the century's ultimate piece of decadence" (20)—this novel allows DeLillo to work out the connection between Nazism and the media. One of the characters says of Hitler:

> Movies were screened for him all the time in Berlin and Obersalzburg, sometimes two a day. Those Nazis had a thing for movies. They put everything on film.... Film was essential to the Nazi era. Myth, dreams, memory. He liked lewd movies too, according to some. Even Hollywood stuff, girls with legs. (52)

DeLillo emphasizes the staginess of Nazi culture:

> This is theatrical, the swastika banners, the floodlights.... You respond to the operatic quality, the great flames. (99)

Hitler is again viewed on the model of Presley: "Like a pop hero. Some modern rock 'n' roller" (147). DeLillo begins to blur the line between the real world and the film world in *Running Dog* when two of his characters go to see Charlie Chaplin in *The Great Dictator*. This cinematic representation of Hitler debunks his greatness by reducing him to the level of Chaplin's little tramp, with whom the great dictator is confused:

> *The barber, or neo-tramp, who is the dictator's lookalike, assumes command, more or less, and addresses the multitudes.*
> *A burlesque, an impersonation.* (61)

DeLillo gives us a postmodern scene: His characters sit in an audience watching Chaplin playing a character addressing an audience by imitating Chaplin's own imitation of Hitler, who is himself presented as playing to audiences throughout the film.

But DeLillo has one last turn of the postmodern screw saved for us. When the film of Hitler finally surfaces, it turns out to be not pornographic at all, but rather an innocent, "almost charming" (235) home movie, made by Eva Braun for the benefit of the children cooped up in the Berlin bunker at the end of the war. And when we see Hitler, he is clowning around, doing an imitation of Chaplin. This is the ultimate postmodern moment: the great dictator mimicking *The Great Dictator*.[13] The result may be "Hitler humanized" (237), but it is also a Hitler considerably reduced in stature, shown in fact as a broken and defeated man, a hollow shell. As with Presley, DeLillo begins to develop parallels between Chaplin and Hitler: "They were born the same week of the same month of the same year" (236). And which one had the original of "*the world's most famous moustache*"? (compare p. 60 with p. 235). As the film rolls on, we begin to understand Hitler as a derivative phenomenon: "he was a gifted mimic. He did imitations" (236). To complicate matters, DeLillo leaves open the question of the authenticity of the film; one of his characters wonders if it really is Hitler in the movie: "Not that I'm convinced it's him" (236). Still, the result is to diminish the aura of Hitler:

> I expected something hard-edged. Something dark and potent.
> The madness at the end. The perversions, the sex. Look, he's
> twirling the cane. A disaster. (237)

in *Running Dog* the ultimate judgment passed on the Nazis is a postmodern twist on the standard condemnation: "That whole bunch, they were movie-mad" (237).[14]

DeLillo certainly ends up cutting Hitler down to size in *Running Dog*, debunking the myth of Nazi grandeur, but does he also end up trivializing Hitler, just as the professors in *White Noise* do? How could the feeble old man shown in *Running Dog* have been responsible for all the atrocities committed by the Nazi regime? To be sure, DeLillo may wish us to be aware that this is Hitler at the end of his career, thereby leaving open the possibility that at earlier stages he was the dark force he is usually thought to be. But still the result of DeLillo's choosing to portray just this moment in Hitler's life is, as one of his characters says, to humanize him. Although Bawer's judgment on DeLillo is far too simplistic, there is some truth in it:

> Jack and Murray compare notes on their respective scholarly subjects, Hitler and Elvis, and discover that the two men were really very much alike. DeLillo's point, throughout, is unmistakable: Hitler was just like us. We are all Hitler. (40)

DeLillo's point is hardly unmistakable;[15] as I have tried to show, his view of Hitler is extremely complicated and subtle. Nevertheless, it is troublesome that at some points DeLillo tends to efface distinctions that elsewhere he appears to take seriously.

5

I began by arguing that DeLillo uses the example of Hitler to show how in postmodern culture an authentic horror can become attenuated in representations of it in the media and the academy. This suggests a significant contrast between the world of Hitler and the contemporary world. But as DeLillo probes the sources of the Nazi regime's power, he sees at work forces that are similar to those he observes in American popular culture. The obsession with sex and violence in rock music is a response to the same spiritual vacuum that Nazi myth and ritual tried to fill. This suggests a significant parallel between the world of Hitler and the contemporary world. For both, the only hope of overcoming a paralyzing self-consciousness seems to be a dangerous return to barbarism. But when one examines DeLillo's portrayal of Nazism more fully and more closely, it seems that what it really has in common with contemporary popular culture is its inauthenticity. Both are forms of simulacrum: mediated and derivative imitations of, prior images of greatness and power. Do we resemble the Nazis in their devotion to dark powers or in their theatrical phoniness? Is the world of Hitler a measure of our postmodernism, or is Hitler already a postmodern phenomenon?

I do not mean to suggest that DeLillo is confused about these issues. Rather, I find him fascinating because he embodies what I see as the dilemma of many serious authors today. I can express the problem in the form of this question: Is DeLillo a postmodern writer or is he a pathologist of postmodernism? I have tried to show that DeLillo is a powerful analyst and critic of those aspects of contemporary life that are usually labeled postmodern. His satiric techniques strongly suggest that he is distanced from what he is writing about. But in order to be a critic of postmodernism, DeLillo must delimit the phenomenon, above all, historically. To be able to call contemporary culture inauthentic, one ought to be able to contrast it with earlier culture that was authentic. In this sense, Jack's father-in-law, Vernon Dickey, asks the key question in *White Noise*: "Were people this dumb before television?" (249). No matter how comic this question sounds, it raises an important issue: Can one point to concrete developments in the contemporary world that suggest a fundamental change in the human condition, such that we might speak of a new phase of history—the postmodern—or perhaps the end of history itself? Could one argue, for example, that the all-pervasiveness of television in the contemporary world has given a profoundly mediated quality to human life that it never had before?

With DeLillo's unerring sense for the texture and feel of contemporary life, he does much to suggest that we have indeed entered a new phase of human existence, with our televisions, our supermarkets, and our academicized culture. Part of DeLillo wants to say that we have lost touch with everything that was authentic in our world and in our culture. But I sense that part of DeLillo wants to say that nothing has really changed; things have always been this way. We have our television, but the Nazi Germans had their movies, and neither culture stood in an unmediated relation to reality. DeLillo is disturbed by the American present, but he is also deeply suspicious of any effort to romanticize a past. Hence Siskind's critique of nostalgia:

> Nostalgia is a product of dissatisfaction and rage. It's a settling of grievances between the present and the past. The more powerful the nostalgia, the closer you come to violence. War is the form nostalgia takes when men are hard-pressed to say something good about their country. (258)

DeLillo's choice of Nazi culture as the image of authenticity that fascinates Gladney seems at first surprising and even shocking, but not if one takes into account his deep doubts about any form of cultural nostalgia. I would argue that he chose Nazism as the subject of a romanticized past in *White Noise* in part to keep his readers distanced from his character's nostalgic impulses.

Near the end of *White Noise*, Gladney's cultural nostalgia is thwarted in another direction. Entering a Catholic hospital, Jack decides to turn from ersatz religion and look for the real thing:

> I said to my nun, "What does the Church say about heaven today? Is it still the old heaven, like that, in the sky?"
> She turned to glance at the picture.
> "Do you think we are stupid?" she said. (317)

To his shock, Jack discovers that the nun does not believe in Catholic dogma. She merely gives the appearance of believing for the sake of those who need not religious faith but the faith that someone else is still genuinely religious. The nun has devoted her life to "the others who spend their lives believing that we still believe" (318). DeLillo gives us another perfect postmodern moment: a nun who is a simulacrum of religious faith. This scene shows DeLillo's inability to keep postmodernism delimited. As its name indicates, postmodernism must be defined in contrast to something else, what came before it. But like many others today, DeLillo keeps wanting to extend the range of postmodernism, above all to keep pushing it farther and farther back into the past, until it threatens to lose all meaning as a distinctive term. This process seems to be the logical outcome of the very concept of postmodernism. If postmodernism is the obliteration of all meaningful distinctions, then in the end it must efface even the distinction between postmodernism and any earlier phase of history.

Consider the moment when Gladney, reading obituaries, wonders whether the great heroic despots of the past—Genghis Khan, Suleiman the Magnificent—thought differently about death than contemporary men:

> It's hard to imagine these men feeling sad about death. Attila the Hun died young. He was still in his forties. Did he feel sorry for himself, succumb to self-pity and depression? He was the King of the Huns, the invader of Europe, the Scourge of God. I want to believe he lay in his tent, wrapped in animal skins, as in some internationally financed movie epic, and said brave cruel things to his aides and retainers. No weakening of the spirit. (99)

Here is Jack's cultural nostalgia at work again. As with his fascination with Hitler, he is attracted to the barbaric Attila because he wants to believe in an authentic form of hero, free of his own fear of death. But DeLillo shows that

Jack's fantasy of Attila is mediated by the cinema: Gladney can picture him only as portrayed "in some internationally financed movie epic." Once again in DeLillo, where we finally expect to find the primitive and the authentic, we get only the postmodern simulacrum, Attila the Hun as movie mogul.[16]

This passage suggests what I mean by saying that DeLillo wavers between criticizing postmodernism and practicing it. Gladney's vision of Attila could be another one of DeLillo's attempts to characterize the postmodern condition, showing how it cuts people off not just from the world of nature but from the authentic human past, as they cannot help assimilating figures out of history to the mediated patterns of their own attenuated existence. But, as we have seen, DeLillo risks the same result in the way he chooses to portray a figure like Hitler. DeLillo himself seems unable to break out of the postmodern circle and offer a convincing alternative to its diminished reality. In short, he can give us a vision of the inauthentic but not, it seems, of the authentic. DeLillo is sufficiently distanced from postmodern existence to want to be able to criticize it, but sufficiently implicated in it to have a hard time finding an Archimedean point from which to do the criticizing. That is why he disturbs critics like Bawer with his unwillingness to take straightforward stands, even against the evil of Hitler. But that is also the reason why DeLillo is one of the representative writers of our age and one of the most illuminating. Even as he shares in the uncertainties and confusions of postmodernism, he helps to place it in historical perspective and give us some idea of how we got to the point where in our day the "imperial self" is born "out of some tabloid aspiration" (268).

Notes

1. The opening stanza of "elvis hitler, jesus satan, and the lazy boys," *Virginia Literary Review* (Spring 1990).

2. "Don DeLillo's America," *New Criterion* 3 (1985): 40.

3. *Running Dog* (New York: Knopf, 1978), p. 220.

4. See Tom LeClair, *In the Loop: Don DeLillo and the Systems Novel* (Urbana: University of Illinois Press, 1987), p. 218.

5. For a similarly bizarre set of parallels, this time between Lord Byron and Elvis, see Camille Paglia, *Sexual Personae: Art and Decadence from Nefertiti to Emily Dickinson* (New Haven, Conn.: Yale University Press, 1990), pp. 361–2.

6. I am not making any of this up. For learning about the existence of Elvis Hitler, I am indebted to a fourteen-year-old named Frey Hoffman, who is just as intelligent and articulate as Heinrich Gladney. For tracing down the

Elvis Hitler album, I wish to thank Elizabeth Hull and the record library of radio station WTJU in Charlottesville.

7. Cf. *Running Dog*, p. 151: "Fascinating, yes. An interesting word. From the Latin *fascinus*. An amulet shaped like a phallus. A word progressing from the same root as the word 'fascism.'"

8. *Great Jones Street* (Boston: Houghton Mifflin, 1973), p. 1.

9. Cf. Paglia, *Sexual Personae*, p. 361.

10. This is the opening of "The Eighteenth Brumaire of Louis Bonaparte." See Lewis Feuer, ed., *Marx and Engels: Basic Writings on Politics and Philosophy* (New York: Anchor Books, 1959), p. 320.

11. *Midnight's Children* (New York: Avon Books, 1982), p. 221.

12. *The Satanic Verses* (New York: Viking, 1988), p. 424.

13. See John Frow, *Marxism and Literary History* (Oxford: Basil Blackwell, 1986), pp. 145–6, and Robert Nadeau, *Readings from the New Book of Nature* (Amherst: University of Massachusetts Press, 1981), p. 180.

14. Curiously, DeLillo uses the same adjective, "movie-mad," of the professors in *White Noise* (9).

15. I for one doubt that DeLillo wishes to claim that "we are all Hitler," but he does seem to suggest in his novel *Players* that a people in some sense gets the leaders it deserves. Commenting on the excesses of governments, one of DeLillo's characters says: "They had too many fantasies. Right. But they were our fantasies, weren't they, ultimately? The whole assortment. Our leaders simply lived them out. Our elected representatives. It's fitting ... and we were stone blind not to guess it. All we had to do was know our own dreams." See *Players* (New York: Knopf, 1977), p. 105.

16. See John Frow, "The Last Things Before the Last: Notes on *White Noise*," *South Atlantic Quarterly* 89 (1990): 422. This essay contains an excellent discussion of the role of the simulacrum in *White Noise*.

FRANK LENTRICCHIA

Tales of the Electronic Tribe

T he first 11 days of the Persian Gulf war have had the feeling of a surreal spectator sport here, with the President constantly flicking television channels in the study off the Oval Office and with other senior officials gathered in semicircles with sandwiches around the television set.... Robert M. Gates, the deputy national security advisor, has found the obsessive television watching at the White House so distracting—and perhaps diminishing to the myth of privileged information—that he refuses to even turn on his office television set now, loyally waiting for reports from the Situation Room.

But even that top-secret intelligence, widely presumed to be fuller and more accurate, has been infected by the television coverage.

"The problem is that it's hard to sort out the information because the CNN stuff has a way of trickling into the intelligence," another Bush advisor said, referring to Cable News Network, the potent new entry in Washington's alphabet soup. "We get the intelligence reports and they include stuff that's on CNN. Then we get another report that seems to confirm what

From *New Essays on White Noise*. © 1991 by Cambridge University Press.

the first report said, but it turns out that they're just using a later
CNN broadcast. CNN confirming CNN."
                                    —New York Times, January 29, 1991

"POSTMODERNISM": Our key term of cultural self-consciousness—a
word we utter from within the dark wood in order to define not merely
contemporary art and literature of the first world, but also who we are, how
we live. One of the characters in Don DeLillo's first novel, *Americana*
(1971)—in witty anticipation of the current controversy over the idea of the
postmodern—says that television came over on the *Mayflower*. If television is
the quintessential technological constituent of the postmodern temper (so it
goes), and postmodernism the ethos of the electronic society, then with
twenty years of hindsight on DeLillo's book we can say that what actually
came over on the *Mayflower* was postmodernism itself, the founding piece of
Americana. "America": imagined rather than geographic space, the very
form of postmodern desire.

In that first novel DeLillo defines American desire as nothing other
than desire for the universal third person—the "he" or "she" we dream about
from our armchairs in front of the TV, under the strong stimulus of Madison
Avenue, originally dreamt by the first immigrants, the Pilgrims on their way
over, the object of the dream being the person those Pilgrims would become:
a new self because a New World. Sitting in front of TV is like a perpetual
Atlantic crossing—the desire for and the discovery of America constantly
reenacted in our move from first-person consciousness to third: from the self
we are, but would leave behind, to the self we would become. Advertising
may have discovered and exploited the economic value of the person we all
want to be, but the pilgrim-consumer dreaming on the *Mayflower*, or on the
New Mayflower in front of television, invented that person.

The distinction between the real and the fictional can't be sustained—
not on the *Mayflower*, not while watching TV, nowhere in America, certainly
not in the burgeoning variety of theories of postmodernism. The
undesirability of the distinction between the real and the fictional is the key
meaning, even, of being an American. To be real in America is to be in the
position of the "I" who must negate I, leave I behind in a real or metaphoric
Europe. So in order for America to be America the original moment of
yearning for the third-person must be ceaselessly renewed. One of the
harsher charges of postmodern theorists (especially of the French type) is
that America has perfected the practice of cultural imperialism; everyone in
the world now—Islamic cultures perhaps excepted—wants to be an
American. As I follow the implications of DeLillo's mythic history of
television, that's exactly what the world's always wanted, long before there

was a political entity called America to be scapegoated for the phenomenon of American desire.

In the third chapter of *White Noise* there is a brief scene that extends this surprising history of television. "THE MOST PHOTOGRAPHED BARN IN AMERICA" is the ostensible subject of the scene; the real subject is the electronic medium of the image as the active context of contemporary existence in America. TV, a productive medium of the image, is only one (albeit dominant) technological expression of an entire environment of the image. But unlike TV, which is an element in the contemporary landscape, the environment of the image *is* the landscape—it is what (for us) "landscape" has become, and it can't be switched off with the flick of a wrist. For this environment-as-electronic-medium radically constitutes contemporary consciousness and therefore (such as it is) contemporary community—it guarantees that we are a people of, by, and for the image. Measured against TV advertising's manipulation of the image of the third person, the economic goals of which are pretty clear, and clearly susceptible to class analysis from the left—it is obvious who the big beneficiaries of such manipulations are—the environment of the image in question in *White Noise* appears far less concretely in focus. Less apprehensible, less empirically encounterable—therefore more insidious in its effects.

The first-person narrator of *White Noise*, Jack Gladney, a college professor, drives to the tourist attraction known as the most photographed barn in America, and he takes with him his new colleague, Murray Jay Siskind, a professor of popular culture, a smart emigré from New York City to middle America. The tourist attraction is pastorally set, some twenty miles from the small city where the two reside and teach, and all along the way there are natural things to be taken in, presumably, though all the nature that is experienced (hardly the word, but it will have to do) is noted in a flat, undetailed, and apparently unemotional declarative: "There were meadows and apple orchards." And the traditional picturesque of rural life is similarly registered: "White fences trailed through the rolling fields." The strategically unenergized prose of these traditional moments is an index to the passing of both a literary convention and an older America. The narrator continues in his recessed way while his companion comments (lectures, really) on the tourist site, which is previewed for them (literally) by several signs, spaced every few miles along the way, announcing the attraction in big block letters. There is a booth where a man sells postcards and slides of the barn; there is an elevated spot from which the crowd of tourists snap their photos.

Gladney's phlegmatic narrative style in this passage is thrown into high relief by the ebullience of his friend's commentary. Murray does all the talking, like some guru drawing his neophyte into a new world which the neophyte experiences in a shocked state of half-consciousness situated somewhere between the older world where there were objects of perception like barns and apple orchards and the strange new world where the object of perception is perception itself: a packaged perception, a "sight" (in the genius of the vernacular), not a "thing." What they view is the view of a thing. What Murray reveals is that "no one sees the barn" because once "you've seen the signs about the barn, it becomes impossible to see the barn." This news about the loss of the referent, the dissolving of the object into its representations (the road signs, the photos), is delivered not with nostalgia for a lost world of the real but with joy: "We're not here to capture an image, we're here to maintain one. Every photograph reinforces the aura."

In between Murray's remarks, Jack Gladney reports on the long silences and the background noise—a new kind of choral commentary, "the incessant clicking of shutter release buttons, the rustling of crank levers that advanced the film"—and on the tourists ritually gathered in order to partake, as Murray says, of "a kind of spiritual surrender." So not only can't we get outside the aura, we really don't want to. We prefer not to know what the barn was like before it was photographed because its aura, its technological glow, its soul, is our production, it is us. "We're part of the aura," says Murray, and knowing we're a part is tantamount to the achievement of a new identity—a collective selfhood brought to birth in the moment of contact with an "accumulation of nameless energies," in the medium of representation synonymous with the conferring of fame, charisma, desirable selfhood. "We're here, we're now," says Murray, as if he were affirming the psychic wholeness of the community. "The thousands who were here in the past, those who will come here in the future. We've agreed to be part of a collective perception."

What will trip up any reader intent on extrapolating DeLillo's views on postmodernism—as if the passage on the most photographed barn were a miniature essay, and a transparent one at that—is the doubly distanced relationship of writer to his materials. If we remember that Murray—a character, after all—does most of the talking, that his talking is filtered through a character of special narrative authority—a first-person narrator—then the question becomes not what does DeLillo think of Murray's ideas but what does Gladney think of them, and only then might we ask how does DeLillo position his thoughts of Gladney's thoughts of Murray. The regress is not infinite, but it is pretty thick and has the effect of throwing readers back on their own resources of judgment without the comfort of firm authorial guidance.

It's hard to miss the excitement of Murray's dialogue, the rhythmic blooding of his ideas:

"What was the barn like before it was photographed? ... What did it look like, how was it different from other barns, how was it similar to other barns? We can't answer these questions because we've read the signs, seen the people snapping the pictures. We can't get outside the aura. We're part of the aura. We're here, we're now."

Hard to call that ironic talk (though elsewhere Murray will show himself to be the devil's own ironist). No satiric voice utters the phrases "spiritual surrender," "collective perception," or "religious experience." Have we somehow come back to the world, beyond the alienation that a number of writers made synonymous with the literature of modernism? The community despaired of by nostalgic modernists located, at last, not in some premodern village of artisans, or some fascist state, but in postmodern society, godless and bereft of tradition though it is? Community sprung wholly from the technology of the image? Can this be serious? What does Gladney think? At the end of Murray's outburst Jack says: "He seemed immensely pleased by this." In light of his caustic treatment of contemporary culture everywhere else in the book, this is a curiously withheld remark, as if he can't quite get a fix on Murray.

The more typical Murray is a subversive whose humor depends on our recognition that postmodern values are the dominant ones of our culture. When Jack tells him that there is something perplexing about someone they know, Murray solves the puzzle with "He's flesh-colored." The typical Jack is the same sort of humorist who enjoys tripping on the postmodern. He asks a worker for a state agency called SIMUVAC (short for "simulated evacuation"), "Are you people sure you're ready for a simulation? You may want to wait for one more massive spill. Get your timing down." People who speak of using the real as a model deserve sardonic treatment. But in the scene of the most photographed barn the typically witty Murray and Jack are strangely absent. Is community a specially honored value of Gladney's, exactly what his irony may not touch? One worth cherishing, wherever it is found? Does the passage on the most photographed barn represent a new literary form comfortably based on the technology of electronics? And shall we now speak of the postmodern idyll?

Walter Benjamin once cited Proust on the phenomenology of the aura as the experience which gives access to tradition: "monuments and pictures" of the past presenting themselves "only beneath the delicate veil which centuries of love and reverence on the part of so many admirers have woven about them." To experience monuments and pictures in this way is to experience intimacy with those who have cared about art history; it is to experience the entry into community, aesthetically mediated over time, as a variegated tapestry of loving response. And it is precisely such experience of community that Benjamin would deny our age of: mechanical reproduction, the age decisively marked by the advent of photography, which is (Benjamin again) the advent of the decline of aura, the loss of tradition and the historical sense.

But Benjamin's deadly camera which returns no human gaze may be the mediator of a new kind of community, wherein all distinctive selfhood is extinguished in a new art form whose mass cultural presence glows at postmodernism's holy place, the site of the most photographed barn. DeLillo's point, unlike Benjamin's, is not the nostalgic one that aura is in decline, but that its source has been replaced. The question he poses in all but words is, What strange new form of human collectivity is born in the postmodern moment of aura, and at what price?

It probably can't be said too strongly. *White Noise* is a first-person narrative—a fact of literary structure that will turn out to be decisive for all that can be said about the book's take on contemporary America and the issues that cluster about the cloudy concept of postmodernism. Like Melville's Ishmael, Twain's Huck, and Fitzgerald's Nick Carraway, DeLillo's Jack Gladney is a sharp observer and commentator who at the same time participates—often to the reader's bewilderment—in an action which fatally shapes him, so that he will not understand with total lucidity what it is he observes, or who he himself really is, or the extent to which he, Jack Gladney, is the less than self-possessed voice of a culture that he would subject to criticism and satire. The major consequence of the book's materials being filtered through a character named Gladney rather than directly through a writer named DeLillo is a complexity beyond the narrator's ken: a terrible complicity in the horrors narrated that may be the real point of the writer's (not Gladney's) discomforting perspective.

Like a number of novels in the mainstream of American literature, *White Noise* appears to be motivated by a double purpose: to write social criticism of its author's place and time, while showing its readers the difficulty of doing so with a clean conscience and an un-self-deluded mind. This sort of doubly motivated writing, from Melville to DeLillo, gives no comfort because while it trades upon the desire to fix what seems most dreadful in our culture it insists on showing us that what especially needs fixing is the intelligent and sensitive fixers themselves. *Moby Dick*, *Huckleberry Finn*, *The Great Gatsby*, and *White Noise* are exemplary first person narratives in the American grain for the reason that their critical authority cannot be abstracted from their trapped and partially subverted first-person tellers; abstracted and then assigned to a kingly sort of storyteller—an omniscient narrator who gives the illusion of being uncontaminated by the issues he would excoriate and who would therefore perform the role of good cultural doctor, safely inoculated from the diseases that plague the rest of us. The reader of *White Noise* may be bewildered, but such bewilderment is the strategic effect of DeLillo's most important formal decision.

Point of view in narrative produces its most immediate effects (especially in the first-person mode) sentence by sentence where it is embodied sensuously in the sound of the storyteller's voice. DeLillo gives us his Jack Gladney in full tonal profile in the brief five-paragraph first chapter of the novel, which begins with a cutting description of an annual autumn ritual at what are called the finer American colleges and universities—the lavish return of students and admiring parents—and ends on a note of poignancy—beyond the reach of the narrator's usual irony: "On telephone poles all over town there are homemade signs concerning lost dogs and cats, sometimes in the handwriting of a child." The opening and closing sentences of a number of this novel's chapters are so unusually weighted with emotive freight that they seem discontinuous and self-sufficient, virtually leaving the text, so much the better to haunt the mind. The last sentence of the first chapter works that way, surprising us as an expression of sheer domestic sentiment unpredictable in context—intriguing precisely because it appears to be ungrounded in the knowing and well-weathered voice that begins the chapter; the voice that takes wicked pleasure in making lists of the bounty that students unload when they return to classes:

> the stereo sets, radios, personal computers; small refrigerators and table ranges; the cartons of phonograph records and cassettes; the hairdryers and styling irons; the tennis rackets, soccer balls, hockey and lacrosse sticks, bows and arrows; the controlled substances, the birth control pills and devices; the junk food still in shopping bags—onion-and-garlic chips, nacho thins, peanut creme patties, Waffelos and Kabooms, fruit chews and toffee popcorn; the Dum-Dum pops, the Mistic mints.

This narrator can read the signs of social class in the commodities we command, and he enjoys passing judgment dryly, the proportions and arrangements that he gives to the items of his list: more items of junk food than anything else, and those, by providing closure to both list and first paragraph, perform a retrospective, if implicit, evaluation of the whole. Those who can possess such things—sports-mad, narcissistic, pleasure-seeking—are the pure American products of a culture addicted to junk food, the representations of a junky, because a mass culture, the human Dum-Dum pops. This narrator (he describes himself as a "witness" to this "spectacle" of return: and he says "spectacle" as if what he sees were one of the primary staged entertainments of his culture), this narrator is tired. He's seen it too many times, for years to be exact. Nevertheless his weariness is disturbing because it is rooted in the banality of everyday life, weariness apparently unavoidable. The key cultural marker in his list (the first of many he will give us) is the innocent little definite article: He says the stereo sets, the hairdryers, and the junk food ("The station wagons arrived at noon" is the way the book begins) because he's evoking generic objects and events, things seen everywhere and all the time—relentlessly repetitious experience being something like the point of mass culture in an advanced capitalist economy. With perception so grooved on the routine, the affective consequence follows rigorously. Gladney's ironies bespeak boredom, an enervation of spirit, and, beneath it all, an intimation of a Hell whose origin lies in the high modernist fear that the life of consciousness, especially its aesthetic possibilities, will become like the mass culture that modernists mainly loathe, often parody, and sometimes even love.

The implicit indictment in Gladney's list of predictable first world wonders is leveled not at all the rich kids and their parents—the power of money inequitably distributed—but at the options of the economically privileged, the triviality of this culture's gifts. Where are the books? Shoved, in Gladney's list, ignominiously between boots, stationery, sheets, pillows, and quilts. Whatever their titles (no doubt best not to know them) these books are things like other things, commodities, too, or—in the most question—begging of all economic terms—*goods*, but not good enough to deserve verbal differentiation (we know them only as "books"), unlike the English and Western saddles, the Waffelos and Kabooms. And what could a book really signify in a series whose rolling rhythms make it hard to tell the difference between an English saddle and a Kaboom? There are many things to be said about living in the United States in the late twentieth century, and Gladney's list, whose deepest subject is cultural democracy, is one of them.

And the torpid Gladney can get no satisfaction when he turns his gaze upon this autumn spectacle's human figures, who find the solidarity of their community in displays of style and stylistic mimicry (in a postmodern culture, a hard thing to distinguish), in striking the easily readable pose, in trading upon their culture's most stable currency, that of the image:

> The students greet each other with comic cries and gestures of sodden collapse. Their summer has been bloated with criminal pleasures, as always. The parents stand sun-dazed near their

automobiles, seeing images of themselves in every direction. The
conscientious suntans. The well-made faces and wry looks. They
feel a sense of renewal, of communal recognition. The women
crisp and alert, in diet trim, knowing people's names ... something
about [their husbands] suggesting massive insurance coverage.
This assembly of station wagons, as much as anything they might
do in the course of the year, more than formal liturgies or laws,
tells the parents they are a collection of the like-minded and the
spiritually akin, a people, a nation.

In the mocking crescendo of his final phrases, Gladney's voice builds to the
corrosive authority of satire. Here is image and style classically, suspiciously
viewed as tricky, seductive surface, style and image as absence of substantial
selfhood, the void at the core. The students have watched too many bad
actors; the remark about "massive insurance coverage" is funny and totally
nasty.

Having seen enough of the spectacle of return, Gladney leaves the
panoramic perch of his office and walks home, noting along the way more
numbing simulcra (the "Greek revival and Gothic churches"). Then
suddenly there is a shift in focus and we feel ourselves for a moment on the
familiar terrain of the realist novel. He tells us he lives at the end of a quiet
street "in what was once a wooded area with deep ravines." This turn from
critical to novelistic observation is enhanced with a moody reverie on the
past pressing into the present; he mentions that now, just beyond his
backyard, there is an expressway, and at night, as he and his wife settle into
sleep, they hear the "remote and steady murmur" of traffic moving past:
haunted, foggy sounds, as if the cars, moving over the place of the old
wooded area, were moving over a graveyard, as if they were giving voice to
something strange, "as of dead souls babbling at the edge of dream."

Before we can measure the effect of this tonal shift—it seems a lament
over modernization—the tone quickly shifts again and the narrator tells us
flatly who he is: chairman of the department of Hitler studies at the College-
on-the-Hill (the "College-on-the-Hill," we know where it is, we know it
well), who invented Hitler studies in America in March of 1968. This piece
of information is followed by the first chapter's oddest sentence: "It was a
cold bright day with intermittent winds out of the east." Straight or deadpan?
A joke about the way we talk these days about the weather, with our voices
indentured to the jargon of what is called meteorology? A joke that stings us
for our inability to muster "real" voice, "real" speech, even about—or is it
especially about?—matters so ordinary? Or is the sentence delivered
unawares, just the way Jack talks sometimes, like a weatherman? Self-parody

or a weird, because unconscious, form of "pastiche," a term whose very meaning assumes an act of deliberation? After inquiring in Jack's sort of voice whether the parents were costumed in cableknit sweaters and hacking jackets, Babette, Jack's wife, makes the point: "Not that we don't have a station wagon ourselves."

Our strolling narrator notes another ritual act: "At Fourth and Elm" (we know those streets) "the cars turn left for the supermarket," as if they never turn right, perhaps because the supermarket is another of this novel's communal sites—and that is why they always turn left. And now the final sentence about the homemade signs concerning lost dogs and cats, in the handwriting of innocence itself, to which Jack, who would seem the innocent's very antithesis, is nevertheless drawn. The Jack who comes to us bearing the satirist's gift of criticism to his culture comes bearing pathos and portents as well. That sentence about the "spiritually akin, a people, a nation" seemed purely caustic, but perhaps it was only partially so. But what could "partially caustic" mean, and how do we define a point of view that can accommodate that sort of tone?

In the usual sense of what it means to say that a novel has plot, *White Noise* has no plot. But plotlessness is itself a controlled effect of this book because until its concluding chapters (when Gladney decides that he will put some plot into his life) the novel is narrated by a man who fears plots in both conspiratorial and literary senses—a distinction hard to make in DeLillo's world—and who therefore resists them, even prays for plotlessness, a life ungoverned by design and intention: "Let's enjoy these aimless days while we can, I told myself, fearing some kind of deft acceleration." That's the surprising first sentence of the fifth chapter through which DeLillo manages to let Jack speak his wish and fear at the same time. The apparently unprepared appearance of the sentence is a sign of the undriven, episodic character of the first third of the book in particular, and its portentous and out-of-the-blue quality is an indication that his narrator is working hard to repress an obscurely grounded anxiety that something horrible is about to happen to him and his family. There really is a story at work in Gladney's life, one he'd prefer not to know about because it's a story over which he exerts no authorial control, a story, nevertheless, he will be caught up in as he tells it from the edges of his consciousness, half-ignorant of what it is he narrates.

"Waves and Radiation," the title of the first of the book's three sections, is composed of twenty brief chapters, most of which seem disconnected from one another. In *White Noise* disconnection is the narrative mark of a mind taking pleasure in its meandering progression, a mind that avoids causal coherence by skipping from topic to topic: his wife, the children—his and hers—who live with them, his students, his colleagues (especially those in popular culture), the supermarket, the shopping mall, television, his ex-wife, the kids who don't live with them, what it's like to live in a small town called Blacksmith. (Murray says, "I can't help being happy in a town called Blacksmith.")

The major effect of "Waves and Radiation" is of leisurely description interrupted every so often by the question that obsesses Jack and Babette— "Who will die first?"—and by those startling sentences that open and close a number of the chapters. Like the one about a man in a rocker on his front porch, glimpsed in passing, who "stares into space"; or the one about Jack's oldest son, only in his early teens, already with a hairline in dramatic retreat; or the one about Jack waking "in the grip of a death sweat"; or the one about the day the youngest child cried for almost seven straight hours, for no reason that anyone, including a doctor, can discern; or the most telling one of all, which opens the ninth chapter. "They had to evacuate the grade school on Tuesday." Such moments in the novel function as terrorized punctuation, a sort of tip of the withheld subjective life of Jack Gladney, teasing signs of something outside his voice, rarely seen, an index to a level in his dense, meticulous, and disquietingly observed description to which Jack can give no overt interpretation because he seems not conscious of how the intensely observed items in his notation all come together to form the motive of his terror, his unwitting theme. "Theme": exactly what you can't observe but must interpret, a barely audible refrain that will clue us in to the function of "Waves and Radiation"—the establishment of the novel's true setting. Not Blacksmith, middle America, but the environment unintentionally produced by advanced technology, the effects of technology, the by-products, the fallout.

The pervasive tension that gives the reader perspective and constant access to the novel's atmosphere of pathos—what DeLillo knows and Jack does not want to know but half-knows—is that character is a function of setting. In *White Noise*, DeLillo rewrites the classic naturalist novel. Unlike, say, Dreiser's Carrie, Jack is endowed with intellectual power, yet in the end he is no less a plaything of his "American environments" (as the popular culture program at Jack's college is called). Jack is a strong reader, a ceaseless professor, but DeLillo opens a space between him and the novel's setting across which Jack's interpretive energy cannot jump. The tension between what DeLillo knows but cannot say directly, and what Jack knows, stimulates the reader to make sense of the novel's setting by connecting widely separated facts of description: Jack notes "our brightly colored food"; he notes the stack of "three-hour colored flame sawdust and wax logs" on his front porch; the fruit bins in the supermarket where "Everything seemed to be in season, sprayed, burnished, bright." Having grasped that embedded series, maybe the reader will draw a connection between it and Jack's brooding question about Heinrich's hairline: "Have I raised him, unwittingly, in the vicinity of a chemical dump site, in the path of air currents that carry industrial wastes capable of producing scalp degeneration, glorious sunsets? (People say the sunsets around here were not nearly so stunning thirty or forty years ago.)" When we eat "our brightly colored food," what else—unwittingly—do we eat? What do the Gladneys inhale for the pleasure of watching the colored flame of their sawdust and wax logs? Is it important that Jack and Babette know exactly why two of their closet doors open by themselves? Jack hears with paranoid apprehension the quiet rumble of the clothes dryer, the radiator, the refrigerator, the thermostat buzzing for unknown reasons. Do these standard friends of the standard American family give off something other than harmless sound? Just how far does our unwittingness extend? Hazardous waste dumps are bad, but at least we know where they are. Electromagnetic radiation (Heinrich will drive this point home) is the menace outside sensory apprehension. "Where do you think all the deformed babies are coming from?" Heinrich asks. "Radio and TV, that's where."

"Waves and Radiation" is all about the white noise, actual and metaphoric, that constitutes the setting of a postmodern life, an environment more or less in focus—less rather than more because not a direct object of perception like traditional novelistic and premodern environments, the city and the country. And the less in focus the environment, the more our paranoia is enhanced, not clinically but as a general (and reasonable) psychic condition of privileged first world citizens. But there is a type of white noise more cultural than technological, another difficult distinction in postmodern context—*more* rather than less in focus, more in focus especially if you're a Jack or a Murray, a type of the intellectual found flourishing (but hardly exclusively so) in the humanities wing of institutions of higher learning: the habitually ironic cultural critic, the urban intellectual guerrilla finely attuned to the presence of the media as powerful shaper of the way we crystallize ourselves for ourselves and for others; who believes in his own freedom just because he knows how the culture industry works; who believes in the West's classic philosophic dictum, that self-knowledge sets us free, though he's generally too cool to say he believes in anything.

When Murray tells us that he "can't help being happy in a town called Blacksmith," he is telling us how happy he is to note, for the delectation of anyone who might be listening, the gap between word and thing, the nostalgia of the name. When Jack asks Murray where he's living, Murray responds:

"In a rooming house.... Seven or eight boarders.... A woman who harbors a terrible secret. A man with a haunted look. A man who never comes out of his room. A woman who stands by the mailbox for hours, waiting for something that never seems to arrive. A man with no past. A woman with a past. There is a smell about the place of unhappy lives in the movies that I really respond to.
"Which one are you?" I said.
"I'm the Jew. What else would I be?"

Murray knows all about the movies, how they shape the texture of what he sees, and he knows how to turn his knowledge into playfulness. But Jack's immediate reflection implies that there is impotence beneath Murray's postmodern ironies, that what comes before the image—though itself maybe movie-generated—is nevertheless painfully real, a sadness and deprivation that motivates the story of Murray's search for the third person of his dreams:

There was something touching about the fact that Murray was dressed almost totally in corduroy. I had the feeling that since the age of eleven in his crowded plot of concrete he'd associated this sturdy fabric with higher learning in some impossibly distant and tree-shaded place.... The small stiff beard, confined to his chin and unaccompanied by a mustache, seemed an optional component, to be stuck on or removed as circumstances warranted.

Is Jack master of himself, this postmodern Longfellow with a Chaplinesque eye for cultural anatomy, who delivers the maxims by which we frighten ourselves?

When times are bad, people feel compelled to overeat. Blacksmith is full of obese adults and children, baggy-pantsed, short-legged, waddling. They struggle to emerge from compact cars; they don sweatshirts and run in families across the landscape; they walk down the street with food in their faces; they eat in stores, cars, parking lots, on bus lines and movie lines, under the stately trees.

The contemplative distance of that meditation and the superiority it implies are deliciously subverted about two hundred pages later when the Gladneys engage in a feeding frenzy in a fast-food parking lot, after times have indeed turned bad for them. But we don't have to wait that long for Jack's culture to exact its revenge. The scene is the bedroom of the adult Gladneys; Babette is about to perform an act that Jack hugely enjoys. She will read to him from their historically wide-ranging collection of pornographic literature. Jack chooses; Babette reads:

> "But I don't want you to choose anything that has men inside women, quote-quote, or men entering women. 'I entered her.' 'He entered me.' We're not lobbies or elevators.... Can we agree on that? ..."
> "Agreed."
> "I entered her and began to thrust."
> "I'm in total agreement," I said.
> "'Enter me, enter me, yes, yes.'"
> "Silly usage, absolutely."
> "'Insert yourself, Rex. I want you inside me, entering hard, entering deep. Yes, now, oh.'"

The funniest moment in the passage occurs not in dialogue, however, but in Jack's immediate interior reflection. "I began to feel an erection stirring," he says. "How stupid and out of context"—that his last hold on nature should be the effect of a quotation. Jack, a parodist of contemporary jargons, and, like Murray, a cultural ecologist, knows better. That is why he says "stupid." But knowledge and wit cannot undo his victimage by the cultural ecosystem: the "eco" of ecology, from the Greek *oikos*, means "house." No "out of context" because no getting outside our cultural house.

Just how far down and in media culture has penetrated is illustrated by the novel's formally most astonishing moment—an effort to represent the irruption of the unconscious—variations on which are played throughout. A deep refrain—like a line of poetic chant, with strong metrical structure—is placed by itself in privileged typographical space, part of no paragraph or dialogue, without quotes and related to nothing that comes before or after: a break in the text never reflected upon because Jack never hears it. It is, of course, Jack who speaks the line because *White Noise* is a first-person novel, and it could therefore be no one else. Jack in these moments is possessed, a mere medium who speaks:

Dacron, Orlon, Lycra Spandex
MasterCard, Visa, American Express
Leaded, Unleaded, Superunleaded

Jacques Lacan said the unconscious is structured like a language. He forgot to add the words "of Madison Avenue."

From the cultural and technological density of the first section of *White Noise* two actions emerge and eventually come together in the near fatal act that shapes the novel's concluding chapters. One of those actions is Jack's effort to learn the significance of an experimental and illegally obtained medication secretly ingested by Babette and known to him only as "Dylar." Not known to him until far into the novel's final section (entitled "Dylarama") is that Dylar is Babette's desperate response to the question "Who will die first?" Madison Avenue captures the unconscious; industrial pollution enhances the beauty of nature (what Jack calls "postmodern" sunsets); Dylar, ultimate postmodern drug, would inhibit fear of death, nature's final revenge on postmodern culture. What we see from a Dylaramic prospect is everyday life in America as a 360-degree display of what are called "controlled substances," America as the culture of the Dylar effect.

The other action that emerges quite literally from the novel's setting is the matter of deep plot, the process that motivates the novel's agents. In the classic naturalist vision of *White Noise*, it is the novel's setting that "acts," the novel's setting that drives the novel's human agents, and by so acting upon them deprives them of their free agency. But *White Noise* is no classic naturalist novel; it is a subversion of the genre played out through the mask thereof. The emerging scenic action of *White Noise* crystallizes all the tiny intimations of disaster that crowd Jack's consciousness, and that come fully into view in the novel's second section, "The Airborne Toxic Event"—the evasive name not of a natural but of a human effect whose peculiarity is that it is the unintended consequence of the desire of the technologically sophisticated to insulate themselves from the enduring cockroach. "The Airborne Toxic Event" is DeLillo's dark comic rebuke of first world hubris, an expression of a controlling structural irony that definitively subverts the conventional critical distinction of character and setting. Setting, in this book, is character become a runaway cancer, intention out of control.

Cutting against the grain of this ecological theme of man as self-victimizer is a countertheme initiated by the romantic poets, elaborated and fully embraced in the high modernist ethos of Yeats, Joyce, Pound, and Stevens: the theme of freedom and dignity aesthetically won, the artist as hero. In the philosophical tradition out of Kant's *Critique of Judgment*, running through the cultural theories of neo-Kantian idealists from Schiller to Marcuse, culminating in literary theory in Northrop Frye's *Anatomy of Criticism*: the theme of aesthetic humanism, modernist culture's last ditch defense of man against the technologies of modernization. In art, so goes the plea, lies the salvation of our humanity—character shielded from setting, free agency and the autonomy of intention restored.

White Noise is a meditative sort of narrative conducted by a cultural anatomist in the wake of Keats, capitalism, and the revolutions in electronics. When Jack thinks, sees, and feels in the categories of art—the book is liberally peppered with such moments—Jack the victim is magically transmuted into Jack the victor, the poised angel of observation whose values are superior to those of the mass culture he anatomizes. The more impressive effects of Jack's aesthetic consciousness come through with a minimum of rhetorical fanfare: They are effects of the counternarrative sort, spatial rather than temporal, produced with quiet painterly eloquence and the haunting precision of black-and-white photography. These are the signature moments of Jack as artist, working in the mode of Antonioni, whose camera eye (with sharp point in *Red Desert*) repeatedly creates painterly and photographic effects, infinitesimally frozen frames, an antinarrative cinema dedicated like Jack's antinarrative narrative to the disquieting image removed from the stream of time, a thing of beauty forever whose power to mesmerize is owed to its menacing context, the story that moves silently underground.

These small moments of the aesthetic image in *White Noise* tend to be put into the background (where they belong and do their insidious work) by big interpretive moments when Jack sees his world demanding to be read, as if his salvation (a recollection of Christian allegory) depended upon it. In this register, Jack's high cultural perspective would redeem him from the cultural ecosystems of the mass media that threaten to rule his consciousness, and would provide a consolation of spirit—the Dylar effect of high culture—even as he faces fatal exposure to the terrible black cloud. Nowhere is Jack's aesthetic power more flashily in evidence than when he lifts the trash bag from the trash compactor: "An oozing cube of semi-mangled cans, clothes hangers, animal-bones and other refuse ... a horrible clotted mass of hair, soap, ear swabs, crushed roaches, flip-top rings, sterile pads smeared with pus and bacon fat, strands of frayed dental floss, fragments of ballpoint pen refills, tooth picks still displaying bits of impaled food." He wonders if he has finally encountered the "dark underside of consumer consciousness." He says, in his revulsion, "the full stench hit me with shocking force," but the stench is not quite full because the stinking chaos is mediated, shaped into the speech of a sharp-tongued familiar. The oozing cube of garbage sits there "like an ironic modern sculpture, massive, squat, mocking."

Constantly shadowing Jack's arty self-consciousness is an unconscious epistemology of consumption. Jack tends to "see" commodities, and with their right names attached. He notes a "camouflage jacket with Velcro closures"; "a family of five [getting] out of a Datsun Maxima"; he tells us that his "newspaper is delivered by a middle-aged Iranian driving a Nissan Sentra"; somebody is wearing a "Gore-Tex jacket"; he feels a "chill pass through the Hong Kong polyester" of his pajamas. In each of these instances funny to us but not to Jack—Jack is the object of DeLillo's wit, the postmodern anatomist postmodernized, and so become the automaton of consumer society: Sometimes the object of Jack's wit, in these instances brand names creep into the syntax of his perceptions. The brand name: the lens of his vision, the source of his power to name and in naming create the world of typical experience. The brand name: a curious human bond, the stuff of community. And not even the cute malapropisms of his kids can escape. One of them says, "It's called the sun's corolla." Another responds, "I thought corolla was a car." The precocious Heinrich rejoins, "Everything is a car." In desperate conversation with Murray—he knows that he's been decisively exposed to the toxic cloud—Jack says, "I want to live," and Murray replies with a brief filmographic description: "From the Robert Wise film of the same name, with Susan Hayward as Barbara Graham, a convicted murderess. Aggressive jazz score by Johnny Mandel." Heinrich was wrong; everything's a movie.

Against such odds Jack's aesthetic sensibility plays to win. Gazing upon his "ironic modern sculpture" he resembles an earlier gazer upon the ironies of spatial art. "What habits, fetishes, addictions, inclinations? What solitary acts? behavioral ruts?" The exact rhythmic echo of Keats's excited questions in the poem about the Grecian urn is parodic, all right, but with a difference. Jack's parody establishes a decidedly deflating commentary on Keats's enthusiasm with its unflattering reduction of the urn to garbage ("Thou shalt remain ... a friend to man"), and its delightfully grotesque translation of Keats's idealized "more happy, happy love" to "I found crayon drawings of a figure with full breasts and male genitals," "I found a banana skin with a tampon inside"—as if to say, look what I, impoverished postmodern poet, have to deal with. At the same time a subtle compact with Keats is made in the covert celebration of the power (Jack's and John's both) of aesthetic redemption, transcendence to the plane of art. Garbage mediated by literary history becomes a kind of literary text. The isolation of the postmodern moment is alleviated as the individual talent makes contact with tradition. That "ironic modern sculpture" of compacted garbage is a figure for *White Noise* itself, whose mocking irony consists in its refusal to let its readers off the hook of self-reliance by giving them an omniscient perspective: never telling them, however subtly, how to live, what to think.

The difficulty of levitating garbage to the plane of art is nothing compared to the problem posed by the toxic cloud. The second section of the novel offers us two narratives: the gripping plot of mass threat, mass evacuation, and mass escape, shadowed by an overplot of sensibility, a narrative whose end is also escape—to make looming death hospitable by making it beautiful. What Jack glimpses in his first look through the binoculars lies at the distant edge of his categories: "a heavy black mass hanging in the air beyond the river, more or less shapeless." Heinrich tells his father that the radio calls it a "feathery plume," but Heinrich, like his father, comments on its strangeness: "Like a shapeless growing thing"—is this the beginning of a sci-fi movie?—"A dark black breathing of smoke." Others in the family inhale the media mediation: "Can you see the feathery plume?" one of the other kids says. What are they "doing about the actual plume," wonders another. The media revises the image: from "feathery plume" to "black billowing cloud" and then, in a forsaking of all concreteness, in a leap to the plane of abstraction, "the airborne toxic event." A character in *Ratner's Star* remarks that we "can measure the gravity of events by tracing the increasingly abstract nature of the terminology." The perfected abstract euphemism, the state's poetry of concealment, offers no consolation; for those who can read it, it tells the awful truth in the very act of cover-up.

The interior narrative of Jack's aesthetic sensibility, never shared in dialogue, represents another kind of journey to abstraction and containment, whose end is neither truth nor lie but conversion of the real for the ends of private consolation. The scene of the toxic spill at the railroad switching yard becomes "operatic chaos"; the thick mist arching over the scene recalls "some grand confection of patriotic music." In the midst of *evacuation*, Jack sees exodus people on foot, sadly burdened with various belongings, crossing a highway overpass. Jack thinks "epic quality"—and suddenly these people become for him "part of some ancient destiny, connected in doom and ruin to a whole history of people walking across wasted landscapes." On the highway he sees the aftermath of a terrible wreck, bloody people, collapsed metal, blood-soaked snow—"all washed in a strong and eerie light," the whole taking on the "eloquence of a formal composition." Passing a hastily evacuated gas station, pumps unlocked, Jack finds himself in a museum, thinking "the tools and pottery of some pueblo civilization, bread in the oven, table set for three, a mystery to haunt the generations." Finally, the thing itself, no longer "shapeless," no longer a "thing" but a literary memory, "like some death ship in a Norse legend," a spectacle assuming its honored place in the "grandness of a sweeping event"—and Jack is reminded by it of the "operatic" scene at the switching yard; reminded of the "people trudging across the snowy overpass," "a tragic army of the dispossessed," reminded, in other words, of the recent aestheticizing history of his own mind.

The narrator tries hard to disillusion himself. "This was a death made in the laboratory ... this was not history we were witnessing." But it *is* history, of a monstrous kind, beyond our traditional categories of familiarization.

Under the duress of the event Jack has told us of his need to experience sublimity whatever the source; to make grand, sweeping, literary sense of the good old-fashioned sort, when there were heroes; to become part of a tradition extending from unnamed Norse poets, to Keats, to himself, deployer of literary and art history, poet's critic. In his most imaginative moment, he leaps into the future to assume the role of archaeologist digging into the ruins his civilization will leave; the imagined dig becoming romantic adventure, conferring mystery while repressing the harsher question: Who or what is responsible for the dispossession of the dispossessed?

Not once does DeLillo permit his narrator reflection upon his own proclivity for ennobling conversion. The implication is that the aestheticizing habit is Jack's personally cultivated state of self-consciousness, which would function as a saving balance to his banal, semi-stupid brand name apprehension of the world. DeLillo's critique of high-cultural Jack is implicit. When the camp of evacuees is threatened by a shift in wind currents, a stampede erupts, which Jack is quick to invest with grandiosity— "like the fall of a colonial capital to dedicated rebels. A great surging drama with elements of humiliation and guilt." Precisely at that moment, his second up-close sight of the toxic cloud, the heroic veneer of his perception is stripped away and Jack's high art becomes a stunning reminder of what it most desires to oppose: media jargon. Jack's aesthetic way is another kind of euphemistic escape, literary feedback doing the work of a mind ill at ease in its setting, straining to get out, and telling us in the process, without meaning to, how beside the point its high cultural values are: telling us, without meaning to, that literary feedback—the cultivated media experience of the highly cultivated—is not much different from mass media feedback, with the difference lying all in the favor of the mass media.

In the hybrid character of Jack Gladney, DeLillo plays a condensed variation on the method of *Ulysses*, with Joyce's high-order phenomenological seismograph, the sensitive Bloom, become Jack, a richly registered impression of postmodern culture, the vehicle of the novel's "naturalistic" surface; and Dedalus also become Jack, the high literary leavening and clarification of chaotic contemporaneity, however sterile. The Jack-as-Bloom socialized in the ambience of the postmodern arts of advertising rebukes the Jack of high art, the Jack-as-Dedalus, with something more believable, more "natural"—another kind of mediation which makes allusions to Norse legend seem absurd. The revenge of mass culture: The cloud "resembled a national promotion for death, a multi-million dollar campaign backed by radio spots, heavy print and billboard, TV saturation."

"We faced each other, propped on elbows, like a sculpture of lounging philosophers in a classical academy." Thus Jack, as he and Babette lie in bed, she about to reveal the sordid little tale of Dylar, he thinking about a trip to ancient Greece via the high Italian Renaissance, remembering perhaps Raphael's *School of Athens*. And after he's been told by a medical technician that tests show traces in his bloodstream of the spilled by-product of the airborne toxic event, and that he should carry his computer-coded results to his doctor (because "Your doctor knows the symbols"), Jack walks out of the clinic directly into the pathos of a nineteenth-century novel: "How literary, I thought peevishly. Streets thick with the details of impulsive life as the hero ponders the latest phase in his dying." This latter, literary reminiscence, then succeeded immediately by unreflective media-speak, in the rhetoric of the weather report: quotation unawares, pastiche undeliberate, no parody intended, no critical distance won. "It was a partially cloudy day with winds diminishing toward sunset."

Precisely at that moment (in Chapter 36) with weatherman jargon welling up through his voice, this human collage of styles—this loquacious product of, and advertisement for, the American cultural ecosystem— appears to free himself by turning deliberate storyteller, by seizing his culture's most powerful medium of the image, the TV commercial, as the stuff of literary narrative and the occasion of intervention. Jack is here postmodernism's own parodic Homer, no longer media subject but media subjugator, telling us the tale of the electronic tribe. The extended family that phones together stays together—a Trimline, a white Princess; a people, a nation:

> That night I walked the streets of Blacksmith. The glow of blue-eyed TVs. The voices on the touch-tone phones. Far away the grandparents huddle in a chair, eagerly sharing the receiver as carrier waves modulate into audible signals. It is the voice of their grandson, the growing boy whose face appears in the snapshots set around the phone. Joy rushes to their eyes but it is misted over, infused with a sad and complex knowing. What is the youngster saying to them? His wretched complexion makes him unhappy? He wants to leave school and work full-time at Foodland, bagging groceries? He tells them he *likes* to bag groceries. It is the one thing in life he finds satisfying.... I like it gramma, it's totally unthreatening, it's how I want to spend my life. And so they listen sadly, loving him all the more, their faces pressed against the sleek Trimline, the white Princess in the bedroom, the plain brown Rotary in granddad's paneled basement hideaway.

"What happens after the commercial ends?" Jack had asked himself earlier, at the beginning of the chapter, when he'd aborted his blow-by-blow replay of that same AT&T ad, "Reach out and touch someone!" And now we know the answer. At the end of the chapter Jack reimagines the commercial in a caustically comic excursion through TV land, which ends with a personal meditation that evokes a traditional ominous symbolism, a key vein of romantic imagery, passing from Poe's story of A. Gordon Pym, trapped hopelessly in the Antarctic, through Joyce's December snows in "The Dead," to Thomas Mann's *Magic Mountain*. Jack's postmodern music begins with a quotation of the classic weather report and concludes with a complex allusion to classic literature's allegorical winters: "Clouds race across the westering moon, the seasons change in somber montage, going deeper into winter stillness, a landscape of silence and ice."

Then one thing more, a single-sentence paragraph which ends Chapter 36: "Your doctor knows the symbols"—a repetition of what Jack had been told by the medical technician who knows the bad news, and who was given to us as a foreshadowing double only a few pages earlier: "He was a mild-eyed fellow with a poor complexion and reminded me of the boys at the supermarket who stand at the end of the checkout counter bagging merchandise." The medical technician, a minor character in Jack's novel (so goes the fiction of the first-person mode) unexpectedly haunts a fiction within a fiction. Jack's masterful send-up story of the TV commercial is undermined by the protean messenger of death who gets inside the safe place of his imagination—assuming the shape of the acne-struck bag boy, messenger of the last word that undoes all words, including those of Jack's parody.

Jack's failure to dominate the art of the TV ad—not his beloved euphemisms of high art—brings him, curiously, closest to himself as a voice whose integrity is sustained against the erosions of all mediation—whether high literary or high Madison Avenue—a brooding presence whose abiding source is death-obsession. The authentic Jack is the vulnerable self who flees himself through the cover-ups of his acute learnedness, his satire, parody, and general all-around wittiness; he is the man who fears for his wife and children—and whose attachment to them is not ironic; whose devotion—the book's deepest mystery, its most shocking dimension—is actually supported by the supermarket ("where we wait together, regardless of age, our carts stocked with brightly colored goods"), by the shopping mall, where his kids become guides to his "endless well-being"—"I was one of them, shopping, at last"—and by the arts of advertising which give him entry into religious solace, even "aura." "Aura": the salient quality that Murray ascribed to our experience of "the most photographed barn"; the emanation of a source, the

nimbus, of the real, the indicator of depth, origin, and authenticity—
everything, in other words, presumably unavailable to the postmodern world
of reproduction, simulation, repetition, and image—suddenly and stunningly
restored by the supermarket, the mall, the poetry of media glut.

That night at the camp for evacuees of Blacksmith, Jack hears one of
the kids mumble something in her sleep; he leans over to catch the meaning,
convinced it will be a revelation of innocence and his route to some
unshakable comfort. She speaks again—this time clearly, as if in ecstatic
chant, a ritualized utterance that he receives not in corrosive satiric
perspective—which would have been the conventional literary payoff in this
moment—but with amazement and awe:

> *Toyota Celica.*
> The utterance was beautiful and mysterious, gold-shot with
> looming wonder. It was like the name of an ancient power in the
> sky, tablet-carved in cuneiform. It made me feel that something
> hovered. But how could this be? A simple brand name, an
> ordinary car. How could these near-nonsense words, murmured
> in a child's restless sleep, make me sense a meaning, a presence?
> ... Whatever its source, the utterance struck me with the impact
> of a moment of splendid transcendence.

Each of these moments—at the supermarket, at the mall, hearing
Steffie talk in her sleep—is delivered with mordantly styled humor because
it's almost impossible for Jack to speak any other way: He's doomed with
critical knowledge of his life's deep support systems. Nevertheless, there is
always something else in the voice, not easy to define because in books of this
sort we don't expect domestic commitment or a sense of wonder on behalf of
the culture's binding power. At such moments in *White Noise*, DeLillo's
readers—sophisticates, like him, of corrosive truth—are given an alternative.
Would we prefer that Jack give up the supermarket, the mall, his family, the
nights gathered around the TV, for another, chilling guarantor of
community, who lurks in the background of *White Noise*, as in the
background of a number of modernist literary monuments—the specter of
the totalitarian, the gigantic charismatic figure who triggers our desire to
give in, to merge our frightened selves in his frightening authority? Hitler,
another kind of epic hero, voice of national solidarity, is the other object of
Jack's awe.

At the novel's end Jack meets Willy Mink, Babette's betrayer, the corrupt
agent of Dylar. The plot that Jack hatches in order to kill Willy Mink
embodies his dream of existential self-determination, precisely what his

culture denies him. But he who would be master of plot, at the end, becomes, again, plot's creature, as he plays, again, the role of the clown of plot.

Willy Mink is what the precariously centered Jack might become, postmodern man's essence, and our culture's re-formation of the meaning of madness. Willy Mink is a voice without a center, a jumbled bunch of fragments from various contemporary jargons, mostly emanating from the TV he sits in front of with the sound turned down, overdosing on Dylar— the pure American product who speaks these sentences:

> Some of these sure-footed bighorns have been equipped with radio transmitters.... The heat from your hand will actually make the gold-leafing stick to the wax-paper.
>
> This is what the scientists don't understand, scrubbing their smocks with Woolite. Not that I have anything personal against death from our vantage point high atop Metropolitan County Stadium.

Willy Mink is the promised end of a journey that began on the *Mayflower*, the shocking *telos* of the third-person ideal, the "I" converted to bits and pieces of language not his own. Sitting in front of the TV, throwing fistfuls of Dylar at his mouth, babbling, Willy Mink is a compacted image of consumerism in the society of the electronic media, a figure of madness, but our figure of madness. Is Willy Mink a just image of postmodern community in America, a sick representation thereof, or both?

America's profoundest philosopher of community, Josiah Royce, believed that true community consisted in collective consciousness of historical process; community as memory of a significant extended past which all members hold in common and as hope for the future—an expectation that the historical process will continue to be a story that possesses sense and coherence, and that the future will, like the past, be a nurturing time for cohesive values and actions. In Royce's rigorous terms, it is difficult to speak of postmodern "community," unless we are willing to take absolutely seriously the proposition that postmodernism came over on the *Mayflower*. If we cannot, then we are left with this rejoinder to Royce: Communities have to start somewhere, a community's collective memory needs to have beginnings to recollect. The era of the shopping mall, the supermarket, the fast-food restaurants, and the ritual family gatherings around the TV is in its infancy. But who knows? One day we might say that at the close of the twentieth century we began to discover the binding power, the comforts of our new Roman Church. Hard to say, before it comes to pass, in all its laws, liturgies, and forms of behavior, that it will do any more damage than the old.

LEONARD WILCOX

Baudrillard, DeLillo's White Noise, and the End of Heroic Narrative

From *Americana*, through *Great Jones Street*, *White Noise*, and *Libra*, Don DeLillo's novels have been concerned with the relationship between American identity and the mediascapes. If the two earlier works were preoccupied with the way in which the American dream is manipulated by the media, the later two chart a world that is mediated by and constituted in the technologico-semiotic regime. In *White Noise* DeLillo's protagonist Jack Gladney confronts a new order in which life is increasingly lived in a world of simulacra, where images and electronic representations replace direct experience. In *Libra*, Lee Oswald is a product of that order; a figure devoted to media self-fashioning, he constructs his life—and indeed his death—from the proliferation of charismatic images and spectacles of a postmodern society.[1]

White Noise and *Libra* particularly, with their interest in electronic mediation and representation, present a view of life in contemporary America that is uncannily similar to that depicted by Jean Baudrillard. They indicate that the transformations of contemporary society that Baudrillard describes in his theoretical writings on information and media have also gripped the mind and shaped the novels of Don DeLillo. For *White Noise* especially—because it most specifically explores the realm of information and mediascape—Baudrillard's works provide an interesting, valuable, and

From *Contemporary Literature* 32, no. 3 (Fall 1991): 346-365. © 1991 by the Board of Regents of the University of Wisconsin System.

even crucial perspective. The informational world Baudrillard delineates bears a striking resemblance to the world of *White Noise*: one characterized by the collapse of the real and the flow of signifiers emanating from an information society, by a "loss of the real" in a black hole of simulation and the play and exchange of signs. In this world common to both Baudrillard and DeLillo, images, signs, and codes engulf objective reality; signs become more real than reality and stand in for the world they erase. Baudrillard's notion that this radical semiurgy results in the collapse of difference, firm structures, and finalities (the "fixities" by which stable meaning is produced) markedly resembles DeLillo's vision of an entropic breakdown of basic rituals and concepts in the informational flow of electronic communication. Moreover, for both Baudrillard and DeLillo a media-saturated consciousness threatens the concept of meaning itself. For Baudrillard, "information devours its own contents; it devours communication," resulting in "a sort of nebulous state leading not at all to a surfeit of innovation but to the very contrary, to total entropy" (*In the Shadow* 97, 100). Similarly for DeLillo, the flow of electronic information obliterates coherent meaning. The very notion of "white noise" that is so central to the novel implies a neutral and reified mediaspeech, but also a surplus of data and an entropic blanket of information glut which flows from a media-saturated society.

But the similarities between Baudrillard and DeLillo do not end here. For both, this increasingly simulational and nonreferential world brings about radical changes in the very shape of subjectivity. For Baudrillard an older modernist order—with its dialectic of alienation and inner authenticity—is eclipsed by new forms of experiencing the self. Lured and locked into the "uninterrupted interfaces" of video screen and mediascape, the subject experiences an undifferentiated flux of pure signifiers, an "ecstasy of communication" in which conventional structures of meaning dissolve and the ability to imagine an alternative reality disappears. A new experience of euphoria, an ungrounded "delirium" replaces the anxiety and alienation of an earlier period. Unlike the earlier experience of alienation, which attested to a coherent private sphere, an interiority of self, this new delirium, a vertiginous fascination with the "instantaneity" and "obscene" visibility of media events, attests to the "extermination of interstitial and protective spaces" ("Ecstasy" 127). Indeed the "communicational promiscuity" of the omnipresent and ubiquitous mass media strips society of its secrets, inhibitions, repressions, and depths and leads inexorably to the hollowing out of the self—or better to say, the dispersal of self, the generalized destabilization of the subject in the era of networks and electronic transmission of symbols ("Ecstasy" 130–31).[2]

Similarly DeLillo sees a new form of subjectivity emerging as the modernist order is eclipsed by the postmodern world. Indeed, an older modernist subjectivity is in a state of siege in the information society. Jack Gladney, the narrator of *White Noise*, is a modernist displaced in a postmodern world. He exhibits a Kierkegaardian "fear and trembling" regarding death and attempts to preserve earlier notions of an authentic and coherent identity by observing the tribalistic rituals of family life. Gladney attempts to "shore up the ruins" of an older order, ironically by chanting advertising slogans as if they were sacred formulas. Yet he often succumbs to the Baudrillardian condition, floating "ecstatically" in a delirium of networks, hyperreal surfaces, and fetishized consumer objects. Gladney's narrative is interspersed with the entropic chatter and snippets of talk shows that emerge from a television that "migrates" around the Gladney household, moving from room to room, filling the air with jingles and consumer advice ("The T.V. said: 'And other trends that could dramatically impact your portfolio'" [61]). His narrative is interpenetrated by brand names and advertising slogans as he chants, "Mastercard, Visa, American Express ... Leaded, unleaded, superunleaded ... Dristan Ultra, Dristan Ultra ... Clorets, Velamints, Freedent" (100, 199, 167, 229). These "eruptions" in the narrative imply the emergence of a new form of subjectivity colonized by the media and decentered by its polyglot discourses and electronic networks. They imply the evacuation of the private spheres of self, in Baudrillardian terms "the end of interiority" ("Ecstasy" 133).

Moreover, for Baudrillard and DeLillo the dissolution of a modernist subjectivity in the mire of contemporary media and technology is integrally connected to another issue: the passing of the great modernist notions of artistic impulse and representation, the demise of notions of a "heroic" search for alternative, creative forms of consciousness, and the idea of art as specially endowed revelation. Such a heroic modernism struggled through extraordinary artistic and intellectual effort to create meaning from the flux and fragments of an atomized contemporary world, to pierce the veil, to reveal underlying truth. But for Baudrillard, the very impulses that gave impetus to this project have dissipated in the contemporary world: "Something has changed, and the Faustian, Promethean, (perhaps Oedipal) period of production and consumption gives way to the 'proteinic' era of networks, to the narcissistic and protean era of connections, contact, contiguity, feedback and generalized interface that goes with the universe of communication" ("Ecstasy" 127). For Baudrillard these heroic Faustian, Promethean, and oedipal impulses to struggle, to illuminate, and to unveil a (repressed) truth give way to "the smooth operational surface of communication" ("Ecstasy" 127); they have all but dissolved in the pure, empty seriality and the decentering forces of a "proteinic" information society.

Similarly, for DeLillo, such heroic striving for meaning has been radically thrown into question in the contemporary world. For at the core of the modernist version of the heroic is the notion of the constitutive power of the imagination, the idea of an autonomous and authentic subjectivity out of which springs vision and illumination. Such is the modernist "epiphany": a moment of profound imaginative perception in which fragments are organized and essence revealed, and (on the level of narrative) in which a hermeneutical core of meaning is contained within a constellation of luminescent images. But *White Noise* suggests such moments of authentic and unfettered subjectivity are being supplanted by a Baudrillardian euphoria or "schizophrenia" which characterizes the experience of the self in the space of the simulacrum. By rendering moments of "heroic" vision and imaginative epiphany as parody and pastiche—as he does in the climactic "showdown" between Gladney and Gray (a.k.a. Willie Mink)—DeLillo implies the exhaustion of late modernist, existentialist notions of heroism. As well, DeLillo's parody and "terrific comedy" (Lentricchia 1) underscore a crisis of representation relating directly to the collapse of patriarchal authority and to the breakup of the oedipal configurations that underpin the heroic narrative itself.

The passing of a heroic modernist "Faustian and Promethean era" and the emergence of a "proteinic" postmodern order is registered in *White Noise* through the narrative voice of Jack Gladney. Gladney sifts through the layers of white noise—electronic media, printed information, traffic sounds, computer read-outs—listening for significance, for a grasp of essence in the flux. In modernist fashion, he struggles in an almost Sisyphean way to glean meaning from the surrounding noise of culture and is drawn toward occasions of existential self-fashioning, heroic moments of vision in a commodified world. When he shops with his family he notes that "I began to grow in value and self-regard. I filled myself out, found new aspects of myself, located a person I'd forgotten existed" (84). And when he hears his daughter Steffie uttering the words "Toyota Corolla, Toyota Celica, Toyota Cressida" in her sleep, his response is "whatever its source, the utterance struck me with the impact of a moment of splendid transcendence" (155).

Yet Gladney's modernist impulse toward authentic selfhood and his quest for transcendental meaning seem oddly out of place in the postmodern world. Gladney's colleague Murray Siskind, a visiting lecturer in "living icons" who lives in a one-room apartment with a television set and stacks of comic books, and who teaches popular culture courses in "Elvis" and "The Cinema of Car Crashes," insists that looking for a realm of meaning beyond surfaces, networks, and commodities is unnecessary; the information society provides its own sort of epiphanies, and watching television, an experience he describes as "close to mystical," is one of them. For Murray television proffers the Baudrillardian "ecstasy of communication," a "peak experience" of postmodern culture. Television, he says,

> welcomes us into the grid, the network of little buzzing dots that make up the picture pattern. There is light, there is sound. I ask my students, "What more do you want?" Look at the wealth of data concealed in the grid, in the bright packaging, the jingles, the slice-of-life commercials, the products hurtling out of darkness, the coded messages and endless repetitions, like chants, like mantras. "*Coke is it, Coke is it, Coke is it.*" (51)

For Murray the postmodernist, the euphoric forms of electronic data and informational flow are to be enthusiastically embraced, and Murray takes it upon himself to be Gladney's tutor in the new semiotic regime. When Murray and Gladney drive into the country to see "The Most Photographed Barn in America," for example, Murray explains the significance of the tourist attraction within the new order of image and simulacrum. Rather than conjuring up associations with a pioneering past or an authentic rural life, the barn has been subsumed into the process of image replication; it is surrounded by tour buses, roadside signs, venders selling post cards of the barn, people taking pictures of the barn, people photographing other photographers photographing the barn. Observing the tourists, Murray points to the postmodern experience of proliferating images without ground: "they are taking pictures of taking pictures" (13). Murray expounds solemnly on the unfolding of a new order where the distinction between reality and representation, sign and referent, collapses: "Once you've seen the signs about the barn, it becomes impossible to see the barn" (12). He explains to the reluctant Gladney the logic of a simulational world where signs triumph over reality, where experience is constructed by and in service of the image, and the ephemeral image takes on its own resplendent, mystical "aura": "We're not here to capture an image, we're here to maintain one. Every photograph reinforces the aura. Can you feel it, Jack? An accumulation of nameless energies" (12).[3]

Yet if Murray savors the flux of images and signs, Gladney is increasingly nonplused by a world without referents, where the responses of an authentic interior self vanish in the undertow of the simulacrum and where media images and spectacles proliferate, terrorize, and fascinate. The "Airborne Toxic Event" (besides registering the postmodern preoccupation with toxic poisoning) depicts a condition where subjective responses are both constructed and validated by radio and television: initially the "toxic event" is reported as a "feathery plume," which induces curiosity and mild alarm; later it is described as a catastrophic "black billowing cloud," evoking fear "accompanied by a sense of awe that bordered on the religious" (127). Increasingly it becomes impossible to distinguish between the spectacle and the real. Even the natural world—the ultimate ground of the "real"— succumbs to a hyperreal condition of multiple regress without origin. Spectacular sunsets (which Gladney refers to as "postmodern sunsets") appear after the release of toxins into the atmosphere, but it is never certain whether the sunsets are caused by toxic chemicals or by the residue of microorganisms subsequently discharged by scientists into the atmosphere to "eat" the airborne chemicals. Exposure to the toxic materials released by the "event" causes déjà vu in the Gladney children (déjà vu itself being a "recollection" without origin), but it is unclear whether this is a "real" symptom or a psychosomatic one resulting from suggestion, since they get the symptoms only after they hear them reported on the radio.

Gladney's encounter with the SIMUVAC (simulated evacuation) underscores most profoundly the simulated or hyperreal world depicted in *White Noise*. SIMUVAC regularly stages efficient rehearsals for coping with real disasters—volunteers play dead and videotapes are sent for prompt analysis. Yet at the evacuation site during the toxic event, Gladney discovers that the SIMUVAC personnel are using the real event to rehearse and perfect a simulation. The world has been turned inside out; simulation has become the ground of the real: "You have to make allowances for the fact that everything we see tonight is real," the SIMUVAC man complains to Gladney; "we don't have our victims laid out where we'd want them if this was an actual simulation.... There's a lot of polishing we still have to do" (139).

Finally the world of *White Noise*—one based on the abstract circulation of information—follows the logic of the utter commutability of signs. Any semiological network can become a hermetic system into which the individual subject can be inserted and which constructs the self. Gladney's German teacher, for example, tells Jack how after his loss of faith in God he "turned to meteorology for comfort" and soon had created a universe of significance from the weather: "It brought me a sense of peace and security I'd never experienced. Dew, frost, and fog. Snow flurries. The jet stream.... I began to come out of my shell, talk to people on the street. 'Nice day.' 'Looks like rain.' 'Hot enough for you?'" (55).

Indeed, Gladney finds himself unwittingly drawn into this order in which the subject is assembled in signs. Gladney is chairman of "Hitler studies" (which in itself suggests a grim nostalgic impulse to recuperate the "real" in an age of simulation) but is nevertheless warned by the chancellor of the university about his tendency to make "a feeble presentation of self"

(17). Gladney begins to wear heavy-rimmed sunglasses to bolster his credibility and changes his name from Jack Gladney to the more distinguished J. A. K. Gladney. Later, when his wife Babette expresses her irritation at the imposing, mirrored sunglasses and asks Gladney to stop wearing them, he retorts, "I can't teach Hitler without them" (221). Any notion of an essential identity is all but erased in this realm of free-floating signifiers and simulation. Yet Gladney is unable, like his friend Murray, to submit himself happily to surface and simulacrum; rather he is plagued by a nagging late modernist, existential sense that he is in "bad faith": "I am the false character that follows the name around" (17).

This crisis of subjectivity that Gladney faces in this hermetic universe of afterimages, ghosts, floating signifiers, and simulacra is compounded by another—his impending death after exposure to the deadly gas "Nyodene D." during the evacuation. Gladney exhibits a modernist angst about death, ruminating about its significance, visiting graveyards, and talking about it with his friend Murray. Yet Gladney's existential crisis is obsolete in the new postmodern order. Gladney's anguished confession, "I want to live," merely evokes from Murray a flight of free association along the intertextual surfaces of popular culture: "From the Robert Wise film of the same name, with Susan Hayward as Barbara Graham, a convicted murderess. Aggressive jazz score by Johnny Mandel" (283). Moreover, even death is not exempt from the world of simulation: the experience of dying is utterly mediated by technology and eclipsed by a world of symbols. The body becomes simulacrum, and death loses its personal and existential resonances. When Gladney is subjected to a computer scan to obtain a "data profile" on his condition, he notes that "it is when death is rendered graphically, is televised so to speak, that you sense an eerie separation between your condition and yourself. A network of symbols has been introduced, an entire awesome technology wrested from the gods. It makes you feel like a stranger in your own dying" (142). And as Gladney later tells Murray, "there's something artificial about my death. It's shallow, unfulfilling. I don't belong to the earth or sky. They ought to carve an aerosol can on my tombstone" (283).

Thus media and technology transform death into a sign spectacle, and its reality is experienced as the body doubled in technified forms: death by "print-out."[4] But if death, the last vestige of the real, the final border of the self, becomes part of the precession of simulacra, what possibilities exist for meaning, value, for the autonomous self's endeavor to create meaning against death's limits and finality? In an order given over to simulation, such heroic impulses can only be rendered as parody and pastiche—the "blank parody" of exhausted or dead forms, the postmodern response to the disappearance of narrative norms that previously figured heroic action.

When Gladney discovers that Babette has contrived to obtain Dylar (a high tech chemical "cure" for the fear of death) by sleeping with the project manager of the group working on the drug's research and development, he resolves to hunt out the project manager—identified by Babette as "Mr. Gray"—and kill him. Such a confrontation has all the makings of a heroic showdown. Yet from the outset Gladney's role of hero in the showdown is undermined in a variety of ways. A note of literary parody is struck even before Gladney meets Gray. After his exposure to Nyodene D. during the airborne toxic event, Gladney is diagnosed by the computerized scanner as harboring a fatal "nebulous mass" in his body. His comments on his own predicament constitute an overt parody of the existential hero contemplating radical freedom against the knowledge of the inevitability of death: "How literary, I thought peevishly. Streets thick with the details of impulsive life as the hero ponders the latest phase in his dying" (281).

When Gladney confronts Gray (identified as Willie Mink), the "residential organizational genius" of the Dylar research group, now a shabby, demented recluse, the scene becomes a pastiche of the existentialist epiphany—a "negative" epiphany which involves a lucid recognition of the absurd and contingent nature of reality, a moment of heroic self-fashioning based on the sudden perception that existence is grounded in nothingness and the individual is utterly free. When he goes to the seedy motel where Mink is living, there is a strong sense of the utter provisionality and freedom which characterizes Gladney's actions: he proceeds by instinct, continually updating his plans. Like Meursault in *l'Étranger*, who experiences a sensory epiphany—an amplified awareness of the play of sunlight and the sounds of water—just before he commits his act of violence, Gladney experiences an intensity of sensation as he enters Mink's room: "I stood inside the room, sensing things, noting the room tone, the dense air. Information rushed toward me, rushed slowly, incrementally" (305). Like Roquentin, who has a visionary moment in *La Nausée*, Gladney experiences with almost hallucinatory intensity the essential pulsating "thusness" of reality, and in so doing believes himself to be experiencing an unmediated vision of pure existence: "I knew the precise nature of events. I was moving closer to things in their actual state as I approached a violence, a smashing intensity. Water fell in drops, surfaces gleamed" (305).

Yet these perceptions are related in a dry, toneless fashion appropriate to pastiche, which Fredric Jameson describes as "the wearing of a stylistic mask, speech in a dead language ... without parody's ulterior motive, without the satirical impulse, without that still latent feeling that there exists something normal compared to which what is being imitated is rather comic" ("Consumer Society" 114). Pastiche implies a world where fragmented or heterogeneous linguistic islands supplant centered, heroic narrative positions, a world where the possibility of unique vision and style has been lost. Thus rather than the parodic imitation of a peculiar and unique style, DeLillo's pastiche involves a play of stylistic mannerisms, from the high modernist heroics of the existential hero to the B-movie heroics of the hard-boiled detective. Even as he approaches the motel, Gladney assumes the voice-over style of the Raymond Chandler hero: "It occurred to me that I did not have to knock. The door would be open" (305). This B-movie quality is furthered by Gladney's insistence upon inflating the narrative as he dwells repetitively on his sensory apocalypse: "Surfaces gleamed. Water struck the roof in spherical masses, globules, splashing drams" (307); "The precise nature of events. Things in their actual state" (310). But these observations of an intensified reality rapidly descend into ludicrous banality, and rather than an epiphany of identity, Gladney undergoes a farcical loss of self:

> I continued to advance in consciousness. Things glowed, a secret life rising out of them. Water struck the roof in elongated orbs, splashing drams. I knew for the first time what rain really was. I knew what wet was. I understood the neurochemistry of my brain, the meaning of dreams (the waste material of premonitions). Great stuff everywhere, racing through the room, racing slowly. A richness, a density. I believed everything. I was a Buddhist, a Jain, a Duck River Baptist. (310)

Moreover, just as the secure narrative position required by the heroic figure is destabilized by pastiche, the revelations of the heroic transcendental ego are ultimately transformed into a postmodern decentering of self, an "ecstatic" Baudrillardian dispersal of consciousness in the world of screens and networks. As Gladney enters Gray's motel room he observes that "I sensed I was part of a network of structures and channels" (305). As the narrative continues, metaphors of the experience of Dasein through which Being coalesces in an existential moment of recognition startlingly shift to metaphors of the world of networks, information, and white noise: "The intensity of the noise in the room was the same at all frequencies. Sound all around.... I knew who I was in the network of meanings" (312). The whole atmosphere, so charged with unusual vitality, now becomes bathed in the eerie glow of television: "auditory scraps, tatters, whirling specks. A heightened reality. A denseness that was also a transparency. Surfaces gleamed" (307).

For Gladney's confrontation with Mink is an allegorical confrontation with postmodern culture itself. Mink is the personification of a new order; a composite man of undecidable ethnicity, he suggests a world where national and ethnic differences have been eradicated in an increasing internationalization of American popular culture. Mink wears Bermuda shorts with a Budweiser pattern on them; he sprawls on his couch "in the attitude of a stranded air traveler, someone long since defeated by the stale waiting, the airport babble" (307). "I had American sex the first time in Port-O-San, Texas," Mink announces; "American sex, let me tell you, this is how I learned my English" (308–9). A repository of Lyotardian "linguistic clouds" of splintered and fractured discourse, Mink repeats phrases, from television weather reports ("And this could represent the leading edge of some warmer air" [313]) to popular geography merged with popular nutrition hints ("This is the point, as opposed to emerging coastlines, continental plates. Or you can eat natural grains, vegetables, eggs, no fish, no fruit" [311]). Mink voices the drone of the mediascapes; more than that he physically resembles a television set. Gladney notes that "his face was odd, concave, forehead and chin jutting" (305–6). Mink is the embodiment of white noise ("His face appeared at the end of the white room, a white buzz" [312]) and of a system in a state of entropic decay: he is exhausted and depleted; he shows "a senile grin" (309). Moreover he is obsessed with his own deterioration, quelling his fear of death by consuming Dylar tablets one after another.

Gladney's existential epiphany now begins to resemble the "peak experience" typifying the postmodern condition—one similar to Baudrillard's description of schizophrenia—the ultimate outcome of an "obscenity of communication" in which the self succumbs utterly to "networks of influence." Baudrillard describes schizophrenia as "the absolute proximity, the total instantaneity of things ... the overexposure and transparence of the world which traverses [the schizoid] without obstacle" ("Ecstasy" 133). In this "delirium" of communication, the schizophrenic exists only as a nodal point or "switching center"; his mental and physical boundaries dissolve in the flow of information as he experiences the cognitive equivalent of white noise.

Alarmingly, Gladney's peak experience rapidly metamorphoses into this Baudrillardian nightmare. Indeed, it becomes similar to Fredric Jameson's description (elaborating on Baudrillard) of the transformation of the expressive energies of modernism into the fragmentation of emotions in the diffuse and discontinuous schizoid world of postmodernism. For Jameson, this schizophrenic experience is one in which the world takes on a "hallucinogenic intensity" ("Cultural Logic" 73). Gladney's experience has this hallucinatory quality, yet if it initially resembles the Sartrean visionary moment in its intensity, its sense of depth, of unmediated reality and pure existence is ultimately a chimera. Rather than an epiphany of identity, it constitutes a dissolution of self, a lifeworld reduced, in Jameson's terms, "to an experience of pure material Signifiers, or in other words of a series of pure and unrelated presents in time" ("Cultural Logic" 72). Gladney is temporally suspended as he continues to revise his plans to kill Mink in a toneless, chantlike fashion, perpetually rewriting a present which seems without link to past and future. And as temporal continuities break down, his experience of the present becomes overwhelmingly vivid: when he shoots Mink he marvels at Mink's blood, sees its color "in terms of dominant wavelength, luminance, purity" (312). Yet in spite of this heightened intensity, the encounter suggests not the existentialist sense that pure existence looms up as artificial words and constructs drop away, but rather the postmodern awareness that words themselves construct reality. The dominant impression of Gladney's account, in fact, is wordiness, a proliferation of words. Words themselves loom up in hyperpresent materiality; when he shoots Mink, not sound so much as words echo around the room: "I fired the gun, the weapon, the pistol, the firearm, the automatic" (312).

But it is Mink himself who most completely suggests the postmodern "schizophrenic" experience in an instantaneous world of discrete and discontinuous moments in which signifiers fail to add up, to produce the "meaning-effect" of an interlocking syntagmatic series. One of the side effects of the Dylar that Mink ingests to eradicate the fear of death (and coextensively the sense of time) is the sort of literalizing attention to words that results from the isolation of signifiers in pure and unrelated presents and the consequent breakdown of the play of meaning along the temporal manifold of the signifying chain. In their condition as jumbled and isolated signifiers, words are ultimately reduced to mere signals which form a mechanical one-to-one relationship with their referent.[5] Thus Gladney, stalking Mink, says "hail of bullets" and Mink runs for cover; when he says "plunging aircraft" Mink folds himself into the recommended crash position.

Gladney ultimately botches his plan to kill Mink and steal the Dylar: Mink devours the Dylar, and Gladney, after wounding Mink, takes him to the hospital. More significantly, the encounter with Mink suggests the untenability of heroic self-fashioning, as Gladney's epiphany collapses into postmodern schizophrenia. Rather than a moment of pure, unfettered subjectivity, Gladney's experience implies the evacuation of the self, as the deep structures of modern experience—as well as modern narrative— succumb to a postmodern crisis of the sign and representation, to "networks of influence," to a discontinuous schizoid world, and to white noise.

But there is yet another way in which *White Noise* figures the impossibility of heroism and the demise of the heroic narrative. Baudrillard's suggestion that the "proteinic" era of networks has replaced not only Faustian and Promethean but oedipal strivings is relevant here. For DeLillo's postmodern world is one of free-floating and endless simulacra, a meaning cut off from all bases. This is a world in which in Lacanian terms the stability of the *nom du père* is subject to doubt, indeed where notions of a centered authority are mere residues from an earlier period. Even religious belief is swallowed in the order of the simulacrum. When Gladney drags Mink to a Catholic hospital after the bungled murder attempt, he asks the resident nun about the Church's thinking on heaven, God, angels, and the saving of souls. Her response is "saved? What is saved? This is a dumb head, who would come in here to talk about angels. Show me an angel. Please. I want to see" (317). The nun informs him that church officials have long since ceased to believe in the "devil, the angels, heaven, hell"; they merely pretend to. "Our pretense is a dedication," she says. "Someone must appear to believe" (319).

This world in which the ultimate, transcendent "name of the father" is simulational implies a crisis in the deeply patriarchal structures of late capitalism, a world in which there is a troubling of the phallus, in which masculinity slips from its sure position. Initially this insufficiency of masculine authority is suggested by Gladney's position as head of a family of five children, most of whom are brought from earlier marriages. This postmodern family is no longer organized around the *nom du père*, rather it is utterly decentered and globally dispersed. Gladney's string of ex-spouses and his collection of children from previous marriages are connected through time and global space by electronic networks. When one of Jack's ex-wives telephones, he comments that "her tiny piping voice bounced down to me from a hollow ball in geosynchronous orbit" (273).

Gladney's attempts to recover patriarchal authority by wearing sunglasses and teaching courses in Hitler notwithstanding, his narrative is hardly authoritative, nor does it carry a sense of mastery. It is a decentered and toneless montage of voices, ranging from outcroppings of media slogans to metaphysical meditations on the meaning of death. But if Gladney's narrative registers the decline of patriarchal authority, the breakup of the order of phallic power is suggested most strongly by the figure of Gray/Mink and the dynamic of Gladney's confrontation with him. Gray seems initially to represent patriarchal privilege and power. He is a scientist, the "project manager" of the research work on Dylar. And he is the man who has usurped Gladney's wife Babette, lured her into bed in a seedy motel room in exchange for the drug. Stung by Babette's confessed adultery, Gladney imagines Gray and his wife in the motel. The figure of Gray initially suggests phallic mastery, a dominance which affirms the masculine gaze and its power of appropriation: "Bedward, plotward. I saw my wife reclining on her side, voluptuously rounded, the eternal waiting nude. I saw her as he did. Dependent, submissive, emotionally captive. I felt his mastery and control. The dominance of his position" (241).

The "bedward, plotward" trajectory suggests the oedipal narrative itself, with Gray representing the corporate father (or "project manager") who has usurped Gladney's "motherly" wife (Babette exhibits "an honesty inherent in bulkiness" [7]). This trajectory also implies the need to bring the narrative logic to its fruition by Gladney's killing Gray and reclaiming his love object. Yet Gray is finally not a figure of centered authority; he is a "composite man," as Babette informs Gladney, and "Gray" is a convenient name she uses to refer to several scientists with whom she had transactions in the research group. Further, Gladney imagines Gray as "four or more grayish figures," vague organization men without potency or phallic power, technocrats devoted to eradicating human emotion, especially the fear of death: "selfless, sexless, determined to engineer us out of our fear" (241). Moreover, oedipal logic gives way to the "proteinic" world of information as Gray appears in Gladney's fantasy as a televised image, a representative and embodiment of a postmodern informational world of networks and circuits: "I sat up late thinking of Mr. Gray. Gray-bodied, staticky, unfinished. The picture wobbled and rolled, the edges of his body flared with random distortion" (241). Finally the "bedward, plotward" trajectory of the oedipal narrative, culminating in the primal scene itself—the moment of consummation between Gray and Babette—is dissipated by the echoes of brand names and a ubiquitous "panasonic" white noise: "[I] heard them in their purling foreplay, the love babble and buzzing flesh. Heard the sloppings and smackings, the swash of wet mouths, bedsprings sinking in. An interval of mumbled adjustments. Then gloom moved in around the gray-sheeted bed, a circle slowly closing. Panasonic" (241).

Similarly Willie Mink (incarnation of the spectral Gray) is associated with the flow of information and with white noise. But as the one-time project manager of the Dylar research group, which is "supported by a multinational giant," he is also connected with a global economy. The Mink/Gray composite in fact is associated both with informational flow and transnational monopoly, a new world of multinational capitalism whose channels of control are so widespread and dispersed that no single authoritative father figure is necessary for its operation. Rather than figuring the power of a centered, authoritative, symbolic father, Mink/Gray represents the "flow of desire" of postindustrial society, a society of services and information in which desire tends less and less to be sublimated and organized within the patriarchal oedipalized family.[6] The figure of Mink/Gray is as amorphous and diffused as the relays and networks of the social desiring machine in the desublimated and postoedipal space of late capitalism. Mink/Gray provides no focal point for an oedipal dynamic that might otherwise underpin the sort of heroic confrontation Gladney undertakes. "This is the grayish figure of my torment, the man who took my wife" (308–9), Gladney resolutely tells himself when he sees Mink. Yet Mink is less a usurper than a repository for the rambling, metonymic discourses of a consumer culture, and Gladney, even if he could carry off a heroic encounter, has nothing substantial to fight. The battle on the heroic terrain of oedipal rivalry and phallic power is abortive: if Gladney symbolically castrates Mink, shooting him in the "midsection" and "hipbone" ("his lap a puddle of blood"), he carelessly allows Mink to do the same to him (Mink shoots him in the "wrist"). Finally Gladney's antagonism toward his opponent collapses; he begins to identify with Mink and regard him as a brother in adversity: "I felt I did honor to both of us ... by merging our fortunes, physically leading him to safety" (315). Both are now figures of the powerless male, and Gladney finds himself, on the way to the hospital, "growing fond" of Mink.

In DeLillo's world, where the *nom du père* is simulational or dispersed in the networks and channels of a multinational capitalism, the crisis of phallic power also suggests a crisis of representation. Roland Barthes observes that narrative provides an "Oedipal pleasure (to denude, to know, to learn the origin and the end)" and that it may be true that "every narrative ... is a staging of the (absent, hidden, or hypostatized) father" (10). But if all narrative has traces or residues of this oedipal dynamic, in DeLillo's postmodern landscape the oedipal configuration lingers as an impossible memory forever closed off to the errant hero. The very basis of the oedipal logic of the heroic narrative is thrown into question, leading to a breakdown in the economy of representation and the collapse of heroic narrative itself.

After the debacle with Mink, Gladney finds himself back where he started—in a world where experience is so technologically mediated and processed that televised courses are offered on basic bodily functions such as "Eating and Drinking: Basic Parameters." Gladney is left in the "ambient roar" of white noise in the shopping center, in the realm of the simulacrum where signs are constantly mutating and reorganizing the consumers' cognitive world: the supermarket shelves having been rearranged, shoppers wander aimlessly, "trying to figure out the pattern, discern the underlying logic, trying to remember where they'd seen the Cream of Wheat" (325).

Thus ends DeLillo's grimly satiric allegory of the crisis of the sign in the order of the simulacrum, the dissolution of phallic power, and the exhaustion of heroic narratives of late modernity. These processes of postmodern culture, the novel suggests, are finally tied up with the issue of death. For the existential "fear and trembling" in the face of death represents that last vestige of subjectivity, that deep alterity which both threatens and delineates the self. Dylar promises to erase the awareness of death—the last absolute truth in a world of simulation, the last traces of the deep structures of a modernist consciousness. Yet as the lab technician Winnie Richards tells Gladney: "I think it's a mistake to lose one's sense of death, even one's fear of death. Isn't death the boundary we need? Doesn't it give a precious texture to life, a sense of definition? You have to ask yourself whether anything you do in this life would have beauty and meaning without the knowledge you carry of a final line, a border or limit" (228–29). Moreover, Gladney himself concurs that death provides an essential boundary that gives shape and meaning to life; "dying," he notes, "cures us of our innocence of the future" (15). And he adds: "All plots tend to move deathward. This is the nature of plots. Political plots, terrorist plots, lovers' plots, narrative plots, plots that are part of children's games" (26).

Gladney's comments imply an awareness that life or narrative "plots" presuppose an end (death), and that it is in the light of an ending that narrative (or life) takes on meaning. The passion for meaning that animates readers is the desire for an end; to eradicate a sense of ending in life or narrative is to extinguish meaning.[7] Yet the sense of boundaries and endings that define the self and give life or narrative meaning (or "heroic" possibilities, moments of self-knowledge, moments of vision) are erased in postmodern society. In a sense the processes under way in DeLillo's contemporary America—the loss of significant existential moments such as angst and the fear of death that register a space of interiority and authenticity—resemble the effects of Dylar. The "delirium" of communication, the arbitrary sign's rapturous loss of referent, and the flow of desire in late capitalism erode a sense of temporal continuity, history, limits, and endings—death included. As Murray Siskind observes, "here we don't die, we shop" (38).

In its concern with the importance of plots and narrative, therefore, *White Noise* suggests that the breakdown of grand narratives (such as the heroic narrative) does not mean a diminished reliance on plotting. Rather the novel implies that we still rely on plots and have recourse to narrative representations of some kind, that narratives still function to construct and criticize our world, that storytelling is ultimately a historical and political act.[8]

Indeed, DeLillo's novels engage historical and political issues; they do not exhibit the ahistoricism and pastiched depthlessness often associated with postmodernism. If his works exhibit the postmodern concern with the unstable nature of subjectivity and textuality, with representation and narrative process, his postmodernism retains the legacy of the modernist impulse to explore consciousness and selfhood and to create an imaginative vision that probes and criticizes its subject matter. If DeLillo uses postmodern devices like parody, pastiche, and parodic intertextual echoes, if he exhibits an interest in the play of language in the postmodern text (exhibited especially in a novel like *The Names*), these devices are deployed with a commitment to interrogate culture in America, to connect the transformations of narrative and subjectivity to cultural and historical processes.[9] Thus his depiction of postmodern culture in *White Noise* is no celebration of the ephemerality of *jouissance*. His vision of the dissolution of an older modernist subjectivity in a "mediated" world is not one of "nomadic" and flexible selves that find liberation in the play of style and image, selves that find release of primary desire from oppressive structures in a ludic postmodern "schizophrenia."[10] Nor is his parodic treatment of the patriarchal structures that underpin heroic-narrative paradigms yet another "deconstruction" that serves to remind us once again of their artifice and to expose naturalized myth, embedded ideology. Rather his novel connects the postmodern delirious and decentered subjectivity to a decentered capitalism and to the array of technological and representational apparatuses in the contemporary world—to the flood of media which disarticulates the subject and which dissolves the Faustian, Promethean, and oedipal impulses, replacing them with a new ecstasy of ever-shifting bricolage, with intersubjectivity as schizophrenic seriality.

In his depiction of a Baudrillardian landscape, therefore, DeLillo differs from Baudrillard in one important respect. Baudrillard's position toward the postmodern world is ultimately one of radical skepticism: finally there is nothing outside the play of simulations, no real in which a radical critique of the simulational society might be grounded.[11] DeLillo's writing, on the other hand, reveals a belief that fictional narrative can provide critical distance from and a critical perspective on the processes it depicts.

Given a world such as that which *White Noise* depicts, a culture based on the mode of information, there seems little chance of returning unproblematically to a modernist sensibility, with its heroic strivings for imaginative unity and an "unmediated" vision. In fact the novel suggests that to go back would be a form of nostalgia, could in fact lead in the direction of "Hitler studies" and a grim recuperation of a mythic unity and an "authenticity" of blood and soil ("the more powerful the nostalgia, the closer you come to violence," says Murray [258]). Yet the final image of Gladney suggests that DeLillo would wish to retain some aspects of the legacy of modernism (as he has done in his writing) in a postmodern world—such as the ideal of a rational, autonomous subjectivity—and that he is highly critical of a commodified, fast-image culture that threatens to bring about "the end of interiority." Gladney's modernist "last stand" is his refusal to submit to the "imaging block," in which the body is irradiated with the information of "ecstatic communication" and in which his impending death is consigned to a technologico-semiological hyperreality:

> Dr. Chakravarty wants to talk to me but I am making it a point to stay away. He is eager to see how my death is progressing.... He wants to insert me once more in the imaging block, where charged particles collide, high winds blow. But I am afraid of the imaging block. Afraid of its magnetic fields, its computerized nuclear pulse. (325)

A failure at heroism, Gladney shops at the supermarket and contemplates his "fear and trembling" about death, an indication that his subjectivity has yet to be completely swallowed up in the hyperreal. DeLillo's sympathies surely must be with his protagonist as Gladney holds tight to his fear of death in a society where the fear of death, like other aspects of the deep structures of subjectivity, is being transformed into images, codes, simulations, and charismatic spectacle; standing in the supermarket check-out line, Gladney ominously notes the "tabloids in the racks" and their tales of the "cults of the famous and the dead" (326).

Notes

I wish to thank David C. Harlan for his helpful comments on this essay.

1. For a discussion of Libra and DeLillo's mediascapes, see Lentricchia 10–29.

2. In this formulation of Baudrillard's position, I am indebted to Crary 285–86 and Kellner, "Baudrillard" 126–27.

3. Here I am indebted to a considerable extent to Lentricchia 7–10.

4. The issue of death provides another comparison between Baudrillard and DeLillo. For both, death is the ultimate signified, the single natural event which ultimately cannot be subsumed into simulacra, models, and codes. As Baudrillard conjectures in *Symbolic Exchange and Death*, "Perhaps only death, the reversibility of death is of a higher order than the code. Only symbolic disorder can breach the code" (*Jean Baudrillard* 122). And for both Baudrillard and DeLillo the symbolic mediations of

contemporary society deprive the individual of an intimate relation with death, with the result that society is haunted by the fear of mortality (Kellner, *Jean Baudrillard* 104).

5. Baudrillard similarly notes the collapse of signification into mere "signals" in postmodern society. For a discussion of Baudrillard and the "signal," see Poster 29.

6. I am indebted here to Dana Polan's discussion of the father figure and transnational capitalism; see Polan 178. For another discussion of the same issue, see Kroker and Kroker 27.

7. For a discussion of the relationship between narrative and death (to which I am indebted here), see Brooks 283–84.

8. Linda Hutcheon argues that much postmodern fiction reflects the view that we are still reliant on narrative representations in our verbal discourses in spite of the demise of grand narratives; see Hutcheon 49. Jean-François Lyotard, of course, argues that "little narratives"—among which are literary texts devoted to a flexible "narrative pragmatics"—operate in the absence of master narratives and are in fact antagonistic to any grand totalizing narrative (20).

9. In an article on *The Names*, Matthew J. Morris similarly argues for a political effectiveness and commitment for DeLillo's postmodernism, despite its interest in language play (121).

10. Here DeLillo differs from Baudrillard. Baudrillard may decry the "obscene delirium of communication," but as Douglas Kellner points out, his more recent works speculate that even though the disappearance of the subject "might create dizziness or even panic," there may nevertheless be "new pleasures and new modes of being awaiting us as we de-subjectify and progressively objectify ourselves" (*Jean Baudrillard* 175).

11. See Kellner, Jean Baudrillard 90.

WORKS CITED

Barthes, Roland. *The Pleasure of the Text*. Trans. Richard Miller. New York: Hill, 1975.

Baudrillard, Jean. "The Ecstasy of Communication." *The Anti-Aesthetic: Essays on Postmodern Culture*. Ed. Hal Foster. Port Townsend, WA: Bay, 1983. 126–34.

———. *In the Shadow of the Silent Majorities ... or the End of the Social: And Other Essays*. Trans. Paul Foss, Paul Patton, John Johnston. New York: Semiotext(e), 1983.

———. *Jean Baudrillard: Selected Writings*. Ed. Mark Poster. Stanford: Polity, 1988.

———. *Simulations*. Trans. Paul Foss, Paul Patton, Philip Beitchman. New York: Semiotext(c), 1983.

Brooks, Peter. "Freud's Masterplot: Questions of Narrative." *Literature and Psychoanalysis: The Question of Reading Otherwise*. Ed. Shoshana Felman. Baltimore: Johns Hopkins, 1982. 280–300.

Crary, Jonathan. "Eclipse of the Spectacle." *Art after Modernism: Rethinking Representation*. Ed. Brian Wallis, New York: New Museum of Contemporary Art, 1984. 282–94.

DeLillo, Don. *White Noise*. London: Picador, 1986.

Hutcheon, Linda. *The Politics of Postmodernism*. London: Routledge, 1989.

Jameson, Fredric. "Postmodernism and Consumer Society." *The Anti-Aesthetic: Essays on Postmodern Culture*. Ed. Hal Foster. Port Townsend, WA: Bay, 1983. 111–25.

———. "Postmodernism, or the Cultural Logic of Late Capitalism." *New Left Review* 146 (1984): 53–92.

Kellner, Douglas. "Baudrillard, Semiurgy, and Death." *Theory, Culture, and Society* 4 (1987): 125–46.

———. *Jean Baudrillard: From Marxism to Postmodernism and Beyond*. Stanford: Stanford UP, 1989.

Kroker, Arthur, and Marilouise Kroker. "Thesis on the Disappearing Body and the Hyper-Modern Condition." *Body Invaders: Panic Sex in America*. Ed. Arthur Kroker and Marilouise Kroker. New York: St. Martin's, 1987. 20–34.

Lentricchia, Frank. "Don DeLillo." *Raritan* 8.4 (1989): 1–29.

Lyotard, Jean-François. *The Postmodern Condition: A Report on Knowledge*. Trans. Geoff Bennington and Brian Massumi. Minneapolis: U of Minnesota P, 1983.

Morris, Matthew J. "Murdering Words: Language in Action in Don DeLillo's *The Names*." *Contemporary Literature* 30 (1989): 113–27.

Polan, Dana. "Brief Encounters: Mass Culture and the Evacuation of Sense." *Studies in Entertainment: Critical Approaches to Mass Culture*. Ed. Tania Modleski. Bloomington: Indiana UP, 1986. 167–87.

Poster, Mark. *Foucault, Marxism, and History: Mode of Production versus Mode of Information*. New York: Cambridge UP, 1984.

ARNOLD WEINSTEIN

Don DeLillo: Rendering the Words of the Tribe

The work of Don DeLillo is not easy to size up. Like a latter-day Balzac or Zola, he seems to have some giant composite plan in mind, an all-encompassing scheme that, when completed, will bear witness to how we lived, worked, played, and sounded in the second half of the twentieth century. DeLillo's zest for rivaling with the *état civil* has led him to some exotic subjects and oddball places: football, professional mathematics, Wall Street, rock music, pornography, terrorism, espionage, the college campus, the nuclear threat, and, more recently, America's founding trauma: the Kennedy assassination.

One finds amid this teeming variety of DeLillo subjects a number of constants that make his work both recognizable and developmental, as if a large argument were gathering force over the course of some nine novels. There is, first of all, the remarkable DeLillo style: cool to the point of being hip, close to the vest, drawn to the jargons and tics of coteries and the argots of professions, informed by the concepts of the media, wry, distant, exquisitely focused on the inane, the bizarre, the surreal, and yet capable of pathos and power.

And then there seems to be a fixed number of DeLillo themes: fascism, espionage, communication, power in all its guises, and finally the antics of the individual subject in his encounter with a systemic world.[1] Whereas

From *Nobody's Home: Speech, Self, and Place in American Fiction from Hawthorne to DeLillo.* © 1993 by Oxford University Press, Inc. Reprinted by permission.

artists such as Coover or Bertolucci conceive of fascism in terms of spectacle, mass movements, and paranoia, DeLillo is more theoretical and cerebral, at once more oblique and more various. *Great Jones Street* chronicles, for example, the career and retreat of an idolized rock star; DeLillo is drawn to the big-business sleaze around the performer as well as the visionary desperation of the lyrics themselves. The figure of Hitler runs in filigree in DeLillo's texts. The much-coveted, sought-after film footage in *Running Dog* is thought to be a pornographic rendition of final events in the bunker, and the novel cunningly interweaves, on the one hand, the obsession with the sexual antics of the doomed Führer, and, on the other, a grainy story of intelligence and counterintelligence, of hired killers and coerced sex.

Hitler reappears as the academic specialty of Jack Gladney in DeLillo's comic masterpiece, *White Noise*, and once again we perceive the reaches of DeLillo's theme by dint of the way he pairs and replicates it, this time in the guise of "twin" academic departments: Gladney's program of Hitler Studies may receive an American complement through the proposal for an Elvis Studies program. Comic fiction though it is, *White Noise* explores to great effect the cult of power and death that fascism entails, and in that light it is surprisingly more informative than the book on Lee Harvey Oswald, *Libra*, in which one expects a full-fledged rendition of Kennedy fascination to complete the series of portraits in power. Instead, *Libra* has a rather different orientation, and it chronicles the special "world within a world" of the CIA and international intelligence communities, thereby adding to the already masterly depiction of such circles and antics in *Great Jones Street*, *Running Dog*, and the extraordinary account of middle-management Americans caught up in Middle Eastern terrorism and cults in *The Names*, a novel of 1982 that is certain to gain in stature as DeLillo's novelistic status becomes clearer to us in the coming years.

But the cornerstone of DeLillo's work, the reason why he deserves inclusion in a study of "freedom of speech" in American fiction, is his peculiar, always fascinating, sometimes visionary concern with language. I have already mentioned his ear for the private jargons and codes of today's technocratic society (he is like Balzac here); at other moments he actually fashions a new discourse (here he is breaking new ground), as in the language of rock music or the project of the eerie questers in *The Names*. At all times DeLillo is concerned to render for us either sounds that we have heard without knowing it—the "white noise" of our Muzak age—or to usher us verbally into those other, unsuspected worlds behind the scenes of business and diplomacy, the academy and the cocktail party. In the tradition of Fenimore Cooper and Balzac, DeLillo is out to guide his readers into verbal precincts they have never entered before, but in his hands that guided tour becomes an explosive and dangerous affair, an encounter with sounds that can kill. Consider, in this light, the view of music-language as pure kinetic energy, as articulated by Bucky Wunderlich, the rock star of *Great Jones Street*:

> The true artist makes people move. When people read a book or look at a painting, they just sit there or stand there. A long time ago that was okay, that was hip, that was art. Now it's different. I make people move. My sound lifts them right off their ass. I make it happen. Understand, I make it happen. What I'd like to do really is I'd like to injure people with my sound. Maybe actually kill some of them. They'd come there knowing that full well. Then we'd play and sing and people in the audience would be frozen in pain and some of them would actually die from the effects of our words and music.... People dying from the effects of all this beauty and power. That's art, sweetheart. I make it happen.[2]

A vertiginous linguistic and cultural meditation is under way here; the manifestations of power and of art are collapsed together, are understood as speech phenomena. Life and death are graphed as language.[3] DeLillo occupies a very special place in my argument about freedom of speech, for his books always circle around the issue of utterance, and they make us understand that language is the *Urgrund*, the ultimate stage on which a society or a culture lives and goes through its antics and its rituals. "Le monde est fait pour aboutir à un livre," Mallarmé wrote, and in DeLillo's work of lingual crises and unheard-of frequencies we may glimpse the *aboutissement* of the reality-as-language equation, but trumped up now in the tribal and technocratic jargons of our media age.

DeLillo's cumulative project resembles at times that of Roland Barthes, especially the Barthes of *Mythologies*, for he is scrupulously attentive to the ways in which belief and passion are displaced, renamed, formatted, and commodified in a materialist age. And he succeeds in these ventures largely because he has the eyes of the anthropologist as well as the ears of the linguist, perceiving the peculiar poetry of everyday rituals and services, chronicling the muffled spiritual impulses concealed within our mundane comings and goings. DeLillo's modernity lies in his sense that our myths are on the surface rather than in the depths, recorded in the print of our newspapers rather than in dark, oneiric scripts. Hence, in *Libra*, the CIA agent's wife, Beryl, no longer writes letters to her friends; she merely cuts clippings out of the papers and sends them instead: "She believed these were personal forms of expression. She believed no message she could send a friend was more intimate and telling than a story in the paper about a violent act, a crazed man, a bombed Negro home, a Buddhist monk who sets himself on fire. Because these are the things that tell us how we live."[4] Our myths are broadcast in the news, on the front pages, but we do not come easily to the realization that these acts of violence and melodrama somehow *speak us*, are devious utterances of our own private wishes and fears. That seems to be DeLillo's major accomplishment, book after book: to enter, as roving eye and roving ear, into and behind the worlds of finance, diplomacy, and violence, and to make us aware that these realms, apparently "argotized" and other, are actually "ghostlier demarcations" of ourselves.

DeLillo first gained a wide audience with *White Noise*, winner of the American Book Award in 1986, chronicle of the terrors lurking in the environment and the family, infused with a deadpan survivalist humor that marks it as one of the landmark fictions of our time. But *The Names*, published in 1982, leaner and more metaphysical than *White Noise*, constitutes the proper entry into DeLillo's world, for it sounds his major themes; an analysis of its exploratory ventures will make it possible for us, then, to hear the fuller resonances and to savor the unusual warmth and pathos of the later text. My consideration of DeLillo will be capped by some remarks on his most controversial work, *Libra* (1988), which both extends his exploration of high-level espionage and leads, in the eyes of some, out of the world of fiction altogether, although we may come to believe that the distinctions between history and fiction have now lost all meaning entirely.

The Names looks, initially, to be in the tradition of American expatriate novels. James, the narrator, is an "international risk analyst" stationed in Athens, and he measures, early on, the gap that separates him and his fellows from the experience of the Lost Generation of the twenties: "The deep terraces spill over with lantana and jasmine, the views are panoramic, the cafés full of talk and smoke into the early hours. Americans used to come to places like this to write and paint and study, to find deeper textures. Now we do business."[5] This declaration gently but firmly marks the distance between modernism and postmodernism, not in terms of writerly codes and imperatives but in the sense of a changed globe, a changed definition of what it means to be "American." Much of DeLillo's interest is devoted to defining the "new" American abroad; no longer the bumbling innocent of Melville or Twain or the Jamesian seeker of refinement or the Hemingway seeker of authenticity or the Fitzgerald seeker of pleasure, DeLillo's people are middle-management types, representing huge multinational conglomerates, trying to cope with a world of precarious allegiances and the ubiquitous threat of terrorism. Jake Barnes knew which Parisian restaurants to eat in, what hotel to stay at in Pamplona; this group has different expertises:

We were versed in percentages, safety records, in the humor of flaming death. We knew which airline's food would double you up, which routes connected well.... We knew which airports were efficient, which were experiments in timelessness or mob rule; which had radar, which didn't; which might be filled with pilgrims making the *hadj*.... We advised each other on which remote cities were well maintained, which were notable for wild dogs running in packs at night, snipers in the business district at high noon. We told each other where you had to sign a legal document to get a drink, where you couldn't eat meat on Wednesdays and Thursdays, where you had to sidestep a man with a cobra when you left your hotel. We knew where martial law was in force, where body searches were made, where they engaged in systematic torture, or fired assault weapons into the air at weddings, or abducted and ransomed executives. (6–7)

The clipped, air-conditioned DeLillo style, larded with savvy particulars, nicely conveys the ironies and absurdities of this new dispensation: on the one hand, "we," the corporate Americans, "were versed," "knew," "advised," and "told each other"; on the other hand, this terrain defies charting and mapping, and from the doubled-up stomach to the running dogs and the man with the cobra, we learn that the natives and their exotica are no longer so manageable. This passage announces a change in America's place in the world, and the earlier pilgrim seeking knowledge is out of place in these precincts. The world—that extended version of the virgin West—is no longer open to explorers and tourists in the same way, and we see that the American bildungsroman has been turned on its head, that the educational scheme has become one of survival. The imperialist self is also in trouble here: DeLillo's people take up little space, have small appetites, are good at standing sideways, and are happy to come out with their skin. The contrast with Hemingway's Paris or even Hawkes's Alaska is striking and revelatory. American hegemony is a thing of the past.

And yet, *The Names* is still in the great quest tradition of Westerners seeking the wisdom and secrets of Europe and the East. Ever since Marco Polo we have known that a little business can also be done on the side, but there is an undeniable spiritual hunger in this text, reminiscent of figures such as Forster and Hesse, and DeLillo's triumph is to encode his quest parable in a mimetic narrative of capitalist maneuvers in the Middle East.

Needless to say, Americans are not the only ones who have to be careful in this territory. The Turkish businessman Vedat Nesim explains to James that his own sphere of operations is a veritable mine field:

"You are a target only outside your country. I am a target outside and inside. I am in the government. This makes me a marked man. Armenians outside, Turks inside. I go to Japan next week. This is a relatively safe place for a Turk. Very bad is Paris. Even worse is Beirut. The Secret Army is very active there. Every secret army in the world keeps a post office box in Beirut. I will eat this shrimp in garlic and butter. Later I will eat profiteroles in thick chocolate sauce. After Japan I go to Australia. This is a place that should be safe for a Turk. It is not." (195)

We shall see, in *Libra*, that Americans are not advantaged over Turks at all, that they too are targets both outside and inside. But the real power of the passage resides in its uncertainty, its staccato list of places and particulars that do not cohere. This is vintage DeLillo style, and the lovely insertion of shrimp and profiteroles perfectly finishes off the old tourist paradigm, a sequence of colorful, discrete items for visiting and ingesting, with a twist: they could kill you.

Rich in exotica, this setting is also rich in secrets and indecipherable codes, in surprises and reversals. But how do we get there from here? Interpretation requires a stable base to which mysteries and enigmas are referred. But DeLillo's people are decentered: "The sense of things was different in such a way that we could only register the edges of some elaborate secret. It seemed we'd lost our capacity to select, to ferret out particularity and trace it to some center which our minds could relocate in knowable surroundings. There was no equivalent core" (94). Such an environment resists all interpretive grids except one: conspiracy. And this is because conspiracies are nothing but purposeful, interconnecting, secret relations that we do not comprehend, and secrets themselves are a nostalgic term for cogency, the cogency that eludes us, from which we as outsiders are excluded. This epistemological imperative has as its flip side paranoia, the certainty that the world is packaged in plots devised by others, in which we ourselves play unwitting roles as targets.

The central (impossible) activity within such a scheme is that of decoding, of getting a grasp on the grammar and the system at hand, so that one's own place in the composite can be understood. In *The Names* DeLillo has presented that paradigm in the purest possible form: the deciphering of languages, the understanding of the Names. And even though DeLillo is not a formally playful writer, has no verbal tricks or pyrotechnics to display, it is hard to think of any Western narrative that matches *The Names* in its exploration of language as high adventure. At the center of this exploration is the novel's chief quester, Owen Brademas, farm boy from the prairies turned archaeologist and eminence grise, in search of ancient inscriptions and the secrets they harbor. This insistent metaphysical tug is convincingly linked to the novel's commercial foreground by the involvement of other, less "pure" characters in Owen's (more or less conscious) mesh: Kathryn (James's wife), who works under his leadership at the dig on the Greek island; Tap (James's son), who is writing a quasi-novel about Owen; and most especially two males who track the tracker into the Greek hinterland: Frank Volterra, who wants to film Owen's involvement with a putative secret cult, and James himself, who becomes Owen's younger alter ego, who helps him complete the pattern. The secret cult at the heart of the matter is, not surprisingly, a language cult.

All of Owen's historical and archaeological pursuits are now transfigured into a project that is profoundly linguistic: erasing the gap between words and things. As if he had absorbed large doses of Saussure and Derrida, DeLillo has imagined a quest for the *natural language*, a language that would eclipse difference, dissolve the space between sign and referent, and install a regime of pure presence. DeLillo's materials become incandescent at this juncture, as if they were acquiring a signifying potency beyond the bounds of ordinary narrative. For instance, Owen explains to Tap the etymology of "character" (the ironies abound here, given that Owen is "also" a "character" in Tap's novel): "Owen says 'character' comes from a Greek word. It means 'to brand or to sharpen.' Or 'pointed stake' if it's a noun" (10). "Character" is on the move here, exiting the realm of the literary or even the print convention and moving in the direction of pure action or pure object. The cult that Owen has come upon exercises the central fascination of the novel because it is devoted to the power of letters, of the alphabet itself. The search for ancient inscriptions reveals itself to be a quest for originary language, language that is immediate and immanent. Such a quest can never be distant from the professional writer's generic interests— one thinks of Emerson's essay on language, or, in a much more sinister vein, of Kafka's story of the penal colony and its fable of body inscription—but DeLillo takes pains to show that even the business interests of the novel are part of a linguistic tradition. After all, as Owen explains, the old inscriptions were nothing but inventories, records of commodities, evidence of the view that "the first writing was motivated by the desire to keep accounts" (35), and with that theory in place James and his middle-management buddies acquire a strange linguistic aura of their own, appear to us as the keepers of a scribal tradition so all-encompassing that all labor ultimately reverts to it.

But the most vexing and arresting link between the secret language cult and the international business community is the common terror that informs both: terrorism as the new global fact of political and economic life, and violent death as the uncanny signature of the cult itself—"terrorists of textuality, agents of literacy's mastery and alienation infiltrating oral cultures," is how Thomas LeClair terms the cult—a signature that betokens nothing less than the fusion of person and place, sign and referent.[6] Here is the terrible synchrony that would erase difference: the cult brutally murders its victims in places where the initials of the place and the person coincide. All the players of the novel are obsessed with these ritual killings because they all know obscurely that their own lives are written out of this archaic grammar, that these ritual murderers are composing a new map and a new human language, by collapsing agent into setting, and by energizing the word so utterly that "character" once again becomes "pointed stake." Finally, one is tempted to posit terror itself as the ground for the psyche in DeLillo, an indwelling creatural horror that underlies all the codes and systems, that endows these books with a muted affective plaint beyond the cool surface ironies. We shall see more of this in *White Noise*.

The beauty of the novel lies in the radiance of its theory, its elegant fusion of esoterica and realpolitik. Yet even to consider *The Names* as a dualistic text is too fixed and schematic, for DeLillo's real game is to transmute all his materials, to achieve that fourth and fifth dimension in narrative that Hemingway was aiming for, in which the newspaper clippings of today not only speak our private myths but keep covenant with the primitive rites of the past. In such a text foreground and background are no longer separable, just as center and circumference become interchangeable. DeLillo's grasp of history confirms his belief in fluidity and plasticity. He is interested in etymology, the flow of names over time, and he is also drawn to the man-made changes, the fate of names such as Persia and Rhodesia, the alphabetical merry-go-round of modern Asia and Africa. Gatsby, we recall, placed San Francisco in the Midwest, but the mobility of the Fitzgerald text never gets much beyond "Biloxi, Tennessee"; DeLillo is bent on staking out a territory that mixes up characters, turns all stakes into pointed stakes, and works according to a directional code and gearshift that wreak havoc. James's friend David is struck that cars come at him in reverse:

> He was always finding himself driving down a narrow street with a car coming toward him backwards. The driver expected him to move, or ascend, or vanish. Eventually he saw what was so fearful about this, a thing so simple he hadn't been able to isolate it from the larger marvel of a city full of cars going backwards. *They did not reduce speed when driving in reverse.* To David Keller, between wives, this seemed an interesting thing. There was a cosmology here, a rich structure of some kind, a theorem in particle physics. Reverse and forward were interchangeable. (65)

Once again we are in classic DeLillo territory, a place for measuring the weather of the mind, a setting of velocities, sensory impressions, and careening lives atilt and akimbo. "To David Keller, between wives, this seemed ... interesting" acquires the mathematical precision of a graph, with its double axes and mysteriously moving lines of force. We are not far from the trope of palm reading, but the face of fortune is no longer static and inscribed once and for all on the hand; instead, all of the elements are lurching in their own ways, propelled in their different channels and circuits, the erotic career and the moving cars melding a textual weave, a vehicular map of lines and intensities that recalls the Fates with their famous scissors.

This new cosmology brings with it a new poetics, a writerly physics in which statements signify doubly, move in forward and reverse. The language of the text becomes especially heated and active as DeLillo closes in (and opens up) on the language quest. Consider, for example, Owen's tale-within-a-tale of the Englishman Rawlinson, who wanted to copy the inscriptions (in Old Persian, Elamite, and Babylonian) on the Behistun rock. The rock being dangerously inaccessible, the Englishman makes use of a Kurdish boy to achieve his ends: "The boy inched across a rock mass that had only the faintest indentations he might use for finger-grips. Fingers and toes. Maybe he used the letters themselves. I'd like to believe so. This is how he proceeded, clinging to the rock, passing below the great bas-relief of Darius facing a group of rebels in chains. A sheer drop. But he made it, miraculously according to Rawlinson, and was eventually able to do a paper cast of the text, swinging from a sort of bosun's chair" (80). This fine passage epitomizes the richness, economy, and multidirectionality of DeLillo's project. We see the language quest in full swing, and we are struck by the physicality of the signs: the boy finding footholds and toeholds in the very lettering itself. The "characters" in play here are close to the "pointed stake," for the writing itself "brands" and "sharpens" not merely the rocky script "in" the passage but especially the colonialist narrative that delivers it, the brutal "inscription" of the Kurdish boy into the Englishman's design, the kind of invisible, systematic exploitation that has conditioned the stage now occupied by James and his cohorts.[7]

Taking still another step away, we see what may be the central paradigm of DeLillo's book: the arduous recovery of a secret script and the complex mediations required to make it happen. In that light this casual scene comes close to being the absent center of the novel. Some two hundred pages later Owen himself will arrive at his final destination, Rajsamand, to read the great stone inscriptions of the seventeenth-century Sanskrit poem, and he will make use of a young Indian boy to speak what he sees: "Together they read aloud, slowing, the man deferring to the music of the boy, pitching his voice below the other's. It was in the sound, how old this was, strange, distant, other, but also almost known, almost striking through to him from some uncycled memory where the nightmares lay, the ones in which he could not speak as others did, could not understand what they were saying" (284). Lines, many lines, are being blurred and erased in these sequences. Owen merges with the boy, with the Indian past, with his own traumatic childhood encounter with speaking in tongues, even his own preverbal fears from infancy, as the text ceases to distinguish between forward and reverse. Nothing remains discrete. The Kurdish boy becomes the Indian boy, who may be thought to fan out into the stalking, listening figures of Frank Volterra and James—Frank with his feverish desire to film the cult murders, James as the indispensable scribe-mediator for Owen, the one who finds Owen dying and takes down his story so it can be passed on.

We cannot fail to see that the getting of the script and the meaning of the script are akin, and that they have a common base in some elemental violence. This unspecified, unlocalizable violence is at the core of the novel, just as it seems to be at the origin of language itself. The ritual murders performed by the cult are nothing less than acts of exorcism and control, for they derive from a belief system strangely parallel to that described by René Girard in *La Violence et le sacré*, a world view that supposes originary violence, a flowing violence that precedes culture and language, that must be decorously channeled through the institutions of sacrifice and effigy if civilization is to be. DeLillo has given a linguistic turn of the screw to this theory of sacrifice, so that the indwelling violence of life is released by acts of verbal synchrony, by moments when the Names assert their all-encompassing authority, erasing distinctions of person and place. Hence, these dazzling murders establish the primacy of the letter above all else, and they remind us that the writer's narrative project is always, at least in some sense, a lethal quest for a magic script, an alchemical script that would liberate the original power of the word by dint of annihilation.

Such moments have an epiphanic, almost nuclear clarity in *The Names*, for they make visible a kind of blinding truth that has almost entirely disappeared from the day-to-day lives of these characters. The major fact of these lives is that they are in the dark and are interchangeable. They are living the reality of forward slipping into reverse. Owen thinks himself a scribe, but the cultists insist he is a member of their group. People cross lines. James infuriates Kathryn by listing his version of her view of his flaws. The Kurdish boy shades into the Indian boy. Andreas confuses James the risk analyst with David the banker.

Yet the benightedness of such a perceptual and conceptual murk is arguably preferable to the fatal light of identity, the moment when the letter speaks. One thinks particularly of Borges in this regard, the Borges of "Death and the Compass," who works with the topos of fatal illumination, of the unity between naming and killing. Here is the sinister side of DeLillo's Pauline meditation about seeing through the glass darkly, about knowing and being known, and in that sense he tells us something about the status of knowledge and information in a computerized, terrorist age. Michaelis Kalliambetsos is murdered at Mikro Kamini. Will the same thing happen to James Axton at Jebel Amman? It very nearly does. James is possibly shot at while jogging in Athens, and David is hit. Mistake? The deadly revelation of the Names is not an archaeological dig, not a whimsical scholarly interlude. To be named, to be revealed in full light, to have total consonance between sound and substance, letter and person, is risky business for risk analysts. James learns, belatedly, from others, that the company he works for, Northeast Group, is a CIA cover, and we see once again DeLillo's brilliance in weaving his strands together. To learn that one's corporate identity is CIA is to learn a new grammar; in many parts of the world it is a death sentence. Remember Vedat Nesim's words: "I am in the government. This makes me a marked man." Branded. Marked by a pointed stake. Like the characters in Beckett's work, especially those of *L'Innommable*, the people of *The Names* are awaiting deliverance, to be spoken at last; but they may not outlive the utterance.

Writing is thus a form of Russian roulette, for letters can be loaded, and when the inscription is right, when the conditions are right, the violence of naming occurs. Melville's Bartleby, we are told after his death, may have been the disabused handler of dead letters. For DeLillo the letter is potent, deadly rather than dead, and his book closes with the final avatar of Owen Brademas, his letter-alike Orville Benton, protagonist of the fiction authored by the boy Tap, last in the series of youths who mediate the script. Orville Benton, through the agency of Tap, lives out Owen's confused stirrings of the encounter with tongues, the preverbal past, "some uncycled memory where the nightmares lay, the ones in which he could not speak as others did, could not understand what they were saying" (284). Savvy postmodernist that he is, DeLillo knows that language precedes its speakers, that it got there first. So Tap uses what he has, does not even attempt to invent some new language. Early on he had, like so many youngsters, his version of pig latin, his "Ob" code.[8] But in the novel he writes, he rearranges (by ignorance?) the letters themselves, breaks (and breaks into) the fixed orthographic armature of the old words to liberate their indwelling violence and energy: "Seal the old language and loose the new!" Orville hears the preacher say, just as Owen remembered it. And it is done: "He was in the middle of a crowd, tongue-tied! There was a daise like a drunkerds skuffling lurch, realing in a corner"

(335). Is this not the nightmarish but vitalizing encounter between self and sign? Using the child's memory of the revival meeting, DeLillo has found words here for the bondage from which we all come, the autism with which we all begin life, the universal crisis of being "in the middle of a crowd, tongue-tied," or, as the theorists remind us today, *infans*, "speechless."[9] The precariousness and the dazzling vistas of this scene are the conditions for one another: the flower and animal worlds press in with "daise" and "drunkerds," and "realing in a corner" perfectly delivers the DeLillo breakthrough, the regrouping of the Letter that removes our conceptual floor, throws us into a "skuffling lurch," while making possible a brave new "real" of its own. Orville is struck by the "glossylalya" he encounters, the way "people burst out in sudden streams," and the initiatory baptism he records is a would-be entry into the flux of the Names, the epic journey into the community of words. This *passage* rivals the Lacanian schemes for depicting our traumatizing and fissuring entry into language, for the journey into words is a (tragic?) exit from things: "He looked in vane for familiar signs and safe places. No where did he see what he expected. Why couldn't he understand and speak? There was no answer that the living could give. Tongue tied. His fait was signed. He ran into the rainy distance smaller and smaller. This was worse than a retched nightmare. It was the nightmare of real things, the fallen wonder of the world" (339).

DeLillo closes his novel on a pre-Babel note, leaving us to ponder the circularity of his materials (Owen the quester is now launched), the beauty of his fashionings: "looked in vane," "his fait was signed" (entailing a French, even a semiotic view of destiny itself), "a retched nightmare" that thrusts, convulsively, the body back into language where it was at the beginning. Tap's narrative is all of five pages long; DeLillo is not redoing *Finnegans Wake*, and he is content, here at the end of his story of death (of Owen, of James's marriage with Kathryn), to close with the voice of the child, to insist on continuum. Orville Benton, exiled into language, finds himself nonetheless entering the "nightmare of real things, the fallen wonder of the world," but his account is shot through with radiance. His journey is to be filled with surprises, a quest rather than a trip, one that lies at the core of this travelogue-fiction and shapes the lives of its "characters," all of them, in the final analysis, risk analysts, lurching into identity and synchrony, stumbling into "a self exposure we are never prepared for no matter how often we take this journey, the buried journey through categories and definitions and foreign languages, not the other, the sunlit trip to the east we thought we'd decided to make" (255). In taking the measure of its political and commercial schemas by reaching to the archaic poetry beneath them, *The Names* testifies to a noble and spirited view of utterance, an art form that is half palimpsest, half travelogue, outfitted with large vistas and dealing in high (pointed) stakes.

If *The Names* recalls, in its exoticism, the great travel and quest narratives of the past, *White Noise* displays DeLillo's no less prodigious gift for focusing his anthropological gaze homeward in order to deliver an anatomy of America the Beautiful in such a way that we discover a world we live in but have never seen, shimmering in its defamiliarized rendition of how the natives work and play. There is no undercover activity, no reportage on slums or cults or youth groups or hired killers or political campaigns. On the contrary, DeLillo sets his sights on the humdrum routines of middle America: the "new" family with its children of previous marriages, the presence of the media, the life of the campus, the threats to the environment, the adventures of consumerism, the management of dread. DeLillo is, of course, not Updike, and *White Noise* is not of the "around-the-house-and-in-the-yard" school of American fiction, nor is its reportage focused on "marriages and separations and trips to Tanglewood."[10] Savvy mix of the planetary and the minute, it is a Drummond-light fiction, out to reveal to us our placedness and our surroundings.

As Murray, the resident guru of the novel, explains to his students, we "have to learn to look as children again."[11] We have to *see*; and DeLillo emerges as a writer of extraordinary perceptions, the Jamesian figure for whom nothing is lost, but a chronicler in a world unlike any James would have selected for notation. A visit to the supermarket (how many novelists take us to supermarkets?) yields this: "A woman fell into a rack of paperback books at the front of the store. A heavyset man emerged from the raised cubicle in the far corner and moved warily toward her, head tilted to get a clearer sightline. A checkout girl said, 'Leon, parsley,' and he answered as he approached the fallen woman, 'Seventy-nine.' His breast pocket was crammed with felt-tip pens" (19). *White Noise* is larded with such moments of zany mishap, given in deadpan style, without exclamation points, and invariably sandwiched into other "bytes" of cultural routine. The episode is finely seen; from the adverb "warily" to the felt-tip pens, it depicts a jungle, a precarious place pinned down with numbers, data, and codes. It is vintage DeLillo in its refusal of pathos, its leveling, egalitarian inclusiveness that calls to mind Whitman's democratic project a century earlier, stripped of all affect but no less canny in its sense of "fit" and "grouping." DeLillo the systems thinker is visible in these evocations, and he shows himself to be a savvy observer of environmental forces, wise about the clutter that surrounds and informs us.

The capacity to be insider and outsider, "to look as children again," enables the author to depict the known world with the eye-opening vision of a Martian visitor, an anthropologist seeking religious patterns in the daily routines of Americans.[12] Let us return to the supermarket:

> Steffie took my hand and we walked past the fruit bins, an area that extended about forty-five yards along one wall. The bins were arranged diagonally and backed by mirrors that people accidentally punched when reaching for fruit in the upper rows. A voice on the loudspeaker said: "Kleenex Softique, your truck's blocking the entrance." Apples and lemons tumbled in twos and threes to the floor when someone took a fruit from certain places in the stacked array. There were six kinds of apples, there were exotic melons in several pastels. Everything seemed to be in season, sprayed, burnished, bright. People tore filmy bags off racks and tried to figure out which end opened. I realized the place was awash in noise. The toneless systems, the jangle and skid of carts, the loud-speaker and coffee-making machines, the cries of children. And over it all, or under it all, a dull and unlocatable roar, as of some form of swarming life just outside the range of human apprehension. (36)

Here is where we have lived, walked with our children, frolicked in the garden where all things are in season, partaken of the artfully arranged, bountiful harvest, wrestled with the filmy bags, arranged children and produce in the carts, taken in the noise, taken out the goods, paid our dues, exited, returned. There is "swarming life" here, and Murray, the expert on cultural studies, thinks it rigorously comparable to the spiritual transactions of Tibetan theology, thinks that is why we make these weekly pilgrimages:

> This place recharges us spiritually, it prepares us, it's a gateway or pathway. Look how bright. It's full of psychic data.... Everything is concealed in symbolism, hidden by veils of mystery and layers of cultural material. But it is psychic data, absolutely. The large doors slide open, they close unbidden. Energy waves, incident radiation. All the letters and numbers are here, all the colors of the spectrum, all the voices and sounds, all the code words and ceremonial phrases. It is just a question of deciphering, peeling off the layers of unspeakability. (37–38)

Let there be no mistake: "peeling off layers of unspeakability" stands for the major activity of this novel, and it is a full-time job, unlike peeling fruit or unwrapping groceries. To see like a child again is to see dimensions, to perceive auras, to grasp the connectedness of what is discrete, the particulars of what seems joined, the odd magic of the material world we have made. DeLillo is the metaphysician of the kitchen and breakfast room, the poet of fast food; he actually looks at our gadgets: "I watched the coffee bubble up through the center tube and perforated basket into the small pale globe. A marvelous and sad invention, so roundabout, ingenious, human. It was like a philosophical argument rendered in terms of the world—water, metal, brown beans. I had never looked at coffee before" (103). There is something literally wonderful about this kind of writing, a kind of conceptual generosity that restores our doings to light and language, brings awe back to the world.

As one might expect, however, it can be a double-edged vision. The routines and trivia acquire radiance, but the "heavy" traditional icons are seen with a more jaundiced eye. This eye is alert to posturing, and it delights in exposing the song and dance of American packaging, the assiduous cultivation and merchandising of Americana. Hence, we have "the tourist attraction known as the most photographed barn in America," about which Murray wisely states, after seeing the array of slides, cards, and camera wielders, "Once you've seen signs about the barn, it becomes impossible to see the barn" (12). DeLillo's project of "innocenting" vision is rigorously counterpointed by the awareness of vision as construct, the awareness of the media's enormous shaping (and occulting) role in the way we see. Part of *White Noise* consists in seeing, like a child, the cultural machinery; the other part consists in examining, like an adult, the "unreal" vistas manufactured by that machinery—"unreal" in the sense that they are mythic constructs, making it "impossible to see the barn." We are dealing with more than the machinations of advertising; DeLillo wants to highlight the inevitable disjunction, *décalage*, between the concepts handed to us by the social order and the retinal evidence our eyes take in. Jack Gladney muses over the American nostalgia for yesteryear when he goes for a check-up at the medical laboratory with state-of-the-art facilities named Autumn Harvest Farms: "Was this an attempt to balance the heartlessness of their gleaming precision equipment? Would a quaint name fool us into thinking we live in pre-cancerous times? What kind of condition might we expect to have diagnosed in a facility called Autumn Harvest Farms? Whooping cough, croup? A touch of the grippe? Familiar old farmhouse miseries calling for bed rest, a deep chest massage with soothing Vicks VapoRub. Would someone read to us from *David Copperfield*?" (275–76). DeLillo is touching here on the conceptual and rhetorical lag that informs all our lives, the ways in which we live in the past, still using Newtonian physics or medieval theology to explain events in our consciousness, busily applying to the present scene a host of models that have been defunct for centuries.

The story in *White Noise* takes place in a lazy college town called Blacksmith, and although DeLillo exploits the ironies made possible by his bucolic setting, he is not about to give us a cultural narrative in the manner of George Eliot. He has put his cultural experts in the book itself, and these folks are abrasively modern, on the lookout for today's icons; their view of rites of passage and cultural self-definition revolves around key queries such as "Did you piss in sinks?" "Where were you when James Dean died?" These folks, some of whom "read nothing but cereal boxes," are the connoisseurs of "American environments," and DeLillo is out to map that environment with the thoroughness of a cartographer-journalist who sees everything twice: both straight and at a tilt. Blacksmith is a town where Old Man Treadwell and his sister are lost for several days at a giant mall, where the technocratic order has made inroads everywhere, not merely in supermarkets and hospitals but in homes and people's minds. The human scale and unit of measure that governs *David Copperfield* (and most modern fiction as well) is eclipsed here, and we are witness to an array of compromises and uneasy truces, of skirmishes and negotiations between humans and their gadgets, humans and their environment. Sometimes it is delicious: "The smoke alarm went off in the hallway upstairs, either to let us know the battery had just died or because the house was on fire. We finished our lunch in silence" (8). This is what Hemingway's separate peace looks like sixty years after World War I. Make no mistake about it: American environments can kill you:

> They had to evacuate the grade school on Tuesday. Kids were getting headaches and eye irritations, tasting metal in their mouths. A teacher rolled on the floor and spoke foreign languages. No one knew what was wrong. Investigators said it could be the ventilating system, the paint or varnish, the foam insulation, the electrical insulation, the cafeteria food, the rays emitted by micro-computers, the asbestos fireproofing, the adhesive on shipping containers, the fumes from the chlorinated pool, or perhaps something deeper, finer-grained, more closely woven into the basic state of things. (35)

One senses that such deadpan writing stems, nonetheless, from an imagination of apocalypse, and DeLillo succeeds in bringing to the surface our repressed fears about cataclysm and nature's revenge, about the hubris of our technological feats and the day of reckoning that is on the way. He is the modern Kafka, the man who is at home in bureaucracy and who sees the lunacy of our engines of civilization and progress; like Kafka, DeLillo is the bookkeeper who starts in the red and goes downhill from there, wise about the myriad ways we are cornered and dispossessed, but at peace with his dark vision, palpably happy to inventory the mess we find ourselves in.

DeLillo also emerges as the poet laureate of the media age, for he understands the crucial role that television plays in the American environment, making it possible for us to savor erupting disasters, to watch, with relative impunity and vicarious thrills, the endless parade of world-class miseries visited on others and visiting us in our living rooms:

> That night, a Friday, we gathered in front of the set, as was the custom and the rule, with take-out Chinese. There were floods, earthquakes, mud slides, erupting volcanoes. We'd never before been so attentive to our duty, our Friday assembly. Heinrich was not sullen, I was not bored. Steffie, brought close to tears by a sitcom husband arguing with his wife, appeared totally absorbed in these documentary clips of calamity and death. Babette tried to switch to a comedy series about a group of racially mixed kids who build their own communication satellite. She was startled by the force of our objection. We were otherwise silent, watching houses slide into the ocean, whole villages crackle and ignite in a mass of advancing lava. Every disaster made us wish for more, for something bigger, grander, more sweeping. (64)

Needless to say, the pleasures of such spectating depend on the feeling of being untouchable. When it begins to look as if Blacksmith is having its own catastrophe, Jack is convinced there must be a mistake: "Society is set up in such a way that it's the poor and the uneducated who suffer the main impact of natural and man-made disasters.... Did you ever see a college professor rowing a boat down his own street in one of those TV floods?" (114). The media play a pivotal role in *White Noise* because they perform the double function of actualizing and derealizing, as if one's experience itself were not real until packaged and narrated and, ideally, served up on the evening news. Thus the folks in Blacksmith will feel a collective resentment when the catastrophe that has their name on it comes, goes, and never makes the news.[13] But it makes the novel.

Eerily paralleling Bhopal in a gentler key, DeLillo has arranged for his bucolic college town a small environmental disaster, to be coolly named the airborne toxic event. A tank car loaded with toxic gases is punctured, and the Gladney family's yearning for a disaster "bigger, grander, more sweeping" is fully satisfied. Here we have the novel's piéce de résistance, and DeLillo's evocation of the event, the evacuation, and the ensuing circus is both hysterical and bone chilling because no reader can escape the feeling that "it could happen here."

The description of the toxic cloud itself, seen in the mad exodus from the town, has the resonance and reach of myth:

> The enormous black mass moved like some death ship in Norse legend, escorted across the night by armored creatures with spiral wings. We weren't sure how to react. It was a terrible thing to see, so close, so low, packed with chlorides, benzines, phenols, hydrocarbons, or whatever precise toxic content. But it was also spectacular, part of the grandness of a sweeping event, like the vivid scene in the switching yard or the people trudging across the snowy overpass with children, food, belongings, a tragic army of the dispossessed. Our fear was accompanied by a sense of awe that bordered on the religious. It is surely possible to be awed by the thing that threatens your life, to see it as a cosmic force, so much larger than yourself, more powerful, created by elemental and willful rhythms. This was a death made in the laboratory, defined and measurable, but we thought of it at the time in a simple and primitive way, as some seasonal perversity of the earth like a flood or tornado, something not subject to control. (127)

LeClair has shrewdly observed that the nuclear cloud—"packed with chlorides, benzines, phenols, hydrocarbons"—is presented in consumerist terms, like a new item on the supermarket shelf.[14] Hence, to be understood, internalized as real experience, this event has to be not only packaged and presented but made over into narrative and thereby rendered consumable; in the "refugee camp" for the evacuees, Jack's son Heinrich provides for his fellows precisely this special human mediation, and in so doing he becomes a boy for his time, peculiarly altered by the disaster, both fulfilled and fulfilling:

> What a surprise it was to ease my way between people at the outer edges of one of the largest clusters and discover that my own son was at the center of things, speaking in his new-found voice, his tone of enthusiasm for runaway calamity. He was talking about the airborne toxic event in a technical way, although his voice all but sang with prophetic disclosure. He pronounced the name itself, Nyodene Derivative, with an unseemly relish, taking morbid delight in the very sound. People listened attentively to this adolescent boy in a field jacket and cap, with

binoculars strapped around his neck and an Instamatic fastened to his belt. No doubt his listeners were influenced by his age. He would be truthful and earnest, serving no special interest; he would have an awareness of the environment; his knowledge of chemistry would be fresh and up-to-date. (130)

With a brilliant sense of economy, DeLillo uses the catastrophe to cash in his chips. Jack's wife, Babette, has been reading tabloid articles to Old Man Treadwell, and here at the camp, under the shadow of the great cloud, these mawkish stories of Marilyn Monroe and John Wayne and Howard Hughes returning from the dead, often in UFOs, to consult with privileged viewers or to advise the president, seem no more implausible, no less credible than the actual events taking place. Murray was doubtless right: we are trafficking with the spirits wherever we go, into supermarkets or out of nuclear disasters. The tabloids are paying their way.

A lesser novelist would have dealt with the airborne toxic event in terms of tragedy and heroism: the individual pitted against the elements. DeLillo exploits this episode for the light it sheds on our deep-seated need to believe in the supernatural. In so doing he gives the disaster the kind of authority it rightfully deserves in *White Noise*, the authority of subject not object, of agent not setting. Here is the American environment at its most potent and demonic. And we realize we've been hearing it all along. "White noise" means, for scientists, "aperiodical sound with frequencies of random amplitude and random interval," whereas in music it signifies "sound produced by all audible sound-wave frequencies sounding together."[15] "Panasonic" was an earlier working title for this novel, and DeLillo has actually embodied this sense of an all-pervasive sound scheme, strangely analogous to what Melville was after visually in his meditation on the whiteness of the whale: a scaled picture of tiny space occupied by humans in the larger spectrum of noise and image made audible or visible or imaginable by the text's semiotic strategy.

The people of Blacksmith are only now comprehending the extent of their powerlessness, but DeLillo has been presenting all along a world view that divides up the power, puts humans in their proper, puny place. He has done this in a writerly fashion by divvying up narrational power, by writing a choral narrative in which the environment—now understood as a cultural rather than a physical force—speaks as much as the protagonists do. The novel is literally stereophonic:

Upstairs a British voice said: "There are forms of vertigo that do not include spinning." (56)

The TV said: "Now we *will* put little feelers on the butterfly."
(96)

The radio said: "It's the rainbow hologram that gives this credit
card a marketing intrigue." (122)

The voice upstairs said: "Now watch this. Joannie is trying to
snap Ralph's patella with a *bushido* stun kick. She makes contact,
he crumples, she runs." (257)

Sometimes this voice is not even discursive, just a list, a sequence of terms
coming from out there: "MasterCard; Visa; American Express" (100). And it
can be used to extraordinary point, as in the melodramatic episode in which
Jack has learned from Babette of her Dylar venture and fear of death:

> We held each other tightly for a long time, our bodies clenched
> in an embrace that included elements of love, grief, tenderness,
> sex and struggle. How subtly we shifted emotions, found
> shadings, using the scantest movement of our arms, our loins, the
> slightest intake of breath, to reach agreement on our fear, to
> advance our competition, to assert our root desires against the
> chaos in our souls.
> Leaded, unleaded, super unleaded. (199)

In striking Joycean fashion DeLillo achieves a tonal and philosophical
counterpoint here that conveys the full force of the agon he is truly drawn
to: the human story of love and passion, rendered with delicacy and power,
juxtaposed against (undone by?) the technological indices of power and fuel,
the marketing slogans that move our vehicles as well as our bodies.

At the end of the novel, when Jack is embarked on his fateful venture
of revenge, the list achieves its darkest eloquence, as if to show that human
madness is matched (abetted? produced?) by social and technological chaos
of even greater import: "Random Access Memory, Acquired Immune
Deficiency Syndrome, Mutual Assured Destruction" (303).

It is hard to imagine individual autonomy or dignity in this view of
things, for the echoing, growling world out there continually noises its
presence and power. And corresponding to this verbal, tonal bullying is an
entire philosophy of the human being as automaton, as complex biotechnical
entity ruled by forces unknown and ungovernable. Jack's son Heinrich is the
youthful but formidable exponent of this weltanschauung, and his debates
with his father on the nullity of human will, direction, and knowledge

provide some of the keenest exchanges of the novel. When asked, innocently, by his father whether he wants to visit his mother for the summer at an ashram in Montana, Heinrich answers with the suavity that Voltaire displayed in *Candide*:

> "Who knows what I want to do? Who knows what anyone wants to do? How can you be sure about something like that? Isn't it all a question of brain chemistry, signals going back and forth, electrical energy in the cortex? How do you know whether something is really what you want to do or just some kind of nerve impulse in the brain? Some minor little activity takes place somewhere in this unimportant place in one of the brain hemispheres and suddenly I want to go to Montana or I don't want to go to Montana. How do I know I really want to go and it isn't just some neurons firing or something? Maybe it's just an accidental flash in the medulla and suddenly there I am in Montana and I find out I really didn't want to go there in the first place. I can't control what happens in my brain, so how can I be sure what I want to do ten seconds from now, much less Montana next summer? It's all this activity in the brain and you don't know what's you as a person and what's some neuron that just happens to fire or just happens to misfire. Isn't that why Tommy Roy [the convicted killer with whom he plays correspondence chess] killed those people?" (45–46)

Heinrich's biochemical, mechanized, will-less view of the human subject is perfectly calibrated to fit in the electronic world where the phone rings and "a woman's voice delivered a high-performance hello. It said it was computer-generated, part of a marketing survey aimed at determining current levels of consumer desire. It said it would ask a series of questions, pausing after each to give me a chance to reply" (48). *White Noise* is ultimately akin to the world of the body snatchers because it registers with great wit and accuracy the shrinking space we occupy, the limited autonomy we enjoy, the technological encroachments we endure, the peculiar hybrids we have become.[16]

Thus we are far indeed from *David Copperfield*, far from the reassuring schemes of psychological fiction that do honor to the human subject even when the going is rough. "La littérature de l'âme," in Barthes's phrase, is in trouble here, and DeLillo is offering to American letters an especially genial version of nonanthropocentric fiction, somewhat the way Robbe-Grillet did in his geometric fashion for the French some thirty years ago. The famed *inner life* of traditional fiction, the commodity that has sustained centuries of humanism, is not doing very well in *White Noise*. If the subject's consciousness is revealed to be a program of firing and misfiring neurons, what is to be said for its body, that place that harbors items such as heart, feelings, desire, and so forth? What is life really like on the "inside"? Jack, on the way to Autumn Harvest Farms, is bringing his most intimate disclosures with him: "I carried with me several specimen bottles, each containing some melancholy waste or secretion. Alone in the glove compartment rode an ominous plastic locket, which I'd reverently enclosed in three interlocking Baggies, successively twist-tied. Here was a daub of the most solemn waste of all, certain to be looked upon by the technicians on duty with the mingled deference, awe and dread we have come to associate with exotic religions of the world" (275). It is the supermarket vision gone "inside" for a stint, replete with filmy plastic bags and shiny, "burnished" specimens on parade. DeLillo is quite the master of the wide-angled shot in these precincts as well, as if Jack's privatist intestinal purview required enlarging, opening up to the roomier expanses of the whole family's waste system, yielding—in good supermarket logic—a more generic view of the inner life; and so Jack, looking for the fabulous Dylar medication that Babette has been secretly taking, inspects the compacted garbage of the week and runs headlong into a familial intimacy and exhibition of artifacts he had never suspected:

> I unfolded the bag cuffs, released the latch and lifted out the bag. The full stench hit me with shocking force. Was this ours? Did it belong to us? Had we created it? I took the bag out to the garage and emptied it. The compressed bulk sat there like an ironic modern sculpture, massive, squat, mocking. I jabbed at it with the butt end of a rake and then spread the material over the concrete floor. I picked through it item by item, mass by shapeless mass, wondering why I felt guilty, a violator of privacy, uncovering intimate and perhaps shameful secrets. It was hard not to be distracted by some of the things they'd chosen to submit to the Juggernaut appliance. But why did I feel like a household spy? Is garbage so private? Does it glow at the core with personal heat, with signs of one's deepest nature, clues to secret yearnings, humiliating flaws? What habits, fetishes, addictions, inclinations? What solitary acts, behavioral ruts? I found crayon drawings of a figure with full breasts and male genitals. There was a long piece of twine that contained a series of knots and loops.... Some kind of occult geometry or symbolic festoon of obsessions. I found a banana skin with a tampon inside. Was this the dark underside of consumer consciousness? (258–59)

Once again, DeLillo's linguistic obsessions are on show. Perhaps this is the "natural language" of the species today. Organspeak. In a culture increasingly worried about industrial and nuclear waste, *White Noise* impudently suggests that we are to be known by our detritus, that our private waste is literally a form of ex-pression, of utterance.

And what do these secrets look like? Drawn, in all of his novels, to the dynamics of espionage and discovery, DeLillo is toiling in the same fields here, even though the terrain is now the family. Jack Gladney is a man who finds calm and peace in watching his children sleep. As he sits gazing at his daughter Steffie, he hears words she is murmuring:

> Two clearly audible words, familiar and elusive at the same time, words that seemed to have a ritual meaning, part of a verbal spell or ecstatic chant.
>   *Toyota Celica.*
>   A long moment passed before I realized this was the name of an automobile. The truth only amazed me more. The utterance was beautiful and mysterious, gold-shot with looming wonder. It was like the name of an ancient power in the sky, tablet-carved in cuneiform. It made me feel that something hovered. But how could this be? ... She was only repeating some TV voice. Toyota Corolla, Toyota Celica, Toyota Cressida. Supranational names, computer-generated, more or less universally pronounceable. Part of every child's brain noise, the substatic regions too deep to probe. (155)

One hardly knows what to make of these renderings, these epiphanic moments when DeLillo transmutes dross into gold, makes out of the pollution of advertising a beautiful postmodern lyricism and tenderness.[17] But we can hardly fail to see that, once again, "outside" has gotten "inside," that the TV is no longer "out there" at all; it is PacMan writ large: we are the machines gobbled up by other machines. Not that DeLillo's people have no "insides" or secrets: Wilder's marathon crying jag points to a dark core of pure affect, perhaps of terror, underneath it all, and DeLillo reveres that ultimate opaque language that is prior to all codes and grammars.

But the famous "inside story" which has been the burden of art and literature for centuries is passing "un mauvais quart d'heure" in this novel, is in fact being mauled into something quite unrecognizable, a series of weights and measures that graphs life and death, sickness and health, in utterly material fashion. Proust once assessed the magnificent absurdity of the thermometer that has a knowledge of our body that we, however self-aware we may be, can never possess. Overexposed to the toxic cloud, Jack Gladney seeks today's soothsayer with his computerized crystal ball. No secrets here:

> "You're generating big numbers," he said, peering at the screen.
>
> "I was out there only two and a half minutes. That's how many seconds?"
>
> "It's not just you were out there so many seconds. It's your whole data profile. I tapped into your history. I'm getting bracketed numbers with pulsing stars."
>
> "What does that mean?"
>
> "You'd rather not know."
>
> He made a silencing gesture as if something of particular morbid interest was appearing on the screen. I wondered what he meant when he said he'd tapped into my history. Where was it located exactly? Some state or federal agency, some insurance company or credit firm or medical clearinghouse? What history was he referring to? I'd told him some basic things. Height, weight, childhood diseases. What else did he know? Did he know about my wives, my involvement with Hitler, my dreams and fears? (140)

This passage is an uncanny and prophetic version of "freed" speech, empowered speech. Language is displaced but overflowing here because the machines and disks and data now speak us, frame us within their printouts, pronounce on our likely and unlikely futures, chart the curves and graph the risks. The subject is having his fortune told. Biology, chemistry, and mathematics have become myth. And business. And available. Our history is something somebody else taps into.

Once we grasp the disproportionate strengths and forces in the conflict DeLillo has staged, the profound imbalance between the human and the technological order, then we are in a position to measure the heroic role allotted to the family. Distinct from every other book DeLillo has written—each one cool and spare in its focus on cultural dynamics—*White Noise* is a singularly warm and effusive novel, filled with the poetry (and cacophony) of human relationships, tinged with melancholy at the fragility of the human, rich with laughter at the comedy of connection. The family is to be understood as a last gasp for consoling order, for human assertion. At least, that is Murray's theory:

> Murray says we are fragile creatures surrounded by a world of hostile facts. Facts threaten our happiness and security. The

deeper we delve into the nature of things, the looser our structure may seem to become. The family process works toward sealing off the world. Small errors grow heads, fictions proliferate. I tell Murray that ignorance and confusion can't possibly be the driving forces behind family solidarity. What an idea, what a subversion. He asks me why the strongest family units exist in the least developed societies. (81–82)

DeLillo indulges fully in the farce of misinformation, and many of the Gladney family conversations seem to be a surrealist version of TV quiz shows, larded with garbled data, built on nonsequiturs, overflowing with runaway, homeless facts. But the truth coefficient of family discourse is ultimately irrelevant to the novel's deeper purposes, and the textural reality of human relationships has a richness and density all its own, utterly independent of the whims of true versus false:

> Babette came in from running, her outfit soaked through. Murray walked across the kitchen to shake her hand. She fell into a chair, scanned the room for Wilder. I watched Denise make a mental comparison between her mother's running clothes and the wet bag she'd dumped into the compactor. I could see it in her eyes, a sardonic connection. It was these secondary levels of life, these extrasensory flashes and floating nuances of being, these pockets of rapport forming unexpectedly, that made me believe we were a magic act, adults and children together, sharing unaccountable things. (34)

Even in the midst of catastrophe this tapestry of woven relationships displays itself, shows the warp and woof of our lives, the threadwork and needlepoint that are the homely but profound art of people living together over time: "It was a period of looks and glances, teeming interactions, part of the sensory array I ordinarily cherish. Heat, noise, lights, looks, words, gestures, personalities, appliances. A colloquial density that makes family life the one medium of sense knowledge in which an astonishment of heart is routinely contained" (117). Thus, many scenes in *White Noise* take place in the kitchen, "where the levels of data are numerous and deep, as Murray might say" (48), or in the bedroom or TV room, all turned into social rooms, places of multileveled exchanges and transactions, material for endless study, response, and delight. DeLillo has gotten a bum rap for coldness and abstraction, for failing to produce rounded, believable characters. The children in the Gladney household have a rare fictional presence, and DeLillo shows himself to be a truly democratic writer, widening our environment in more ways than one, letting the TV and the toxic cloud speak, but also broadening the community of human players, expanding our sense of communal enterprise, making us see just how varied and surprising our actual natural resources are. There is nothing maudlin about this, nothing even programmatic in the family-versus-destiny vein. Just a deepened sensitivity to sight and sound, an uncanny appreciation for the odd integrity of little folks and big folks. And this is a modern family: children from prior marriages, former spouses dropping in, youngsters flying out, Chinese takeout on Fridays, joint sprees at the supermarket and the department store.

Once again, DeLillo succeeds in avoiding the sentimental, in acknowledging the stress and paranoia of family while nonetheless depicting its richness, its gratifying reality as environment, human this time instead or chemical or media based. Jack Gladney is an astonishing character in the way Leopold Bloom is, by dint of his capacity to imagine the other fellow, to take the world as real rather than as screen for his own fantasies. But unlike Joyce's protagonist, he is animated by fiercer loyalties and he is rewarded by familial pleasures that Bloom has lost: the sight of children sleeping, the routine skirmishes with them, the endless tugs that give heft and rhythm to one's place on the planet. Listening to Heinrich hold forth about the toxic environment, the father in Jack wants to counter: "I wanted to tell him that statistical evidence of the kind he was quoting from was by nature inconclusive and misleading. I wanted to say that he would learn to regard all such catastrophic findings with equanimity as he matured, grew out of his confining literalism, developed a spirit of informed and skeptical inquiry, advanced in wisdom and rounded judgment, got old, declined, died" (175). There is an exquisite balance in these lines between love, admiration, and irony, including self-irony. Such passages are no less eye-opening, no less exploratory than the anthropological trips to the supermarket, and they go a long way toward positing a center of gravity for *White Noise*.

Much of the novel's power derives from the elemental conflict it stages between the family unit, on the one hand, source of poetry and frail structure against chaos, and the omnipresence of death on the other, death depicted magisterially by DeLillo in an astounding array of colors and hues. The airborne toxic event merely makes public and communal and visible an ongoing presence of destruction that has been making private visits for some time now. Known variously as the reverse Darwinism that punishes survivors, or the brutal myoclonic jerk that wracks the body out of sleep, as the secret goal of all plots, or the terror just beneath the surface in all plane flights, as the secret origin of our sense of déjà vu, or the staple material of the media which fascinates the living, or indeed as the beyond depicted earlier in the *Egyptian Book of the Dead* and felt to be gathering apocalyptic force in the "floods, tornadoes, epidemics of strange new diseases" (136) seen in the hilarious Beckett-like countdown that Vernon pronounces over the entropic decay of his body, Death is of course the major white noise of DeLillo's scheme, the ubiquitous, lurking, palpable dread that is anatomized in this novel. Society's greatest weapon for warding off death is technology, but we have here a vision of technology gone amok: computers that replace our history with pulsing stars and bracketed numbers, toxins that escape to form a great Norse death ship and threaten entire communities, medications such as Dylar that are intended to eradicate the fear of death but instead give rise to death plots of their own.

If technology represents the West's failure to conquer death, fascism represents its supreme effort to serve it. The concern with fascism runs throughout DeLillo's work, but only in *White Noise* does it achieve its true proportions. Not only do the surging crowds that massed around the speeches of Hitler and Goebbels make an eerie return in the evacuation and cosmic threat of the airborne toxic event (with Heinrich playing the role of a child-führer in the improvised camp/*Führerbunker*), but Hitler is finally understood to be a magic talisman against death itself, the kind of epic figure to whom "helpless and fearful people are drawn," not so much larger than life as "larger than death" (287). Fascism is ultimately the conversion experience for Jack Gladney, his transformation from "dier" into "killer."

DeLillo brilliantly plays his German card to the full in *White Noise*, moving from the innocuous metamorphosis of Jack into a more menacing, dark-glassed J.A.K., then accelerating into the fuller homicidal reaches of the Hitler persona. Jack's transformation is insistently coded in linguistic terms, ranging from the rudimentary German lessons to the final descent into Germantown and murder.[18] Recalling, strangely yet precisely, Roman Polanski's gradual and meticulous enmeshing of his people at last in Chinatown (in the film of that name), a place where we do not know who is who, DeLillo propels his lovable protagonist into a crazed search for revenge that takes him to the Dylar czar in Germantown, one Willie Mink, who has had sex with Babette as the condition for giving her the notorious pill for removing fear of death. Germantown, like Chinatown, is the metaphoric heart of the text, the center of the labyrinth, where Jack Gladney finally goes "inside." In this book, with its view of the subject under siege both inwardly (misfiring neurons, decaying organs, death sentence) and outwardly (the environmental invasions, cultural, climactic, media, electronic, nuclear), with Babette's prohibition of the very term "entering" ("We're not lobbies or elevators," she says [29]), it is disturbingly appropriate that Willie Mink define his nefarious enterprise as an inside room: "The point of rooms is that they're inside. No one should go into a room unless he understands this" (306). If there is anything *White Noise* teaches its readers, it is a respect for the dignity of surfaces, and we sense something outright invasive in the strange poetry of DeLillo's end gambit. The author persistently images Jack's "entry" in liminal and nuclear terms: "I was moving closer to things in their actual state as I approached a violence, a smashing intensity" (305); "I continued to advance in consciousness. Things glowed, a secret life rising out of them" (310). Willie Mink is the living embodiment of white noise, the originary generator of waves and rays, the source itself of the static and babble of technology that has punctuated this text in its choral refrains. Here there is light, and at last the murk of the human lifts, dissolves: "Water struck the roof in elongated orbs, splashing drams. I knew for the first time what rain really was. I knew what wet was. I understood the neurochemistry of my brain, the meaning of dreams (the waste material of premonitions). Great stuff everywhere, racing through the room, racing slowly. A richness, a density. I believed everything. I was a Buddhist, a Jain, a Duck River Baptist" (310). But this entry into truth, this blinding light, dismantles all human constructs, those of being and those of doing. Willie Mink is, in his very syntax and utterances, the death of narrative:

> "She wore a ski mask so as not to kiss my face, which she said was un-American. I told her a room is inside. Do not enter a room not agreeing to this. This is the point, as opposed to emerging coastlines, continental plates. Or you can eat natural grains, vegetables, eggs, no fish, no fruit. Or fruit, vegetables, animal proteins, no grains, no milk. Or lots of soybean milk for B-12 and lots of vegetables to regulate insulin release but no meat, no fish, no fruit. Or white meat but no red meat. Or B-12 but no eggs. Or eggs but no grains. There are endless workable combinations." (310–11)

We wind up inside the machine. This realm of interchangeable mechanical systems, the very speech of computer-generated discourse, spews forth a kind of biotalk of "endless workable combinations," but it is alien to human connection, to the human and syntactical linkages that alone figure life in this death-obsessed book. Jack Gladney submits to the fascist lure, becomes a killing machine deep in Germantown.

And, in a turn of pure genius, DeLillo chooses this moment to illustrate the virtues of Dylar, a drug that cannot ward off death but can, instead, produce magic language, turn words into deeds. The text at last speaks German. Jack merely *says* "Hail of bullets," and Mink ducks; says "Fusillade," and Mink takes cover behind the toilet. We are close, here (albeit in Marx Brothers fashion), to the quest for potent language that is at the center of *The Names*, finally and fatefully moving past the mediations of signs into the very pith of violence and terror. It is here that we appreciate the mellowness of *White Noise*. DeLillo indeed underscores in this later text the lethal character of "natural" language, but he goes on to display his abiding commitment to the network of human players, the clowns who use and misuse the verbal codes. The verbal and metaphysical fantasia is cut short here, as Jack wounds Mink, takes him to the hospital, returns the stolen car, and reenters the bosom of his family. The life-affirming rhythm of comedy prevails, and the book closes with an image of immersion into the flow, this time entailing the child Wilder's entry onto the freeway, into the traffic, as if to show that life moves everything and everyone into its gravitational pull, that the child—so long viewed adoringly by his parents as magically suspended in time—is no more a talisman against death than Dylar or technology or fascism. And life continues its round. Even the products on the supermarket's shelves are rearranged.

Lacking the philosophical and linguistic boldness of *The Names*, lacking even more sorely the affective density, surreal humor, and cultural satire of *White Noise*, *Libra*, the fictional 1988 account of the making and unmaking of Lee Harvey Oswald, is nonetheless a story that DeLillo seems almost destined to have written. Building on the essay "American Blood: A Journey Through the Labyrinth of Dallas and JFK," published in *Rolling Stone* in 1983, *Libra* is, in some strange way, DeLillo's version of elegy, conceived almost entirely in terms of media and technology, in honor of America as Humpty-Dumpty, irremediably fissured on November 22, 1963, blinded by "six point nine seconds of heat and light" no less devastatingly than Oedipus was, with the searing intensity of a nuclear explosion.

Reminiscent of Dowell, the narrator of Ford's *Good Soldier*, who sees his work as the labor of a scribe following the sacking of a city, DeLillo's "bookman" Nicholas Branch, retired senior analyst at the CIA, is in the fifteenth year of his assignment to write the secret history of the Kennedy assassination, a task he will never complete, given the endless and increasing flow of computerized data that surrounds and threatens to bury him: the facts, the theories, the biographies, the histories, the countless trails and crossings, a retrospective weave that makes Oedipus's fateful encounter at his crossroads look achingly clean and clear in its spelling of origins and ends. Here, then, is DeLillo's model of the aftermath, the deluge: slain president, lost innocence, and a special purgatory of epistemological murk, of never again seeing clear, of permanent exile in the realm of information glut and data overload. From this morass there can be no credible deliverance, no redeeming truth. Only fiction remains, and that is the project he undertakes here: to understand Lee Harvey Oswald as a fiction, as a theory, in his own eyes, in the eyes of those who used him, in the eyes of history. Ultimately DeLillo has written a Sophoclean parable about the shaping of a life and the limits of knowledge, and this parable is luminous as a fable about the resources of fiction after the fall, the freedom of speech when vision is gone.

Libra is bound to disappoint readers looking for the portrait of an era. It pays attention to the pro- and anti-Castro elements, the ripple effect of the Bay of Pigs, the intricate shadow worlds of the CIA, the plotting and counter-plotting within its many factions, but everything is muffled and undercover, far from the strident realities of news media, national opinion, the fresco of a nation in trauma. Unlike Coover's *Public Burning*, DeLillo's DeLillo's book is not seriously concerned with the themes of American politics, not even with the paranoia and lunacy that he has chronicled so magisterially in earlier books. He is not even interested in Kennedy—and this amazes, given his persistent zeroing in on figures of power. He is only mildly interested in Jack Ruby—and this amazes too, given his brilliance in rendering ethnic types like Ruby (in fact, the few pages devoted to Ruby in *Libra* have a gratifying heft and flavor unlike anything else in the book). DeLillo's prey is the elusive Oswald, the Libra figure who could go either way, who is seeking to find his form, to leave his imprint, the man who defined happiness in a letter to his brother as "taking part in the struggle, where there is no borderline between one's personal world and the world in general" (1). Like a (thwarted) latter-day Hegelian, Oswald is trying to develop his world consciousness, to merge his destiny with the forces of history. As Nicholas Branch pores over Oswald's dealings with the CIA and the KGB, his education in New York and New Orleans, Minsk and Moscow, his lifelong efforts to be mover rather than pawn, surveyor of systems rather than cipher or dupe, the rich parallels and concatenations of American fiction begin to come into focus. Lee Harvey Oswald, putative candidate for regicide, is actually *Homo americanus*, a man trying to forge his identity, utterly at home in our line of figures that starts with Wakefield and passes through Gatsby and Joe Christmas en route to beleaguered types such as Coover's version of Richard Nixon and Rick Blaine. Such a figure haunts, seems (both to himself and others) fictive and even ghostly, engages the narrative imagination: behind the pallid Oswald we can discern the enigmatic Bartleby, the unmoored Doel Bundren, the riddling Misfit, the disembodied Beloved. The world of *Libra* is the labyrinth where Nobody lives, and like so many American texts it displays the desperate countermeasures of art to encroach on the real, to offer rhyme as a bid for reason. As readers, therefore, we are in strangely familiar territory: once again, our desire to see clear is thwarted by the novelist's insistence on doubles and shadows, ranging from the twinning high jinks of *Puddn'head Wilson* to the transformational antics of Anderson, Faulkner, and Hemingway, right up to Hawke's twin islands and the house of games negotiated by Coover's 3-D man and his fictive Chaplin. In these gambles we see the irresistible double game of the American writer, the craft and craftiness of the writer as rendition of, and an alternative to, coercion. These are the generic features of self-making and freedom of speech in the American novel.

Libra plays by these rules but operates, nonetheless, a small but crucial paradigm shift. The shapers are now in the text and in the world. The writer's power has passed into the creation. Libra completes DeLillo's series of conspiracy texts, of subjects encountering systems and environments beyond their control. The fate of Oswald is emblematic of the enmeshed, fettered self, trapped in others' designs. Libralike in its own uncertain allegiances, in search of its fit. *Libra* is the deadpan tragicomedy of information gathering, whether it be Branch's investigation, Guy Bannister's detective agency, Oswald's cross-cultural education, or the surveillance performance of the top secret U-2 aircraft. And the results are always the same: much data, little truth.

But the data itself we now understand to be made rather than given; planted, posited, put there to be "discovered." Thus Libra offers a prophetic vision of theory empowered, turned demiurgic, of models leaving a lab of the Frankenstein scenario becoming routine business within the intelligence community, and beyond it. The shapers are in the system, and the central conceit of DeLillo's book is the *making of a man*, not by self-determination but by paste and glue. An entire American tradition of self-making (vitally embodied in most of the works studied here) is now biting the dust. Win Everett (rebuffed CIA veteran of the Bay of Pigs) has a grand design, and it consists of fabricating a life, doing "the whole thing with paper" (28), planting a paper trail, enlisting his disaffected cohorts in the project of selecting from the ranks of the living "a name, a face, a bodily frame they might use to extend their fiction into the world" (150). Life will yield to design:

> He would put someone together, build an identity, a skein of persuasion and habit, ever so subtle. He wanted a man with believable quirks. He would create a shadowed room, the gunman's room, which investigators would eventually find, exposing each fact to relentless security, following each friend, relative, casual acquaintance into his roomful of shadows. We

lead more interesting lives than we think. We are characters in
plots, without the compression and luminous sheen. Our lives,
examined carefully in all their affinities and links, abound with
suggestive meaning, with themes and involute turnings we have
not allowed ourselves to see completely. He would show the
secret symmetries in a nondescript life. (78)

One can almost taste the pleasures produced by plotting, the great
opportunity to make good on design and intelligence, to bring the world to
order by imposing one's fiction. But this subtle Jamesian view of complexity
and pattern is quickly escalated into a Grand Guignot frenzy of uncontrolled
intrigues, of cancerous and anarchic schemes instigated by competing
factions and individuals, each intent on imposing its own design, making
reality its own way. The result is a world of pure carnival, abounding in
doubles and replicas: multiple Kennedy's and Oswalds, clones, plants, look-
alikes, masks. This histrionic, baroque profusion of images and effigies has
its dark side. Here is how agent David Ferrie, former Eastern Airlines pilot,
fully hairless, interested in young boys, defines himself: "Forty-five. Perfect
astronaut age. I'm the dark scary side of John Glenn. Great health except for
the cancer eating at my brain" (65). And DeLillo's project has the same
lurking "who is who?" terror that doubles have implied ever since Jekyll and
Hyde. Suzanne, the child of one of agents, is never clear of "the dark scary
side," and she goes to sleep with her special Little Figures of a clay man and
a clay woman: "The little Figures were not toys. She never played with them.
The whole reason for the Figures was to hide them until the time when she
might need them. She had to keep them near and safe in case the people who
called themselves her mother and father were really somebody else" (366).

       Role playing, double roles, effigies, double selves, no selves: this is the
utterly unplayful world of espionage. The Little Figures with multiple
identities. Stalin's name was Dzhugashvili; Trotsky's name was Bronstein.
Lee Harvey Oswald will take on pseudonyms-Alek, Leon, O.H. Lee, and
Osborne- but he is most fully revealed by the name Hidell:

       Take the double-e from Lee.
       Hide the double-l in Hidell.
       Hidell means hide the l ...
       Don't tell. (90)

The vision of Libra and the DeLillo metaphysics are best summed up by the
Dallas disc jockey Weird Beard:

"I know what you think. You think I'm making it up. I'm not making it up. If it gets from me to you, it's true. We are for real, kids. And this is the question I want to leave with you tonight. Who is for real and who is sent to take notes? You're out there in the depths of the night, listening in secret, and the reason you're listening in secret is because you don't know who to trust except me. We're the only ones who aren't them. This narrow little radio band is a route to the troot. I'm not making it up. There are only two things in the world. Things that are true. And things that are truer." (266)

If *Libra* comes across as a frustrating book, oddly weightless even in its density, it is because the theatrical world of doubles and covers has finally become spectral and triumphant (true and truer), an affair of voices in the night, clones in the day, aliases and acronyms. Oswald's concept of happiness is the erasing of the "borderlines between one's own personal world, and the world in general" turns out to be simply the erasing of one's own personal world, the disappearance of self altogether into the world's designs.

Six point nine seconds of light and heat, of unbearable clarity, when all the phantoms traveling their separate routes converge and collide, from which now, unsuspected amalgams emerge. Ruby finds himself wedded to Oswald. "The indistinct Oswald merges in death with the spy-doubles Powers, the owned U-2 pilot: "It is the white nightmare of noon, high in the sky over Russia. Me-too and you-too. He is a stranger, in a mask, falling" (440).

These epiphanic lines epitomize DeLillo's achievement. The nightmare is our daytime reality. The stranger, in a mask, is falling, but his estrangement is inseparable from ours. "Me-too and you-too". That is why DeLillo takes the risk of closing his novel with Christlike accents: three times Oswald asks Marina to live with him in Dallas, and three times he is denied; Marguerite Oswald refers pointedly to biblical precedent—"If you research the life of Jesus, you see that Mary mother of Jesus disappears from the record once he is crucified and risen" (453)—as she makes her final utterances. Buried on the ground in a final alias, as William Bobo, Lee Harvey Oswald is the exemplary victim of our culture, the No Man whose story is one long anti-bildungsroman, a "how-not-to" book on social purposiveness, an ongoing disappearing act that registers, in full, the forces that cause us to disappear. Here is the definitive portrait of the American Nobody, the man seeking to construct himself while being constructed by forces beyond his ken. With this text we come to the last of our self-made-men, but-in true DeLillo fashion-forward and reverse have become interchangeable: everything is going the other way now, and this man is made by others, converted neatly from life into fiction. Only he never knew.

The agent Parmeuter's wife, Beryl, watches, along with much of the nation, Oswald's televised death, and she feels the terrible pull of this man's fate: "He is commenting on the documentary footage even as it is being shot. Then he himself is shot, and shot, and shot, and the look becomes another kind of knowledge. But he has made us part of his dying" (447). Shot by revolver and camera, Hidell is exposed and undone, is witness to his own execution, shares in the packaging and distribution of his own death, leaves us his dying as a legacy for the living. Like Bartleby dying in the Tombs, or Joe Christmas dismembered, the final mystery of No Man does not die with the victim but passes on, living, into our lives and dreams.

NOTES

1. The best and fullest account of DeLillo's fiction is Thomas LeClair, *In the Loop: Don DeLillo and the Systems Novel* (Urbana: U of Illinois P, 1987). LeClair not only situates DeLillo in the company of postmodernists and deconstructionists but also invokes a galaxy of contemporary thinkers— Bateson, Wilden, Hofstader, Serres, Lyotard et al.—in articulating the notion of the "systems" novel. For a different effort to align DeLillo generically, see John Johnston, "Generic Difficulties in the Novels of Don DeLillo," *Critique*, 30, no. 4 (1989), 261–75.

2. Don DeLillo, *Great Jones Street* (New York: Vintage, 1983), p. 105.

3. DeLillo himself has characterized Wunderlich's trajectory as a move "from political involvement to extreme self-awareness to childlike babbling" (Thomas LeClair, "An Interview with Don DeLillo," *Contemporary Literature*, 23, no. 1 [1982], 22), and it is clear that this particular curve is an arresting one for the author.

4. Don DeLillo, *Libra* (New York: Penguin, 1989), p. 261. Subsequent references are to this edition and are cited in the text.

5. Don DeLillo, *The Names* (New York: Vintage, 1983), p. 6. Subsequent references are to this edition and are cited in the text.

6. LeClair, *In the Loop*, p. 194. LeClair's reading of *The Names* focuses, quite provocatively, on the tensions between orality and literacy, or intimacy and alienation. For a suggestive and alert early reading of *The Names*, see Fredric Jameson's review in *Minnesota Review*, no. 22 (1984), 118–22. Interestingly enough, Jameson finds the specific language argument itself, especially concerning the cult, at once senseless and de rigueur as postmodern trademark.

7. It is in passages such as this that we can best observe the ideological savvy of *The Names*. DeLillo is demonstrably getting his point about exploitation across, but he is content to let his plot carry it, without sinking into a political debate. This is why John Kucich's charge of racism and misogyny, in "Postmodern Politics: Don DeLillo and the Plight of the White Male Writer," *Michigan Quarterly Review*, 27, no. 2 (1988), 328–41, seems both harsh and insensitive.

8. See Matthew Morris, "Murdering Words: Language in Action in Don DeLillo's *The Names*," *Contemporary Literature*, 30, no. 1 (1989), 113–27, and Paul Bryant, "Discussing the Untellable: Don DeLillo's *The Names*," *Critique*, 39, no. 1 (1987), 1629, for further discussion of the "Ob" language of the text.

9. DeLillo is fascinated with babbling: "Babbling can be frustrated speech or it can be a purer form, an alternative speech. I wrote a short story that ends with two babies babbling at each other in a car. This was something I'd seen and heard, and it was a dazzling and unforgettable scene. I felt these babies *knew* something. They were talking, they were listening, they were *commenting* ..." (LeClair, "Interview," p. 24). The episode in *White Noise* about Wilder's crying must derive from this interest.

10. This mockery of domestic fiction is DeLillo's, cited by LeClair, *In the Loop*, p. 208.

11. Don DeLillo, *White Noise* (New York: Vintage, 1985), p. 50. Subsequent references are to this edition and are cited in the text.

12. When asked about the importance of Wittgenstein to his work, DeLillo replied: "I like the way he uses the language.... It's like reading Martian. The language is mysteriously simple and self-assured. It suggests without the slightest arrogance that there's no alternative to these remarks.... Wittgenstein is the language of outer space, a very precise race of people" (LeClair, "Interview," p. 26).

13. See Michael Messmer, "Thinking It Through Completely: The Interpretation of Nuclear Culture," *Centennial Review*, 34, no. 4 (1988), 397–413, for a provocative perspective on DeLillo's book. Messmer draws suggestively on Jean Baudrillard's notion of "simulacra" and Umberto Eco's "hyperreality" in order to discuss the image-status of nuclear issues, and he turns, not surprisingly, to *White Noise*, with its airborne toxic event and its SIMUVAC (simulated evacuation) technicians, for striking textual support.

14. LeClair, *In the Loop*, p. 219.

15. I owe these definitions to LeClair, ibid., p. 230.

16. Here is the area of the novel (and of DeLillo's achievement) that LeClair very seriously misreads. His systems-analysis thesis requires that old-fashioned notions of cause and effect and so on be challenged by the newer looping models of the systems thinkers, and this in turn leads him to

posit a kind of generational warfare in *White Noise*, a resistance on the part of the parents to come to terms with the "newer" thinking of the young (as embodied in the theories put forth by Heinrich). I think one has to be tone-deaf to miss the (gentle) humor and irony in DeLillo's evocation of these delicious conversational duels, and to position the author on either side of this "debate" (which it is not) is to bypass the poignancy and seriousness of the family theme altogether. See ibid., p. 209, for LeClair's version.

17. Needless to say, those who do not like DeLillo anyway may agree with Bruce Bayer, "Don DeLillo's America," *New Centurion*, 3, no. 8 (1985), 34–42, that the rendition of the human family and its secrets is utterly arid, pretentious, cerebral, clichéd, and unpersuasive. About this specific example of the Toyota Celica utterance, Bayer claims, "How does DeLillo get away with such stale gags?" (39). Bayer cites probably half the passages I hold up for praise as evidence of DeLillo's tendentiousness and failure as a writer. Anyone who agrees with him is not likely to be converted by me.

18. DeLillo arranges a perfect fusion between the German plot and the erotic plot in the lovely little scene in which Howard, the German tutor, puts his finger into Jack's mouth in order to position his tongue properly, producing thereby a moment of shocking erotic intimacy.

MARK CONROY

From Tombstone to Tabloid:
Authority Figured in White Noise

Although the setting for Don DeLillo's novel *White Noise* is a small midwestern college town, there are surprisingly few descriptions of the countryside. There is, certainly, "the most photographed barn in the world," well-known chiefly for being well-known; the countryside is glimpsed as the residents of Farmington and Blacksmith flee the airborne toxic event; and, at the novel's conclusion, a spectacular sunset is on view near the highway, courtesy of the local sky's chemical recomposition. Such scenes, however, are scarcely bucolic, having as much to do with the acids of modernity as with the sort of rootedness one is expected to feel in the country. There is one exception: "the old burying ground" (97). Here the novel's hero, J. A. K. (Jack) Gladney, visits the ancestral dead; and no tourists, refugees, or sightseers get in his way. Three small American flags are "the only sign that someone had preceded me to this place in this century" Gladney notes as he tries to decipher the "barely legible" headstones with their "great strong simple names, suggesting a moral rigor." He listens to the dead: "The power of the dead is that we think they see us all the time. The dead have a presence" (97–98). Yet the dead "are also in the ground, of course, asleep and crumbling. Perhaps we are what they dream" (98). Whether or not that is true, the dead, along with death itself, are what Gladney dreams.

This caesura in the storyline, so reminiscent of the famous graveyard scene opening Dickens' *Great Expectations*, figures as that scene did a quest

From *Critique* 35, no. 2 (Winter 1994): 96–110. © 1994 by the Helen Dwight Reid Educational Foundation.

for identity through the reading of tombstone names. But the names of Gladney's own parents do not appear, either on these tombstones or indeed anywhere else in the novel; and because the town where he lives is itself only the latest in a series for him, there is no reason to impute a search for personal roots to his visit. Its ancestor worship is of a vaguer sort. It is as if Gladney's homage is not to his personal forebears, but to the idea of the past as a source of authority for the present. For it was always the dead who offered the surest claim to authority for the living and the surest means of defeating death itself. One respected those who had died, hoping, perhaps superstitiously, that death for oneself would mean accession to a dynasty and not mere extinction.

Gladney's life has been in severe drift for many years, but his malaise may best be seen as a crisis of authority. His life is falling apart because it needs several registers of traditional authority in order to stay together. And all of them are coming under attack in the America of DeLillo's text: not from revolution, of course, but simply from those acids of modernity.

White Noise dramatizes through the Gladney family and the Gladney career the current fate of several traditional forms of cultural transmission. Each harnesses the living to the dead in its own fashion, and thus each has its own version of immortality. This immortality is assured by means of a certain narrative that figures, in its own form, the way an individual's present life is bonded to the past: a bonding that in recompense grants the individual a role in that narrative's version of the future.[1]

There are roughly speaking four master narratives of cultural transmission in Jack Gladney's universe: the familial, the civic, the humanist, and the religious. The familial relates people to their forebears through the blood tie; the civic to their community, its tradition and duties; the humanist to that patrimony of Western learning held in trust by the university; and the religious to that larger lineage from the ancestral dead. Despite the tensions among these narratives, it is fair to say that the tendency of them all is, broadly speaking, religious, because loyalty to the ancestral dead (with its consequent hope for immortality) finally grounds them all. Fittingly, Gladney relies upon all of these legitimating lines: lines that are tangled, if not cut, by the world presented in this text.

For a start, the narrative of Gladney's family line is an errant one; it has offspring from each of four marriages to its credit. One suspects its family tree would have many branches but no trunk. The parent figures ("parents" seems not to indicate the role properly) are Jack and his wife Babette; but they do none of the passing on of wisdom that is supposed to be the older generation's portion. Instead, the television seems to be the chief source of information and even guidance; its urgent messages frequently interrupt the narrative of *White Noise*, but they seem more like that from which any other learning is the interruption.

Heinrich, Gladney's son by a previous marriage, is the closest thing the family has to a repository of learning, because he is "plugged in" to things scientific. It is important that nobody knows whether Heinrich is generally right or not: he is merely the possessor of scientific discourse, and that is enough to unseat the parents as sources of moral authority. When he insists at the dinner table that the "radiation that surrounds us every day" is "the real issue," the adults try to denigrate the matter, but they worry he is right (174).[2] When they try to regain the field by throwing out remembered fragments from old history and civics classes ("how a bill becomes a law," "Angles, Saxons and Jutes," and so forth), they conjure up only "a confused rush of schoolroom images" (176). Such Gradgrind-like touchstones are all they can come up with. It is only when Babette appears on TV teaching her posture class that her family pays her the reverential attention customarily accorded the wise. It is clear that the apparition of her person on that medium is the chief reason for everyone's newfound respect. With this exception that proves the rule, the people in charge in the Gladney household tend to be the children. After all, Jack's ultimate threat in trying to force Babette to reveal her secret life is the wrath of her daughter Denise, who has figured out her lies. "I will unleash your little girl," Jack swears, reversing the cliché "Wait till your father comes home." Babette has been "bad," and Denise will punish her for it.[3]

Heinrich's own moment of apotheosis, oddly reminiscent of Jesus's appearance in the temple, occurs with the onset of the airborne toxic event, which finds him "at the center of things, speaking in his new-found voice" to a growing crowd "impressed by the boy's knowledgeability and wit" (130–31). In this hour of crisis, Heinrich's sort of knowledge, however spurious, is evidently what people feel is needed. The scene has its exact analogue in the same section when Gladney himself awaits information on his exposure to the event from the much younger keyboard operator for SIMUVAC: "I wanted this man on my side. He had access to data. I was prepared to be servile and fawning if it would keep him from dropping casually shattering remarks about my degree of exposure and chances for survival" (139). In addition to the superstitious undercurrent of thought here, this passage also indicates how the moral authority subtly shifts. The sort of experience transmitted from older generation to younger—with his four marriages, for instance, Gladney has in one sense a great deal of experience, though it does not add up to much—yields to "access to data," the sort of wisdom this young keyboard operator can give or withhold. Admittedly, Gladney almost implies he would rather the data be withheld than given; but either way, the authority has passed to the younger generation in this encounter.

As for the narrative of community, the small town of Blacksmith, despite the "moral rigor" suggested by its "simple name," is largely a backdrop for the careers of the professors at the College-on-the-Hill, the phony establishment where Gladney pursues his work. The towns poor upkeep and general shabbiness are noted in passing: "Some of the houses in town were showing signs of neglect. The park benches needed repair, the broken streets needed resurfacing. Signs of the times" (170). Such signs are little noticed nor long remembered by the host of "New York émigrés," even by one so otherwise sensitive to signs as media medium Murray Jay Siskind, adjunct professor at the department of American Environments. Murray and his colleagues claim to have come to the Midwest in search of "American magic and dread," but in reality are grateful just to have a peaceful night's sleep (19). By and large they get it, too, because Blacksmith is almost as sleepy as the old burying ground. With the airborne toxic event that occupies the center of the novel, the town bids fair to become an old burying ground itself.

Granted, the event and its aftermath provide a certain renewal of civic spirit in Blacksmith. The SIMUVAC mockup of a toxic event, with townspeople including the Gladneys' young girl Steffie playing victims; or the spectacular sunsets the townspeople view, probably made possible by residue of the airborne event—these are the venues wherein community enacts itself. In both instances, the death of the community is what is enacted by that community. Significantly, the one point during the airborne toxic event where the townspeople evince any solidarity in outrage occurs when they discover that their plight did not make the newscast: "What exactly has to happen before they stick microphones in our faces and hound us to the doorsteps of our homes, camping out on our lawns, creating the usual media circus? ... Our fear is enormous. Even if there hasn't been great loss of life, don't we deserve some attention for our suffering, our human worry, our terror? Isn't fear news?" (162). Apparently this community sees its victimhood as the only way to present itself to itself or others. The possibility of mounting some political opposition to the conditions that produce the event in the first place is not even considered. When the residents of Blacksmith, under the aegis of SIMUVAC, are asked to play victims, it is an expression of civicism in its most perverse form. For in playing victims, they would in reality only be playing themselves. In a similar pattern to that where parents become authorities at such time as they appear on TV, the residents of Blacksmith ("citizens" seems too strong a term) are willing to enact the death of their city in order to achieve media recognition for it. The exercise is justified by the idea that enacting it makes it less likely to happen; but this odd notion is just as likely a cover for the feeling that somehow a media apotheosis assures immortality more readily than commitment to a community and loyalty to its fate. In any case, even this projected event is cancelled for lack of interest.

As for spiritual lineage, the one religious venue mentioned in the novel is the Congregational church basement now used for Babette's posture class. Jack says of her students that he is "always surprised at their acceptance and trust, the sweetness of their belief. Nothing is too doubtful to be of use to them as they seek to redeem their bodies from a lifetime of bad posture. It is the end of skepticism" (27). The childhood faith in redemption of souls is here transferred to the body, along with the hope of triumphing over death. The one religious figure in the novel is a nun who materializes in a hospital in Iron City, and although she deigns to treat Gladney for his gunshot wounds, she is hardly out of *Going My Way*: "It is our task in the world to believe things no one else takes seriously ... If we did not pretend to believe these things, the world would collapse" (318). She proceeds to insist that even though Gladney wants her to believe in the "old muddles and quirks ... great old human gullibilities," it is all a pretense: "Those who have abandoned belief must still believe in us. They are sure that they are right not to believe but they know belief must not fade completely.... We surrender our lives to make your nonbelief possible" (319).

When Gladney encounters this nun, the scene has particular force because she mirrors in her profession the sort of bad faith he feels in his. Gladney's career is a living mockery of every ideal of liberal humanism. His world-historical concerns have been boiled down in convenient kitsch form to something he has christened "Hitler Studies." As part of this new career move, he has changed his name from Jack to "J. A. K. Gladney, a tag I wore like a borrowed suit" (16). To round out the Inspector Clouseau effect, he has added some weight, "an air of unhealthy excess, ... hulking massiveness," as if physical girth could somehow confound itself with intellectual solidity (17). Finally, a pair of dark glasses, along with the ceremonial robes that all faculty of College-on-the-Hill are, preposterously, required to wear, completes the donnish getup, which converges in some sinister fashion upon the Hitler persona. Gladney adds, as an afterthought, that he is himself "the false character that follows the name around" (17).

The protagonist's self-awareness is precisely what makes this fakery especially painful. When he calls neurologist Winnie Richards brilliant, she replies that everyone in the academy calls everyone else that. But he demurs: "No one calls me brilliant. They call me shrewd. They say I latched on to something big" (188). He is a charlatan, in brief, and unfortunate enough to realize it. He does not even know German, though he tries to learn a smidgen for the conference over which he presides. Furthermore, all of the figures with whom he interacts have the same con artist aura about them: Murray, Albert (Fast Food) Stompanato, indeed all of the self-styled media analysts who inhabit American Environments.

Gladney is never presented in Socratic dialogue with his classes; but his flights of rhetorical exuberance in lecture have little to do with the Third Reich, and everything to do with his own neuroses and obsessions: "I found myself saying ... 'All plots tend to move deathward. Political plots, terrorist plots, lovers' plots, narrative plots, plots that are part of children's games. We edge nearer to death every time we plot....' Is this true? Why did I say it? What does it mean?" (26). In addition to being significant for the deathward plot of the novel, this passage suggests the vague nature of Gladney's instruction: why did he not ask himself these questions before finding himself saying these things? Perhaps because authority, at least in the world of this text, is above and before all positional; and the words uttered by Jack become portentous rather than silly by virtue of his having spoken them. The professoriate, like the media idols they study and strive to emulate, gain authority not from any innate ability or from credentials but from personal magnetism or, failing that, the mere fact of having the enunciative role. One suspects that in the world of *White Noise*, the students never think to wonder whether what Gladney, Siskind, and the others have to say is true, or even serious. The mantra-like words Siskind uses to seal so many of his pronouncements are a symptom of this self-referential authority. If his interlocutor seems at all skeptical of some outrageous formula of his, he will simply retort, "It's obvious." And why is it obvious? Nowhere in the book do his interlocutors ever think to ask this.

There is for both Gladney and Siskind an additional source of precious professorial authority: charisma by association. Both are making their careers by attaching themselves, as critics are wont to do, to some eminent figure, whose glory they parasitically procure. Thus Gladney, who did for Hitler what it is Murray's ambition to do for Elvis (or is Elvis doing it for Murray?), enters, Murray's class and begins a running colloquy where the personal, *National Enquirer*-like tidbits about Elvis are contrapuntally answered by similar data about Hitler's life. Gladney senses the debt in which he is placing Siskind: "His eyes showed a deep gratitude. I had been generous with the power and madness at my disposal, allowing my subject to be associated with an infinitely lesser figure, a fellow who sat in La-Z-Boy chairs and shot out TVs. It was not a small matter. We all had an aura to maintain, and in sharing mine with a friend I was risking the very things that made me untouchable" (73–74).

This reflection establishes two essential features of Gladney's moral authority: that it is based upon aura rather than intellect (the aura alone is what makes him untouchable, and not any scholarly eminence); and that the aura in turn arises from the association of the professor with some legendary figure (so that to link Elvis to Hitler is to share Gladney's power with Siskind). Small wonder that when Gladney, minus his gown and sunglasses, happens upon one of his colleagues from the college in the department store, he is told with brutal relish that he is a "big, harmless, aging, indistinct sort of guy" (83). (It puts the newly infuriated Gladney "in the mood to shop," and so to illustrate what one could call DeLillo's Law of Consumption: that people expend money in direct proportion to their fear of death or dishonor.)

Perhaps Jack's laying on of hands also indicates a passing of the humanist's baton from world-historical interests, even if sensational ones, to the simulacra of the mass media. The phony theme park aura of the College-on-the-Hill, its professors forced to wear silly gowns (and, to judge by Gladney, loving it), depicts American humanistic learning at its most compromised and meretricious. Even Murray himself is a bit embarrassed by its character: "there are full professors in this place who read nothing but cereal boxes" (10). Whatever can be said in denigration of Hitler studies, there remains an irreducible consequentiality to that event in world history, whereas the consequences of the Elvis "event" are chiefly, perhaps solely, symbolical ones. Thus, Gladney's gracious gesture has the effect of debasing the liberal humanist lineage even further than his Hitler Studies program has already done.

Gladney, whose role in cultural transmission is short-circuited in his own family and community, plays a dubious role even in the culture he claims to hand down as a humanist. In such fashion, all of the forms of cultural transmission, with their attendant stories, are one by one failing Gladney, in part because he is failing them and in part because the modern situation is such that nobody can any longer properly honor them.

The void left by the traditional narratives prompts the desire for other stories, other lineages by which to insure immortality. As Heinrich's fifteen minutes of fame imply, the discourse of science could be one such story; but its results in the narrative are not encouraging. It is true that science produces, with the airborne toxic event, a new form of death, which Murray rightly describes as "growing in prestige and dimension" and possessed of "a sweep it never had before" (150). (In other words, he describes it, characteristically but in this case saliently, as in essence a media event: a TV miniseries, say.) But the toxic event can ennoble only the spectacle of death itself, not the fate of any person who may die.

When it comes to rationalizing the event it has brought forth, science fares little better. Though "a death made in the laboratory," the event is regarded in a "simple and primitive way, as some seasonal perversity of the earth ... something not subject to control" (127). Even were it accessible to the generality, a merely scientific explanation is not enough to transfigure the process of death, to sublate it as earlier narratives of cultural transmission were able to do. Science by its nature cannot provide the promise of immortality that earlier stories, always implicitly religious regardless of their specific lineages, were once able to render.

Instead the rumors spawned by the event transfigure the specter of death more than the possible rationales of scientific discourse. The many rumors and farfetched explanations resurrect a kind of folk culture, because the "toxic event had released a spirit of imagination. People spun tales, others listened spellbound.... We began to marvel at our own ability to manufacture awe" (153). This is awe of a highly self-referential sort, with a consequent tinge of falsity—but awe nonetheless. Among the things marveled at are items from the various tabloids on hand in the shelter—many of which, speaking of manufactured awe, feature some twist whereby an oncoming disaster is rendered magically harmless or salubrious, much in the manner of *Close Encounters of the Third Kind*, a film popular when *White Noise* was written. To be sure, Heinrich is listened to with awe as well; but his story is not received as if it were different in kind from those in the tabloids.[4]

The flourishing rumor mill revives, however briefly and freakily, the spirit of community in Blacksmith. At least as crucial is the void those stories are vainly pressed to fill. For it becomes evident in the airborne toxic event that although science has evolved new and sweeping means of wreaking death, it has not found a way of ennobling or explaining it. The result is that superstition and rumor must begin anew their time-honored task: "The genius of the primitive mind is that it can render human helplessness in noble and beautiful ways" (140).

Perhaps scientific discourse renders this helplessness in noble ways as well. Still, it is fair to say that neither ghoulish Heinrich nor reclusive misanthrope Winnie Richards are sterling exemplars of the spiritual uplift on offer from scientific discourse.

If anything, the scientific advance chiefly on display in this world—the event itself, with its attendant SIMUVAC teams and medical studies—reduces the people further to infantilism, primitive fantasy, and dependence upon the system as if upon a deity. Indeed, throughout the novel, DeLillo charts a recursive movement whereby the large, impersonal forces of technology first produce death-dealing consequences and then offer themselves as palliatives to the fear of death they have aroused. TV and radio may produce deformed babies, and they certainly thrive on the specter of death; but that fact does not keep everyone, including Dylar dealer Willie Mink, from using those media to annul their fears. Gladney himself, a mess beneath his outsize costume of gravitas, becomes almost tearful when a teller machine shows his checking account balanced: "The system has blessed my life" (46). Such a blessing, as Gladney soon finds when confronting his SIMUVAC technician, is a conditional gesture, always capable of retraction.

The first two sections of this three-part novel relate the process by which Gladney comes to realize that his favored means of immortality will no longer do. Early on DeLillo linked the fear of death to the relationship between Babette and Jack: "Which of us will die first?" is a perpetual fear of them both. By a natural passage he comes to associate her initial stealthy drug-taking, in the cause of reducing her fear of death, with some deeper unfaithfulness. It is typical of this novel where the children frequently assume parental functions that his daughter Denise, a close reader of the Physicians Desk Reference, is "on to" her mother long before Gladney is convinced; but soon the incriminating Dylar vial is uncovered. This discovery leads him to extort from his wife the confession that she slept with her distributor to obtain the illegal drug.

Gladney's subsequent rage at his wife's infidelity is doubled by his revulsion at the scientific rationale behind the notion that a drug that "specifically interacts with neurotransmitters in the brain that are related to the fear of death" can "induce the brain to make its own inhibitors" (200). His reply to the thought of being "the sum of [one's] chemical responses" is to wonder what "happens to good and evil in this system? Passion, envy and hate? Do they become a tangle of neurons? ... Are we being asked to regard these things nostalgically?" And most prophetically for the novel's climax: "What about murderous rage?" (200). Gladney's decision to fell his wife's lover, as deranged as it is, springs as much from the need to see the deeper impulses not as things of nostalgia but as forces with a mythic vigor. Rather than chemical reactions to be suppressed with neurological nostrums, "passion, envy and hate" are to Gladney fundamental things. The Dylar drug Babette takes to ward off the fear of death does not really work, although it appears to be addictive. Science, it seems, can no more end the fear of death than it can redeem the fact of death: Babette's Dylar is as powerless as was good posture, her other means of physically curing a spiritual ill. However, it must be added that Gladney's counterattack—the pistol—also uses the magic bullet that preceded Dylar and is, in its own way, just as mechanistic a solution. Fittingly, the pistol is a gift from his father-in-law, representative of an earlier, less sophisticated generation. Going after her supplier thus strikes a blow in two directions: it reasserts Jack's traditional role as husband, in the most old-fashioned of ways to be sure, but it also defeats, by implication, a proferred scientific solution to a moral problem.

The moral simplicity of Jack's retribution is complicated by the fact that he believes himself to be dying and his own death to be less likely if he kills someone else. Babette's father provides the practical means, but—again fittingly—it is Murray Jay Siskind who gives the casuistical theory that justifies the gun's use: "It's a way of controlling death. A way of gaining the ultimate upper hand. Be the killer for a change. Let someone else be the dier. Let him replace you, theoretically, in that role. You can't die if he does. He dies, you live" (291).

Such a theory, it is clear, is wholly symbolical—or, if you prefer, superstitious. Indeed, Murray himself draws an analogy to burial rites. In addition to affirming the morally human against the inhumanly technological, Gladney has recourse to the earlier, more primitive technologies of his father-in-law's generation and to earlier magical forms of rationale. In a paradox that goes to the heart of the complicity between advanced technology and primitive superstition, it is postmodern Murray who delivers the most primitive argument of all, invoking "some prehistoric period" when "to kill was to live" (292).

In trying to reassert his former authority as head of his household and as spokesman for humanist values, Gladney entrusts himself to superstition in its most regressive form. Making as if to assert his ascendancy, he in fact succumbs to a "prehistoric" mode of action. His crime of passion is already an ancient sort of activity: his reasons for it, as propounded by Murray, are even more primitive. And by the way, Murray's argument dramatizes the true nature of his analyses of mass culture's waves and radiation. His cult of the child, that prime target of TV demography, and his resulting desire to transcend the rational in some McLuhanesque way take on an especially sinister character here.

Gladney inhabits a world where advanced technology cohabits with the most primitive of superstitions; where indeed the former encourages the latter. His plan to go to Iron City and shoot Willie Mink partakes of his briefer journey to the old burying ground, as an attempt to revisit an earlier, more straightforward time. Gladney nurses the additional hope that by enacting this particular old-fashioned narrative, he can create the conditions under which the other abandoned or decaying narratives can once again compel belief. For in attacking Willie Mink, he is after larger game too, especially in the symbolic terms of this novel.

It is Willie Mink who has convinced Babette that the fear of death can be overcome by a pill, and it is not without point that his speech is a salad of phrases from TV, that other ubiquitous modern drug: "Did you ever wonder why, out of thirty-two teeth, these four cause so much trouble? I'll be back with the answer in a minute" (312). Living stateless in a motel, watching TV and downing Dylar pills, answerable seemingly to none of the traditional narratives, Mink appears the perfect candidate for a comeuppance: "Transient pleasures, drastic measures" (304). With death imminent, he will pay for his freedom from those narratives by the stark terror with which he will be forced to greet his own demise. His constant popping of Dylar pills, in this respect, is to Gladney a hopeful sign.

But, this primitive solution does not work. Despite the archaic symbolism of the revolver bequeathed from his father-in-law and the immemorial character of his crime of passion, Gladney cannot make his own narratives live by making Willie Mink die. He is too much a part of the world of Willie Mink to be a proper antagonist. He freely admits he is as terrified of death as is his wife; and in succumbing to a magical solution, his own superstition seems no alternative to the sort that is rampant throughout the book.

The revenge narrative takes the form of that purveyor of folklore, the tabloid story. Gladney's plan to leave his car in the driveway of blind Old Man Treadwell who lives for the tabloids (304) emphasizes the connection. He is attempting by sheer brute force to gain back the moral authority that he is losing; but his plan, a combination of superstition, tabloid aggression, and faith in technology, represents not a regaining but a collapse of his authority. Finally, he is too good to follow through on his plan: "I looked at him. Alive. His lap a puddle of blood.... I felt I was seeing him for the first time as a person. The old human muddles and quirks were set flowing again. Compassion, remorse, mercy" (313). The precivilization scenario of which Americans are so enamored, that *mano a mano* fight between two antagonists, cannot be the moment of truth for Gladney. In the ensuing hospital scene, with its cynical nun, it becomes clear that what holds for the old Adam will also be true of the tale of redemption.

When Gladney seeks the ancient story of vengeance, he rejects the sheltering stories of family, polis, and learning: all the approved forms of cultural transmission. However, he has not stepped outside religious or mystical narrative. Even the formula Murray confers like a benediction— "He dies, you live"—resonates as a bargain uncannily like that offered by Christ. So his journey into the elemental emotions of passion, envy, and hate confront him for the first time in the text with the religious subtext underlying all of the other narratives, including Gladney's *crime passionel*. The nun understands his crying need to believe, to submit to authority in order to save his hopes of immortality. But she is less than sympathetic, telling him scornfully, "You would come in from the street dragging a body by the foot and talk about angels who live in the sky" (320).

In the absence of a straightforward, old-fashioned solution to modernity's muddle, what is left of the old narratives that provide a source of authority, a reservoir of legend and story, and the hope of immortality? What is left is, quite simply, celebrity. In an ironic fashion, the picture Gladney espies on the wall, "of [John F.] Kennedy and the Pope in heaven," provides the clue (317). But the heaven they are really in is that reserved for media idols: the Parnassus of the famous. Believing in heaven may be hard, even (or perhaps especially) for the designated believers such as Gladney's German nun. But belief in personality, and in the perpetual renewal of personality by the mass media, is still possible.

Indeed, celebrity is time and again the object of what cultic power is left in the world of *White Noise*. Relevant here is the lengthy discussion among the faculty of American Environments, where Alfonse Stompanato, the chairman, rounds on other participants asking them where they were when James Dean died, as if challenging their bona fides (68–69). Few things may unite Elvis Presley and Adolf Hitler, but star status in film is surely one of them. Orestes, Heinrich's friend, wants to get in the Guinness Book of World Records in the worst way; and Heinrich's mass murderer pen pal has gotten famous in the worst way. In the familial reverence that greets Babette (when on TV), or the reaction of Gladney's daughter Bee to the fact that passengers in the near-crash of an airplane will not be on TV ("They went through all that for nothing?" [92]) we see that being on television is apotheosis to those who otherwise merely watch it.

The technology that brings them into the home may be as alien and inscrutable as that of Dylar or the airborne toxic event, but the celebrities themselves, at least, are people, only with that charismatic glow that contact with mass media lends. The honored dead in the society of this novel are not those named upon illegible tombstones in the old burying ground, but those whose visages have been fixed in the media constellation. With the waning of the old stories of lineage and immortality, the best guarantor of immortality is now not scriptive, let alone discursive; it is iconographic: the televised image, the radio voice. This, and not the old burying ground, is the postmodern dynasty of the dead.

The religious narrative in this new world is thus preserved, but applied to human celebrity rather than to angels or gods. The near crash of the airplane demonstrates how the elaboration of technical means has the paradoxical effect of rendering people more and not less infantilized, dependent upon reassurance from images of authority (their grateful response to such reassurance at this point is to assume the fetal position). The thaumaturgical figure of the chief steward as he comes down the aisle after the plane averts disaster is itself proof enough that faith in authority is being rewarded (90–92). Thus does the iconography of authority outlive its legitimating stories.

As a result, the significance of the fact that it is not European History that Gladney teaches but Hitler Studies becomes clearer. Hitler, after all, was a figure who took unto himself the authority of death; and the reports of his death, like Elvis's, were long thought greatly exaggerated. Given what Gladney says about him in the only glimpse the reader has of his teaching, his approach to his topic is biographical, anecdotal, and psychoanalytic—in short, an academic variant of the approach tabloids and fan magazines take toward celebrities. Celebrity, a hit parade of historical personalities and great men, becomes his way of defining the liberal-humanist heritage.

The family is retained, but now its purpose is not to change children into adults (the traditional function of the family) but rather to insure that adults remain children (the consumer paradigm). The childlike faith in celebrity transfers nicely to the products that in many ways the celebrities resemble. The barn in Farmington stands as the emblem of this transformation of the country's past into a theme park culture: it is called "the most photographed barn in America," and thus meets the celebrity criterion of being well-known chiefly for having been well-known.

It is a commonplace to view *White Noise* as a critique of American materialism, and to a degree, this is true. But that too easy term must be defined and explained. What DeLillo is most conscious of is how the more elaborate forms of spirituality that preceded consumer culture still inhere, in a degraded and superstitious form, within the consumer culture. If the materialism in DeLillo's universe can be given a spiritual inflection, then, it would be a certain kind of Manichaeism: one where spiritual status is marked off by association with the right food and clothing, or proximity to holy ones.

Similarly, the Americans of *White Noise* pursue the right consumer items and try to connect with celebrities, or with celebrity itself, in the hope that proof of spiritual election will follow. Gladney's frantic accretion of weight, wives, and consumer items comes increasingly to be seen as symptomatic of his fear of death, his desire for a talisman to ward it off. (When Gladney has convinced himself that he is dying, he begins to throw out the things he has bought, with the same mania with which he acquired them.[5])

In the twilight of the earlier narratives of immortality, no rational paradigm presents itself to Gladney and the others, least of all one of science or technology. Instead, the products of modern technology become themselves fetish objects: the miracle drugs, the Promethean airplanes, the electronic temple of modern media. Indeed, it is a corollary of the Manichaean emphasis upon personhood, upon the physical as prerequisite for spiritual authority, that the mere fact of one's positioning by the mass media is itself the sign of election. The moral dimension to the publicity— whether it is achieved through mass murder, in the case of Heinrich's pen pal, or through good deeds—becomes secondary to the fact of election itself.[6]

Similarly, the collective worship of these gods produces a community of a sort, but not one that bears much relation to the old story of civicism. Rather, the result is a community of spectators who enact and view their own possible demise. Such is this way of defining the residents of Blacksmith that even their airborne pollution becomes an opportunity to "go to the overpass all the time" and sit in lawn chairs "watch[ing] the setting sun," now enhanced by toxicity. "The sky takes on content, feeling, an exalted narrative life," Jack tells the reader. But as with TV, the crowd comes to look, not converse: "We find little to say to each other" (324). The glow of the sunset, like that of TV, is the source both of fascination and anxiety; and like moths to a flame, the people of Blacksmith go to bask in the glow of the very thing that could do them the most harm.

By novel's end, Gladney has assumed the passivity that is characteristic of the other townspeople. He has been doubly victimized by modernity: his exposure to the airborne event has increased his awareness of his own mortality; and the hegemony of science's story, whose audience numbers his own wife, has weakened the traditional narratives that were his refuge. The weary irony with which Gladney narrates the closing supermarket scene indicates that what the preceding events have taught him is only the exhaustion of previous narrative promises of immortality, not any bright new hope.[7] Only as that quintessentially passive figure, the consumer, does Gladney have the faint glimpse of immortality now allowed him.

In that spirit he revisits the supermarket, a virtual omphalos for so many *White Noise* episodes. Here, it is not only through the "holographic scanners" installed in the checkout counters that "the dead speak to the living" (326). The bread of life is available, to be sure, but so are the lineage to the ancestral dead, the celebrities, and the attendant hope of immortality. These spiritual essences are embodied in the only discursive form remaining in Gladney's world: the tabloid. Through its liturgy, the customer may participate in the American celebrity cult while also consuming American products. Here the profane consumer items in one's cart mingle with the viaticum promised by the sacred image and text of the tabloids.

If the supermarket is indeed the point of intersection between profane consumption and sacred celebrity, it is the tabloids that make it so. The things of the body are cared for, as always, by the supermarket; but so are the things of the spirit. Denied the ability to touch the saints of the mass media directly, the consumer may instead read these devotional tracts. All of Gladney's protective irony cannot conceal the fact that, with the failure of his other narratives, he has no recourse but to look to the tabloids for support, as do all the others. He can no longer read his own immortality in the old stories, so instead of the inscriptions on the tombstones of the Old Burying Ground, Jack Gladney is last seen reading the covers of the tabloids:

"Everything we need that is not food or love is here in the tabloid racks. The tales of the supernatural and the extraterrestrial. The miracle vitamins, the cures for cancer, the remedies for obesity. The cults of the famous and the dead" (326).

NOTES

1. The informed reader may see a certain family resemblance between these stories, which are passed down culturally and which in turn are about their own process of being passed down, and those *grands récits* spoken of by Jean-François Lyotard in his *The Postmodern Condition*. Lyotard has indeed inflected much that I present here, but anyone who tries to find any one-to-one corollary between his narratives and those herein described will be disappointed. For one essential thing, his metanarratives have an Enlightenment provenance, whereas mine (the liberal humanism narrative, I would insist, included) antedate that period and its concerns. Even the civic narrative, seemingly drawn from the Revolutionary War, really stems from far earlier sources such as ancient Greece, at least in DeLillo's text. The closest thing in *White Noise* to an Enlightenment narrative would be the discourse of science: but even those who find it compelling treat it with the sort of veneration accorded magic, not rational inquiry.

2. For what it is worth, recent writings of Paul Brodeur on the effects of extremely low frequency radiation, of the kind emitted from electrical wires and VDT terminals, suggest Heinrich may have in fact been on to something.

3. Tom LeClair, in his *In the Loop: Don DeLillo and the Systems Novel* has pointed out in this regard that the parents in *White Noise* are in fact much more in need of "what they trust are protective and safe relationships" than are their children. Babette, he notes, sees the children as "'a guarantee of our relative longevity.'" As a result, "the children are more willing to face threats to existence than are their parents," thus becoming "a threat—an inescapable threat, because Babette and Jack have sealed them into the nuclear structure" (216–17).

4. Nor is this mere stupidity on their part. As LeClair mentions, the "waves and radiation" of scientific discourse "are beyond the capability of 'natural' perception: knowledge of them cannot be had without the aid of technological extensions of the nervous system" (225). Or, we might add, without faith.

5. For more on this link between the accretion of objects and Jack's fear of death and his ironic reversal of throwing things out, see LeClair, 214–15.

6. John Frow, in his "Notes on *White Noise*," discusses at length and with much cogency the central place of the mass media in this book. He

attributes the substitution of media simulacrum for "real-life" experience as just one more postmodern feature in the mode described by French writer Jean Baudrillard, among others. He understands that DeLillo's novel constructs "a new mode of typicality" where general "representations ... are then lived as real," yet "so detailed" as not to be "opposed to the particular" (418).

Frow is correct to note the constant *reversio* whereby the media, in purporting to "represent" some aspect of existence, in fact put forth a model to be imitated. As he says, "Real moments and TV moments interpenetrate each other" quite a bit in this text (421). But he is too hasty, I suspect, in ascribing this reversal to the sheer profusion of signs in the contemporary world, in foreswearing on DeLillo's behalf any "sentimental regret for a lost world of depths" (427). Whether or not Frow feels admitting the palpable undertow of nostalgia in *White Noise* might make it seem insufficiently postmodern, I think he fails to assess the hollows, the felt absences of once viable stories. It is these hollows that role models for celebrity—and the products they endorse (and that endorse them)—are expected to fill in DeLillo's world.

7. LeClair notes that Gladney draws no conclusion from the miraculous survival of his youngest, Wilder, after the child rides his tricycle across a busy expressway. He sees this as a sign of Gladney's new maturity. This is possible. But its inclusion in the first place suggests to this reader that Gladney hopes to see it as a "good omen," without retaining by this point any larger narrative frame within which to justify that hope; that in short, it is another index that Gladney has indeed succumbed to superstition, as well as the final instance of that recurrent DeLillo chiasmus whereby adults look to their children for guidance, rather than vice versa. (The Gladney family's death-defying trips are made to the same expressway where Wilder performs his feat.)

WORKS CITED

Brodeur, Paul. *Currents of Death*. New York: Simon, 1989.

DeLillo, Don. *White Noise*. New York: Penguin, 1985.

Frow, John. "Notes on *White Noise*." *South Atlantic Quarterly* 89 (Spring 1990): 413–29.

LeClair, Tom. *In the Loop: Don DeLillo and the Systems Novel*. Chicago: U of Illinois P, 1987.

Lyotard. Jean-François, *The Postmodern Condition*. Trans. Geoff Bennington, and Brian Massumi. Minneapolis: U of Minnesota P. 1984.

JOHN N. DUVALL

The (Super)Marketplace of Images: Television as Unmediated Mediation in DeLillo's White Noise

Fascism sees its salvation in giving [the] masses not their right, but instead a chance to express themselves. The masses have a right to change property relations; Fascism seeks to give them an expression while preserving property. The logical result of Fascism is the introduction of aesthetics into political life.

> Walter Benjamin, "The Work of Art
> In the Age of Mechanical Reproduction"

We know that now it is on the level of reproduction (fashion, media, publicity, information and communication networks), on the level of what Marx negligently called the nonessential sectors of capital ..., that is to say in the sphere of simulacra and of the code, that the global process of capital is founded.

> Jean Baudrillard, *Simulations*

Don DeLillo's *White Noise* comically treats both academic and domestic life. Yet both of these subjects serve primarily as vehicles for DeLillo's satiric examination of the ways in which contemporary America is implicated in proto-fascist urges.[1] In making this claim, I do not mean to erase the enormous differences between contemporary America and Europe of the

---

From *Arizona Quarterly* 50, no. 3 (Autumn 1994): 127-153. © 1994 by the Arizona Board of Regents.

1920s and 1930s, particularly Germany and Hitler's National Socialists, which DeLillo's novel invokes. The United States, of course, neither maintains an official ideology of nationalism and anti-Semitism, nor overtly silences political opposition through storm-trooper violence and state control of the media. Nevertheless, our national mythology that tells us we are free, self-reliant, and autonomous citizens, when enacted as moments of consumer choice, produces a cultural-economic system that, in several Marxist and post-Marxist accounts of postmodernity, is more totalizing than Hitler's totalitarian regime. German fascism prior to World War II was a modernist phenomenon, linked to monopoly capitalism.[2] DeLillo's American proto-fascism, however, functions in what Fredric Jameson has identified as the cultural logic of multinational or late capitalism in which the social, the political, and the aesthetic flatten out into what Jean Baudrillard calls the simulacrum.[3]

White Noise performs its critique not simply because its central character and narrator, Jack Gladney, is Chair of the Department of Hitler Studies at an expensive liberal arts college, but rather because each element of Jack's world mirrors back to him a postmodern, decentralized totalitarianism that this professional student of Hitler is unable to read. Jack's failure to recognize proto-fascist urges in an aestheticized American consumer culture is all the more striking since he emphasizes in his course Hitler's manipulation of mass cultural aesthetics (uniforms, parades, rallies). This failure underscores the key difference between Hitler's fascism and American proto-fascism: ideology ceases to be a conscious choice, as it was for the National Socialists, and instead becomes in contemporary America more like the Althusserian notion of ideology as unconscious system of representation. In *White Noise* two representational systems in particular produce this unconscious: the imagistic space of the supermarket and the shopping mall coincides with the conceptual space of television.[4] Both serve the participant (shopper/viewer) as a temporary way to step outside death by entering an aestheticized space of consumption that serves as the postmodern, mass-culture rearticulation of Eliot's timeless high-culture tradition. Because of this linkage, the *market* within supermarket serves as a reminder that television also is predicated on market relations. The production and consumption of the electronic image of desire is a simulacrum of the images (aesthetically displayed consumer items) contained in the supermarket and the mall. This hinged relationship between the supermarket and the television is signaled by the twin interests of Murray Jay Siskind, the visiting professor in the Department of American Environments at the College-on-the-Hill. Siskind, a student of the "psychic data" of both television and the supermarket, acts as an ironized internal commentator on the family life of the Gladneys as both shoppers and television viewers. Siskind's celebration of the postmodern becomes highly ambiguous because, against his celebrations, *White Noise* repeatedly illustrates that, within the aestheticized space of television and the supermarket, all potentially political consciousness—whether a recognition of the ecological damage created by mass consumption or an acknowledgment of one's individual death—vanishes in formalism, the contemplation of pleasing structural features.[5]

From the perspective of Walter Benjamin, this aestheticizing tendency in American culture suggests why it is appropriate that Jack should teach only classes—as the college catalogue describes it—on the "continuing mass appeal of fascist tyranny" (25).[6] For Benjamin, aestheticizing the political is a defining feature of fascism. Speaking particularly of German fascism, he notes in the epilogue to "The Work of Art in the Age of Mechanical Reproduction" that "the violation of the masses, whom Fascism, with its *Führer* cult, forces to their knees, has its counterpart in the violation of an apparatus [the media] which is pressed into the production of ritual values" (243). Although the main thrust of the essay is Benjamin's celebration of the way in which reproductive technologies function to destroy aura in high-culture objects, he senses, in the passage just quoted, a countercurrent to his argument, which he elaborates in a note; that countercurrent is the link between mass reproduction and the reproduction of the masses. "In big parades and rallies, in sports events, and in war, all of which nowadays are captured by camera and sound recording, the masses are brought face to face with themselves" (253). Benjamin, in complicating his notion of mechanical reproduction, points the way toward DeLillo's America, where giving oneself over to a formal contemplation of the image matrix of either television or the supermarket denies one's insertion in the political economy and functions as but another version of Hitler Studies; it is learning how to be a fascist, albeit a kinder, gentler one. DeLillo's characters, as several instances of television viewing and shopping reveal, consistently fall into a suspect formal method when they interpret events in their world; such instances provide an important context for understanding both Murray's teaching of postmodernity and the specificity of American proto-fascism.

The conclusion of "The Airborne Toxic Event," the second section of the novel, typifies DeLillo's meditation on television as a medium constructive of postmodernity. Having fled their homes to avoid contamination from a railroad tanker spill, the Gladneys, along with the other residents of the small college town of Blacksmith, become quarantined evacuees in Iron City. At the end of the first day of their quarantine, "a man carrying a tiny TV set began to walk slowly through the room, making a speech as he went" (161). Like some tribal priest with a magic charm, the man "held the set well up in the air and out away from his body and during the course of his speech he turned completely around several times as he walked in order to display the blank screen" to his audience:

> "There's nothing on network," he said to us. "Not a word, not a picture. On the Glassboro channel we rate fifty-two words by actual count. No film footage, no live report. Does this kind of thing happen so often that nobody cares anymore? Don't those people know what we've been through? We were scared to death. We still are. We left our homes, we drove through blizzards, we saw the cloud. It was a deadly specter, right there above us. Is it possible nobody gives substantial coverage to such a thing? Half a minute, twenty seconds? Are they telling us it was insignificant, it was piddling? Are they so callous? Are they so bored by spills and contaminations and wastes? Do they think this is just television? 'There's too much television already—why show more?' Don't they know it's real?" (161–62)

John Frow notes that "the most horrifying fact about the evacuation is that it isn't reported on network television" (182).[7] What is perhaps most horrifying about this absence of mediation is that, for those who experience the disaster, it is precisely this mediation (and this mediation alone) that could make their terror immediate. Because the evacuees are attuned to the forms, genres, and in fact the larger aesthetics of television, they experience a lack, a sense of emptiness. Strikingly, in the world of *White Noise*, immersed in multiple and multiplying representations, what empties experience of meaning for the evacuees is not the mediation but the absence of mediation. During the TV man's speech there comes a point at which his incredulity— and clearly he speaks for all his listeners—crosses a boundary line where understandable dismay at not being represented on network television becomes satire through the overdrawn particularity of his desired scenario; yet despite the satire, the speech accurately registers how fully mediated the evacuees desire the moment to be:

> "Shouldn't the streets be crawling with cameramen and soundmen and reporters? Shouldn't we be yelling out the window at them, 'Leave us alone, we've been through enough, get out of here with your vile instruments of intrusion.' Do they have to have two hundred dead, rare disaster footage, before they come flocking to a given site in their helicopters and network limos? What exactly has to happen before they stick microphones in our

faces and hound us to the doorsteps of our homes, camping out on our lawns, creating the usual media circus? Haven't we earned the right to despise their idiot questions?" (162)

The problem the tv man articulates, deaf of course to the humor of his own speech, is how in the present one relates to one's fear. The evacuees intuit that their encounter with the poisonous chemical cloud far exceeds the bounds of the everyday. Their terror, however, cannot register in a Romantic sublime where origin is still attributable to the Godhead. The awe and terror of this man-made disaster can only be validated through the electronic media.[8]

What makes this speech humorous is that no one actually would articulate the situation as the tv man does. His language, however, gives voice to a portion of the postmodern unconscious. The masochistic desire to be exploited that passes as the collective desire of his audience seems almost as perverse as the Puritan desire to be scourged by God. And perhaps this analogy is not as strange as it seems. Just as the Puritans sought affirmation of their position through a sign from God (his chastisement) that would stabilize their sense of themselves (the chastisement, after all, meant that God found them worthy of his paternal attention and hence argued strongly that they were among the saved), so do DeLillo's postmoderns seek affirmation through television, the GRID who/that really cares and affirms the legitimacy of their terror. Those who encountered the airborne toxic event intuitively know that television is not a mediation; it is the immediate. Television, the intertextual grid of electronic images, creates the Real.

But if the tv man envisions television as some ideal unmediated mediation for the victims of the chemical spill, how would that same disaster, had it been televised, play at the receiver's end? A way to answer this question is suggested by one of the tv man's own questions: "Do they have to have two hundred dead ... before [the media] comes flocking to a given site ... ?" After concluding his speech, the tv man quite appropriately turns and looks into the face of Jack Gladney because Gladney's vacant gaze serves as a displaced reminder of the answer to the tv man's question; *White Noise* implies that the audience for the tv man's desired broadcast of the evacuees' story would be, figuratively, the Jack Gladney family, since they typify the American family's consumption of television images. The Gladneys' television habits illustrate the way the electronically reproduced image consistently empties its representations of content, turning content into pure form that invites aesthetic contemplation.[9] Each Friday night, Jack's wife, Babette, insists that the family gather to watch television. The attempt to create a family ritual is usually a failure—each would prefer to do something else—but one Friday their viewing begins with a repeated image of a plane crash, "once in stop-action replay" (64). The evening crescendos in a never-ceasing orgy of human suffering that mesmerizes the Gladneys:

> Babette tried to switch to a comedy series about a group of racially mixed kids who build their own communications satellite. She was startled by the force of our objection. We were otherwise silent, watching houses slide into the ocean, whole villages crackle and ignite in a mass of advancing lava. Every disaster made us wish for more, for something bigger, grander, more sweeping. (64)

The answer, therefore, to the tv man's question, then, is yes—at least two hundred dead, preferably more. Network and cable news programs, competing for a market, operate under capitalism's demand to make it newer, thus turning "news" into another genre of entertainment. As a form of entertainment, the distance between television news and the tabloids, a recurring presence in *White Noise*, collapses. Jack may find ridiculous those who believe in the tabloid stories, yet his own belief is predicated on distortions generated by his news medium of choice.

As disaster becomes aestheticized, another boundary blurs, that between television news' representation of violence and violence in film, creating a homogenous imagistic space available for consumption. Murray's seminar on the aesthetics of movie car crashes is a case in point. Jack is puzzled by Murray's celebration of car crashes "as part of a long tradition of American optimism" in which "each crash is meant to be better than the last" (218). Murray's advice on interpreting such filmic moments—"look past the violence" (219)—asserts that meaning resides in form, not content.. And though Jack finds this advice strange, that is precisely what he and his children do instinctively when they watch television—they look past the violence and the human suffering of disaster and see only aestheticized forms, enhanced by repetition and technological innovation, such as slow-motion, stop action, and frame-by-frame imaging of plane crashes. Undoubtedly, the television coverage of Desert Storm confirms DeLillo's novelistic vision. Vietnam may have been the first televised war, but Desert Storm was the first war with good production values. Each network competed for its market share through high-tech logos and dramatic theme music as lead-in to their broadcasts. But not even the networks could compete with the technological splendor of American "smart" bombs, equipped with cameras that broadcast the imminent destruction of targets (and, incidentally, people). Never has death been simultaneously so clearly near and so cleanly distanced for the viewing public, turning the imagistic space of television into something more akin to a video game.

The repeated images of disaster that the Gladneys enjoy holds death at bay and participates in DeLillo's meditation on death in this novel. But what is more at issue is the sharply divergent role television plays for those who are televised and those who consume the image. The heart of the tv man's anger is that for those who experience disaster, the presence of the media makes the experience "real"; that is, as part of our cultural repertoire, people know, like the tv man, that the media is supposed to be interested in marketing disaster. Therefore, the airborne toxic event cannot be a real disaster if the media shows no interest. Stripped of their imagistic knowing, the "victims" (but perhaps they aren't, since there is no media interest) are left without any way to understand their terror. The tv man hopes to enter the Real through imagistic representation but the Real can be received only as aesthetic experience and entertainment.

DeLillo's assessment of the postmodern media is reiterated in several other moments in *White Noise*. In discussing with his son Heinrich a mass murderer with whom his son carries on a game of chess via their correspondence, father and son reveal a clear sense of the genre of the mass murderer as depicted by the media. Jack's questions reveal the *langue* or the general system; Heinrich's answers, the *parole* or particular articulation:

> "... Did he have an arsenal stashed in his shabby little room off a six-story-concrete car park?"
>
> "Some handguns and a bolt-action rifle with a scope."
>
> "A telescopic sight. Did he fire from a highway overpass, a rented room? Did he walk into a bar, a washette, his former place of employment and start firing indiscriminately? ...
>
> "He went up to a roof."
>
> "A rooftop sniper. Did he write in his diary before he went up to the roof? Did he make tapes of his voice, go to the movies, read books about other mass murderers to refresh his memory?"
>
> "Made tapes." (44)

To all of Jack's many questions, Heinrich shows how Tommy Roy Foster signifies within the system "mass murderer." The questions and answers follow through a series of information that any story on a mass murderer must have—number of victims, killer's life history, type of weapon, site of killing, and posited motive. The genre then is predictable and formulaic. It is pleasurable because it is formulaic. The final gesture in the mass murder story is, of course, the hypothesis, the reason for the killing, always woefully inadequate to the mystery and fascination of the killer's "real" motives. (Oddly, the assumption that a mass murderer must have real intention, however deviant, saves the concept of intention for everyone else; our meanings may be fluid and ambivalent but surely the mass murderer is motivated by a singular fixed purpose.) The answer to Jack's final question— "How did he deal with the media?"—is telling: "There is no media in Iron City. He didn't think of that till it was too late" (45). Here, as with the discontent of the tv man, the only thing that confirms the reality of experience is its construction as media event. Jack's and Heinrich's understanding of the aesthetics of mass murder underscore how deeply mediated that knowledge is.[10]

One of the effects of this intensely mediated knowing is a specious tv logic predicated on formalist interpretations of television. After returning to Blacksmith from the evacuation in Iron City, Babette can think about pollution in these terms:

> Every day on the news there's another toxic spill. Cancerous solvents from storage tanks, arsenic from smokestacks, radioactive water from power plants. How serious can it be if it happens all the time? Isn't the definition of a serious event based on the fact that it's not an everyday occurrence? (174)

But the illogic of Babette's argument is not that much greater than Jack's before the evacuation. He believes that disasters "happen to poor people who live in exposed areas," probably, one might add, the same people who rely on the tabloids rather than the television for their news. Jack remains calm, confident that his socio-economic status will protect him: "Did you ever see a college professor rowing a boat down his own street in one of those tv floods?" (114) Logic has been replaced by aesthetics, or perhaps more accurately it is a logic based on aesthetic perception.

Television, however, does not stop at structuring the conscious thinking of DeLillo's characters. More invasively, television and its advertising subliminally shape their unconscious. *White Noise* reminds us how closely related are the subliminal and the sublime. Listening closely to one of his daughter's sleeping verbalizations, Jack finally discerns the syllables that "seemed to have a ritual meaning": Toyota Celica. Jack is left with "the impact of a moment of splendid transcendence" (155). But if we recall Benjamin's concept of aura, then we can see Jack's false transcendence as a key moment in the production of consumers, those who, then take their individual experiences of shopping as constitutive of the auratic self. Aura for Benjamin is a negative concept because it cloaks the work of art in its cultic and ritual function (225–26). For Jack and his family, reproducibility may have removed the aura of the work of art, but art's magic function has merely migrated to the marketing of consumer goods. The irony is clear: at the very time when reproduction destroys the false religious aura of high culture, those same techniques of reproduction establish tradition and aura in mass culture. If modernist art rushed in to fill the void created by the death of God, advertising has stepped in to fill the space vacated by modernism.[11]

Jack certainly creates a ritualistic formula in his narration, repeatedly interjecting trios of brand names, always three products of the same kind. These interjections serve as clear bits of a modernist technique, stream-of-consciousness, used to portray the postmodern.[12] Such moments, inasmuch as they signify within the code "modernist fiction," invite one to tease at the signifying chain. One of these trios occurs, for example, when Jack describes a recurring conversation he and Babette have:

> She is afraid I will die unexpectedly, sneakily, slipping away in the night. It isn't that she doesn't cherish life; it's being left alone that frightens her. The emptiness, the sense of cosmic darkness.
> MasterCard, Visa, American Express. (100)

The apparently unmotivated series, however, has a logic of its own. Thinking of the "cosmic darkness," Jack's series unconsciously masters the moment. Mastery over death is what he strives for in his study of Hitler. He also wants to avoid death and loneliness and here is his exit visa for his vacation from such troubling thoughts. His transportation? A powerful locomotive, clearly, the American Express. Forms of credit, as, we shall see, are crucial to Jack's function as a consumer, and it is through consumption that individuals in DeLillo's novel repress the fear of death. That each trio names specific brand names pushes us towards Jean Baudrillard's sense of consumption as a socially signifying practice that circulates coded values.

In *White Noise*, one might say, DeLillo fuses ideas from the earlier Baudrillard of *Consumer Society* with those of the post-Marxian Baudrillard of "The Orders of Simulacra." The earlier Baudrillard takes a number of categories of traditional Marxist analysis and shifts the focus from production to consumption, yet retains a Marxist perspective by seeing consumption as "*a function of production*" ("Consumer" 46). Thus, in analyzing consumption as a signifying practice, Baudrillard speaks of consumers as a form of alienated social labor and asks who owns the means of consumption ("Consumer" 53–54). DeLillo's novel proves an extended gloss on Jean Baudrillard's notion of consumer society. Baudrillard counterintuitively proposes that the broad range of consumer choices in today's shopping malls, which appear as the embodiment of individual freedom, is actually a form of social control used to produce the consumers that capital crucially needs.

Jack falls into his role as a consumer when his auratic self as Hitler scholar is threatened by a chance encounter with a colleague off campus. Without his academic robe and dark glasses, the colleague notes that Jack is just "a big, harmless, aging, indistinct sort of guy" (83). This deflation of self puts Jack "in the mood to shop" and the ensuing sense of power and control is immense:

> We moved from store to store, rejecting not only items in certain departments, not only entire departments but whole stores, mammoth corporations that did not strike our fancy for one reason or another.... I began to grow in value and self-regard. I filled myself out, found new aspects of myself, located a person I'd forgotten existed. Brightness settled around me. (83–84)

Jack replaces his inauthentic Hitler aura with the equally inauthentic aura of shopping, which he experiences, however, as authentic.[13] His sense of power in the mall, a physical space as self-contained and self-referential as the psychic space of television, is illusory for if Jack "rejects" one corporation, another is surely served by his purchases.[14] Jack says, "The more money I spent, the less important it seemed. I was bigger that these sums. These sums poured off my skin like so much rain. These sums in fact came back to me in the form of existential credit" (84). For Baudrillard, credit is a key element in the social control generated through consumption:

> Presented under the guise of gratification, of a facilitated access to affluence, of a hedonistic mentality, and of 'freedom from the old taboos of thrift, etc.,' credit is in fact the systematic socioeconomic indoctrination of forced economizing and an economic calculus for generations of consumers who, in a life of subsistence, would have otherwise escaped the manipulation of demands and would have been unexploitable as a force of consumption. Credit is a disciplinary process which extorts savings and regulates demand—just as wage labor was a rational process in the extortion of labor power and in the increase of productivity. ("Consumer" 49)

Credit allows Jack the exercise of auratic power, allowing a middle-class college professor to become briefly a conspicuous consumer like the wealthy parents whose children he teaches. Not surprisingly, Jack, the scholar of Germany's great dictator, imagines himself a little dictator in a benevolent mood: "I was the benefactor, the one who dispenses gifts, bonuses, bribes, *baksheesh*" (84). At the conclusion of the family shopping spree, the Gladneys, exemplary alienated consumers, are not satisfied; they "drove home in silence ... wishing only to be alone." The final sentence of the chapter connects the mall as aestheticized site of consumption to television's imagistic space. In what appears to be an attempt to come down from the intensity of the shopping spree, one of Jack's daughters sits "in front of the TV set. She moved her lips, attempting to match the words as they were spoken" (84).[15]

If the Baudrillard of *Consumer Society* is pertinent to *White Noise*, the later Baudrillard of *Simulations* is even more so. Starting from Walter Benjamin and Marshall McLuhan, Baudrillard shifts the focus of technique away from a Marxist sense of productive force and toward an interpretation of technique "as medium" ("Orders" 99). Taken to its extreme, "the medium is the message" becomes Baudrillard's hyperreal, where the "contradiction between the real and the imaginary is effaced" ("Orders" 142). Jack Gladney lives in a world of simulations, modelings of the world tied to no origin or source. The clearest example is SIMUVAC: this state-supported organization, created to rehearse evacuations through controlled models of man-made and natural disasters, uses the chemical spill in Blacksmith as an opportunity "to rehearse the simulation" (139). But SIMUVAC is just the edge of the wedge. At the Catholic hospital in the Germantown section of Iron City, where Jack takes Mink after both are shot, Jack discovers what amounts to SIMUVFAITH. The nuns who serve as nurses, Jack learns, pretend to believe in God for the non-believers who need to believe that someone still believes. One nun tells Jack, "Our lives are no less serious than if we professed real faith, real belief" (319), because the simulated belief serves the same structural function vis-à-vis the non-believer as actual belief. Jack himself is SIMUPROF. At "the center, the unquestioned source" (11) of Hitler Studies, Jack, who invents an initial to make his name signify in the system of scholarly names, successfully lives the era, sure of the imaginary and the real; he is the world-famous scholar of Hitler who can neither read nor speak German.

II

While Jack is the ostensible teacher of fascism's appeal, he has much to learn about the subject from his Jewish "friend" Murray, who sees more clearly the possibilities of fascism for profit and pleasure. To focus on Murray's role might well seem unproductive. He is comic, a man who sniffs groceries, another of DeLillo's almost Dickensian eccentrics, as Murray's colleagues in the Department of American Environments most certainly are. Yet under the umbrella of DeLillo's meditation on the continuing mass appeal of fascist tyranny, Murray helps link the novel's various elements of matter—the media, shopping, the construction of aura—and points to the ways each of the preceding serve in the contemporary to allow individuals to imagine and to repress their sexuality and their death. These mirrored spaces of consumption, the television and the supermarket, are brought into sharper relief by Murray's explicit commentary; his interpretations are Baudrillardian, yet the very elements of simulation that make Baudrillard sad make Murray glad. Although Murray shows himself to be a shrewd semiotician of contemporary America, he is more than a character who comments on the action. Murray is an agent of action, the character whose goals and desires, more than any other's, become the occasion for plot. Much of *White Noise*, as Frank Lentricchia notes ("Tales" 97), is plotless, a fact not surprising given that the narrator, Jack, believes that "all plots tend to move deathward" (26).[16] We have to turn to Murray Siskind to discover the desires that motivate plot, a sub(rosa)plot, if you will.

Siskind is the true villain of *White Noise*. Seductive and smart, he nevertheless encourages and fosters the worst in Jack. Murray is the man who would be Jack. Murray's very openness about his goals makes it hard to see the antagonistic role he occupies, yet Murray covets Jack's power within the college. In Chapter 3, Murray flatters Jack at length about his achievement:

> "You've established a wonderful thing here with Hitler. You created it, you nurtured it, you made it your own. Nobody on the faculty of any college or university in this part of the country can so much as utter the word Hitler without a nod in your direction, literally or metaphorically. This is the center, the unquestioned source. He is now your Hitler, Gladney's Hitler.... I marvel at the effort. It was masterful, shrewd and stunningly preemptive. It's what I want to do with Elvis." (11–12)

But Murray is already more Jack than Jack because Murray understands and sees the possibilities of professional aura in ways Jack does not. It is entirely appropriate that this scene is immediately followed by Jack's taking Murray to a local tourist attraction, "the most photographed barn in America" (12).[17] Murray's interpretation of the site reflects back on his reading of Jack's creation of the college as origin and source of Hitler Studies. Surrounded by people taking pictures of the barn, which is not billed as the oldest or the most picturesque but simply as the most photographed, Murray claims:

"No one sees the barn…. Once you've seen the signs about the barn, it becomes impossible to see the barn…. We're not here to capture an image, we're here to maintain one. Every photograph reinforces the aura. Can you feel it, Jack? An accumulation of nameless energies…. Being here is a kind of spiritual surrender. We see only what the others see. The thousands who were here in the past, those who will come in the future…. What did the barn look like before it was photographed? … What was the barn like, how was it different from other barns, how was it similar to other barns? We can't answer these questions because we've read the signs, seen the people snapping the pictures. We can't get outside the aura. We're part of the aura. We're here, we're now." (12–13)

John Frow quite rightly points out that Benjamin's hope that mechanical reproduction would destroy the pseudo-religious aura of cultural artifacts has been subverted and that, instead, "the commodification of culture has worked to preserve the myth of origins and of authenticity" (Frow 181). Here, as elsewhere in the novel, the myth of authenticity that is aura comes into being through mediation, the intertextual web of prior representations. Jack may object to his son corresponding with a mass murderer, but Jack's textual pleasure turns on his reading and writing about the world's most photographed mass murder, Adolph Hitler. The difference underscores the role of mediation: Heinrich's mass murderer failed to enter the media loop, while Jack's mass murderer is "always on" television (63) in the endless documentaries that our culture produces about the twentieth century.[18]

The most dangerous element of the most photographed barn, finally, is the tourists' collective spiritual surrender precisely because it is a desired surrender. Here is the continuing mass appeal of fascism writ large. It is what Murray understands and Jack does not—the barn is to those who photograph it as Hitler Studies is to Jack; in both instances, an object of contemplation serves to legitimize the myth of origin, which creates a sense of purpose, which in turn serves to mitigate the sting of death. Murray, in a much more critically distanced way, sees the possibilities for institutional power and control by plugging into the aura of the world's most photographed rockabilly singer.

In addition to coveting Jack's position at the college, Murray also quite openly wants to seduce Babette. Even before he meets her, Murray's discussion about women prepares us for his relation to the Gladneys. He tells Jack: "I like simple men and complicated women" (11). Although Jack portrays Babette as a simple woman, the novel proves otherwise. Jack believes, for example, that "Babette and I tell each other everything" (29), yet he will learn later that her fear of death has driven her to answer an ad to become an underground human subject for an experimental drug, Dylar, that blocks the fear of death. Moreover, she gains access to the drug by having sex with the project coordinator, Willie Mink. The Gladneys, then, provide Murray ample range to take his pleasure: Jack is simple, failing entirely to understand the source of his own power, while Babette is more complex than Jack acknowledges. In his use of pornography—Babette reads pornographic texts to add spice to their lovemaking—Jack is straightforwardly heterosexual. Murray, however, despite his professed love of women, exhibits a more polymorphous sexuality, choosing as part of his reading matter *American Transvestite* (33). From the outset Murray announces his reason for being in Blacksmith: "I'm here to avoid situations. Cities are full of situations, sexually cunning people" (11). Yet clearly, Murray is one of those cunning people, a world-weary sexual sophisticate, who outside the evacuation camp bargains with a prostitute to allow him to perform the Heimlich maneuver on her (152)! Murray's seduction is a double one, in which he seduces Jack with his interpretive skills, all the while waiting for the chance to seduce Babette.

Murray's seduction of Jack yields tangible results because Jack soon proves willing to sanction Murray's bid to establish Elvis Studies by participating in an antiphonal lecture in which the two men speak of the similarities between Elvis Presley and Adolph Hitler.[19] Afterwards Jack recognizes what is at stake: "It was not a small matter. We all had an aura to maintain, and in sharing mine with a friend I was risking the very things that made me untouchable" (74). Even as Jack shows an awareness of his action, his language suggests the way Murray has infiltrated his thoughts, for Jack's choice of "aura" to describe his power is Murray's word and clearly depends on Murray's previous articulation of the concept while viewing the barn.

Murray's seductions are dangerous because he plots to supplant his rivals. At the college, this means Dimitrios Cotsakis, a colleague in the Department of American Environments, who has a prior claim on teaching Elvis Presley. On the sexual front, this means Jack. But after Cotsakis dies accidentally over the semester break, that leaves only Jack as an obstacle to Murray's desires. Significantly, Murray relates the news of Cotsakis' death to Jack at the supermarket, a key site of consumption. At this moment, Jack has a quasi-mystical experience:

> I was suddenly aware of the dense environmental texture. The automatic doors opened and closed, breathing abruptly. Colors and odors seemed sharper. The sound of gliding feet emerged

from a dozen other noises, from the sublittoral drone of
maintenance systems, from the rustle of newsprint as shoppers
scanned their horoscopes in the tabloids up front, from the
whispers of elderly women with talcumed faces, from the steady
rattle of cars going over a loose manhole cover just outside the
entrance. (168–69)

He responds to another's death because Jack is acutely aware that, as a result
of his exposure to the airborne toxic event, death lives inside his own body,
but the heightened perception Jack experiences again needs to be read in
light of Murray's earlier interpretation of the supermarket. In Chapter 9,
Murray runs into the Gladneys while grocery shopping and directs the
majority of remarks directly to Babette:

This place recharges us spiritually, it prepares us, it's a gateway or
pathway.... Everything is concealed in symbolism, hidden by veils
of mystery and layers of cultural material. But it is psychic data,
absolutely. The large doors slide open, they close unbidden.
Energy waves, incident radiation. All the letters and numbers are
here, all the colors of the spectrum, all the voices and sounds, all
the code words and ceremonial phrases.... Waves and radiation.
Look how well-lighted everything is. The place is sealed off, self-
contained. It is timeless.... Dying is an art in Tibet. A priest walks
in, sits down, tells the weeping relatives to get out and has the
room sealed.... Here we don't die, we shop. But the difference is
less marked than you think. (37–38)

Although Murray is trying here to seduce Babette with his interpretive
prowess, it is Jack's consciousness that becomes scripted by Murray. The
pattern is clear in the novel: Murray's interpretations become Jack's
convictions; Murray's speculations, Jack's experiences.

Given this pattern, it makes sense that the crucial moment of Murray's
seduction of Jack should occur through an interpretation.[20] Confronted with
the distinct possibility that his life will be shortened through his contact with
the chemical cloud, Jack becomes increasingly depressed. Jack's three means
of repressing death are television, shopping, and Hitler scholarship. During
the academic year, Murray through his conversations has problematized
Jack's relation to the first two, activities Jack shares with most Americans.
During a long peripatetic conversation, Murray points out Jack's logically
contradictory uses of Hitler to conceal himself in a transcendent horror in
order to be outstanding in his professional life. Jack uses Hitler as a shield

against death, and the correctness of Murray's interpretation is perhaps clearest when Jack, before going to face what he believes to be the Angel of Death (actually his father-in-law come on an unannounced early morning visit) grabs his copy of *Mein Kampf* (244). By exposing Jack's last best defense mechanism, Murray takes this simple man and shatters the very ground of his being. Having emptied Jack of his means of repressing death, Murray posits the best of all possible ways to respond to the fear of death: "think what it's like to be a killer. Think how exciting it is, in theory, to kill a person in direct confrontation. If he dies, you cannot. To kill him is to gain life-credit. The more people you kill, the more credit you store up. It explains any number of massacres, wars, executions" (290). Murray's theory of killing for life-credit substitutes for Jack's now untenable sense of shopping for existential credit. Although Murray emphasizes throughout their long conversation that his observations about the efficacy of killing are speculative, the point of his argument is to convince Jack of its correctness. To Jack's objection that if the world is composed exclusively of killers and diers, then he is clearly a dier, Murray asks: "Isn't there a deep field, a sort of crude oil deposit that one might tap if and when the occasion warrants? A great dark lake of male rage?" (292) Jack notes that Murray sounds like Babette and indeed she refuses to identify the man she had sex with on precisely those grounds (225). If Murray sounds so much like Babette, the possibility arises that Murray has succeeded in his intentions with Babette, pillow talk breeding the similar expression. Whether Murray has already bedded Babette, an intent of Murray's seduction would seem to be the following: if he can get Jack to commit a murder, Jack, if caught, would eliminate himself from both the college and from Babette's bed. Murray is a killer, even if his pleasure is psychological rather than visceral.

Beneath the happy exterior of Murray Siskind, the scope of his sinister intentions play far beyond the specific seductions of Jack and Babette. In an analysis parallel to Baudrillard's sense of alienated consumption, Murray tells his students that "they're already too old to figure importantly in the making of society" because they are "spinning out from the core, becoming less targetable by advertisers and mass-producers of culture." The result is "to feel estranged from the products you consume" (49–50). Murray's lesson here, as elsewhere, is intended to seduce his students, just as he seduces Jack, into the postmodern flow. To follow Murray's celebration of the postmodern, however, grants him his desired mastery over others. Significantly, Murray only buys the generic items at the grocery, food packaged in black and white wrappers and, crucially, not advertised and hence not part of the signifying systems of culture Murray seeks to decode. They are outside the media and the very postmodern culture he ingenuously praises.[21] Everyone shall enter the postmodern flow—everyone except Murray, who will remain distanced precisely in order to plot, interpret, and control.

But truly to give oneself over to the imagistic flow of consumer information in the age of electronic reproduction is to become Fredric Jameson's schizophrenic, Willie Mink, who in exchange for sex gave Babette the experimental drug Dylar designed to eliminate the fear of death.[22] Jameson reminds us that if "personal identity is itself the effect of a certain temporal unification of past with one's present" and if "such active temporal unification is itself a function of language," then "with the breakdown of the signifying chain ... the schizophrenic is reduced to an experience of pure material signifiers, or, in other words a series of pure unrelated presents in time" (27). Mink, whose subjectivity has been voided almost entirely and replaced by the signifying chain of television's language, watches television with the sound off when Jack comes to kill him. Mink's language, except for momentary lapses into thought, is a series of non sequiturs, word-for-word transcriptions of television moments:

> To begin your project sweater ... first ask yourself what type sleeve will meet your needs.

> The pet under stress may need a prescription diet. (307)

> Now I am picking up my metallic gold tube.... Using my palette knife and my odorless turp, I will thicken the paint of my palette. (309)

Even Mink's brief moments of quasi-lucidity are dialogized through the discourse of tv sports, weather, and late-night B movies. Before one of "Mink's" utterances, Jack becomes aware of "a noise, faint, monotonous, white" (306). Throughout the novel, the voice of the television intrudes at odd moments, almost as if the television were a character. During a conversation between Jack and his daughter Bee on Christmas Day, for example, the television is on and at times seems to enter the conversation, though without purpose: "The TV said: 'Now we will put the little feelers on the butterfly'" (96). Such moments represent instances when the television, which is always on in the Gladney home, briefly catches Jack's attention. My point here is that when Jack enters Mink's motel room and hears the faint white noise—the hum of the tv—we are not surprised to hear the voice of television. The shock is that the "it said" of television become the "he said" of Mink; Mink is the voice of television. Metaphorically, then, Jack's sexual nemesis has always already been near to him and Jack is no closer now to the source of his pain and anger than he was before he confronted Mink.

Jack, who comes to the motel room in hopes of confronting origin—
the origin of his male rage and the originator of a drug that will eliminate his
fear of death—finds instead only an Oz-like shell of power and authority.
Mink, a pill-popping wreck, offers no satisfying target of vengeance because
there is no core or center to his personality. One of the side-effects of Dylar
is a heightened sensitivity to suggestion, a fact that creates part of the scene's
humor. Jack uses this symptom to terrorize Mink, saying such things as
"falling plane," "plunging aircraft," and "hail of bullets," eliciting an
exaggerated, mime–like response from Mink (309-11). Although Jack's
suggestions and Mink's responses are humorous, their effect finally is
disturbing, for here in displaced form is the tv man's dream of unmediated
mediation revealed as postmodernity's schizophrenic nightmare. Mink
experiences the mediation of Jack's language as pure material signifier—
immediate and real. However exaggerated the exchange may be, we see in
Mink's responses how media produces the consumer. Mink quite literally is
the little man behind the screen of the great and powerful Oz. And the screen
is tv.

DeLillo's name for the drug, Dylar, and the title of the third section of
the novel, Dylarama, serve, it seems, as an indirect way of reminding us that
Americans already have a more successful version of the drug Mink failed to
produce. In *White Noise*, television itself, that means of forgetting death
through aesthetization, is Dylar, an imagistic space of consumption that one
accesses by playing dial-a-rama, turning the dial/dyl to the channel of one's
choice. Such "choice" is illusory, however, since whatever channel one
selects, the subliminal voice of advertising stands ready to produce the viewer
as consumer in "substatic regions too deep to probe" (155).

Mink's role as a subject consumed by television recalls, oddly enough,
Murray's relation to the electronic image. Other than the time he is on
campus, Murray, like Mink, spends much of his time in a rented room sitting
before the television. Nothing, however, could appear more different than
the two characters' relation to the television image. Mink's viewing is more
than passive. There is no distance for him; he is almost another piece of
electronic hardware through which television's messages flow. Murray on the
other hand attempts complete critical distance in his television viewing to
produce his totalizing interpretations of postmodernity. Despite Mink's
deterioration near the end of *White Noise*, he tells Jack, in the discourse of a
Hollywood mad-scientist's confessional moment, "I wasn't always as you see
me now" (307). Like Murray, Mink was a metaphorical killer, the designer of
a plot. Mink sought control and totalizing power over death through his

work on Dylar, just as Murray seeks power and control in his seductions of his students and friends. Even after the Dylar project had been discredited, Mink on his downward slide still managed another plot, the seduction of Babette, the same woman Murray wants to seduce. Mink's failure to produce a drug that would block the fear of death casts an odd light on Murray's plot to eliminate Jack, which in the end is also a failure. Instead of a relation of polar opposites (Murray actively distanced, Mink passively absorbed), it might be more useful to see Murray as a point in a continuum moving toward Mink.

Both Murray and Mink dislodge the signifier's context. When Jack tells Murray, "I want to live," Murray replies, "From the Robert Wise film of the same name, with Susan Hayward as Barbara Graham, a convicted murderess" (283). How different is Murray's shifting of context from Mink's claim: "Not that I have anything personal against death from our vantage point high atop Metropolitan County Stadium" (308)? The difference between Murray's motivated shifting of context and Mink's unmotivated leaps seems to figure the difference between structuralism and the poststructuralism. Murray the structuralist semiotician seeks totality in his reflections on the forms of postmodern media; Mink the true postmodern can only register with a zero degree of interpretation the play of American culture's signifiers.

DeLillo's homologous reflections on the way the mediations of television map the realm of desire in the space of the supermarket and the shopping mall now seem prescient in ways that one could not have seen in 1985, the year *White Noise* was published. The Home Shopping Network combines exactly the intertwined spheres of desire that DeLillo's novel so suggestively connects. Today, personal aura is only a phone call away. As DeLillo contemplates the effects of mediations that pose as the immediate, *White Noise* posits the fear of death as the ground of fascism; such fear creates desire for God/the father/the subject, the logos/text, and the telos/intention. Hitler, Elvis, the most photographed barn, television, shopping all manifest a collective desire for "Führer Knows Best," a cultic aura to absorb the fear of dying. To acknowledge the continuing appeal of fascism, we need look neither to David Duke's strong showing in the 1991 Louisiana governor's race nor to Republican campaign strategists, who interpret the Los Angeles riots, precipitated by the court-sanctioned police mugging of Rodney King, as a sign that family values are weak.[23] As *White Noise* argues, the urge toward fascism is diffused throughout American mass media and its representations.

NOTES

1. Paul Cantor also wishes to show how DeLillo in *White Noise* "is concerned with showing parallels between German fascism and contemporary American culture" (51). He has a brief but interesting discussion of DeLillo's repeated use of Hitler in his fiction prior to *White Noise* (40–41).

2. For Neumann, "monopolistic system profits cannot be made and retained without totalitarian power, and that is the distinctive feature of National Socialism" (354). Neumann's belief that democracy would destabilize monopoly capitalism, however, does not anticipate the totalizing power of multinational capital.

3. The DeLillo of *White Noise* is a satirist practicing his art in an age in which the possibility of satire is problematic. One cannot turn to older definitions of the term and speak of implicit moral standards, if one acknowledges the death of the author (not to mention the subject) and the end of master narratives. Jameson's own assessment of postmodernism does not allow parody, much less satire, since he has answered his own key question—has the "semiautonomy of the cultural sphere ... been destroyed by the logic of late capitalism"?—affirmatively:

> the dissolution of an autonomous sphere of culture is ... to be imagined in terms of an explosion: a prodigious expansion of culture throughout the social realm, to the point at which everything in our social life—from economic value and state power to practices and to the very structure of the psyche itself— can be said to be 'cultural' in some original and yet untheorized sense. (48)

Jameson's totalizing sense of the postmodern, in which every political gesture is reabsorbed by the system and the possibility of critical distance is erased, has been DeLillo's subject matter not simply in *White Noise* but for much of his fictional career. What Jameson sees as "the expansion of multinational capitalism ... penetrating and colonizing those very precapitalist enclaves (Nature and the Unconscious)" is at the heart of DeLillo's assessment of an American proto-fascism embedded in mass cultural representations. Yet the problem remains for DeLillo as a satirist: if he insists that the world is wholly mediated, what distinguishes the novel as a medium and the electronic media he criticizes? If one grants that there is no absolute difference between a novel and a television show, one can nevertheless see *White Noise* participating in the paradoxical nature of postmodern aesthetics that Linda

Hutcheon describes: "the masterful denials of mastery, the cohesive attacks on cohesion, the essentializing challenges to essences" (*Poetics* 20). So that, despite the totalizing picture of postmodernity that DeLillo portrays in *White Noise*, the parodic impulse of the novel prevents it from being completely co-opted by the cultural logic it delineates, since "postmodernist parody is a value-problematizing, denaturalizing form of acknowledging the history (and through irony, the politics) of representations" (Hutcheon, *Politics* 94). Interestingly, DeLillo's fiction since *White Noise* has muted the overt satire and turned toward what Hutcheon calls historiographic metafiction. *Libra*, *Mao II*, and most recently "Pafko at the Wall" have all blurred the lines of history and fiction and self-reflexively pointed to the discursively constructed nature of history.

4. Eugene Goodheart suggestively links these spheres of consumption when he notes that "the two main sites of experience and dialogue are the supermarket and the TV screen" and that the supermarket is "a trope for all sites of consumption" in the novel (121–22). Thomas J. Ferraro asserts that Don DeLillo's fiction "lies at the cutting edge of mass-culture theory because he struggles to imagine how television as a *medium* functions within the home as the foremost site for what sociologists call our 'primary' social relations" (24). Ferraro's sense of the ways in which television "reconstructs the nature of reality itself" (26) aligns his reading with the postmodernism of both Jean Baudrillard and Fredric Jameson.

5. Michael Valdez Moses, who reads *White Noise* against Heidegger, argues that "the technological media ... alienate the individual from personal death" by "imposing an increasingly automatic and involuntary identification with the camera eye," which creates the illusion "that the witnessing consciousness of the individual television viewer, like the media themselves, is a permanent fixture possessing a transcendental perspective" (73).

6. Cantor, meditating on this course description, argues that DeLillo wants to suggest "that the spiritual void that made Hitler's rise possible is still with us, perhaps exacerbated by the forces at work in postmodern culture" (49).

7. Frow's assertion is part of a larger claim about *White Noise* and DeLillo's relation to the postmodern. Frow sees DeLillo representing the postmodern sublime, a sublime in which our terror derives from "the sense of the inadequacy of representation ... not because of the transcendental or uncanny nature of the object but because of the multiplicity of prior representations" (176). Frow convincingly argues that DeLillo is sensitive to the intensely mediated nature of contemporary experience.

8. Fredric Jameson, in opposing the postmodern sublime to that of Edmund Burke and Kant, suggests that "the *other* of our society is ... no

longer Nature at all, as it was in precapitalist societies, but something else which we must now identify" (34). And though Jameson resists simply substituting technology for Nature as the horizon of aesthetic representation, he does see such reproductive technologies as the computer and television as "a distorted figuration ... of the whole world system of present-day multinational capitalism" (37).

9. Michael W. Messmer, using Baudrillard's and Eco's articulation of the hyperreal, argues that the blurring of boundaries between the real and the simulation creates "a distancing which is conducive to the fascination which DeLillo's characters experience as they witness disasters through the medium of television" (404).

More pointedly, Goodheart notes: "We repeatedly witness the assassination of Kennedy, the mushroom cloud over Hiroshima, the disintegration of the *Challenger* space shuttle in the sky. Repetition wears away the pain. It also perfects the image of our experience of it. By isolating the event and repeating it, its content, its horror evaporates.... The event becomes aesthetic and the effect upon us anaesthetic" (122).

10. Jack later repeats exactly Heinrich's line when he picks up his daughter at the airport. Moments before, terrorized passengers deplane from a flight that had experienced a four-mile drop. Jack's daughter wonders where the television crews are, but Jack tells her, "There is no media in Iron City." Her response, though inflected as a question, is actually a statement, one that repeats the lesson of Heinrich's mass murderer and the TV man's outrage: "They went through all that for nothing?" (92). Once again *White Noise* reminds us that the medium of television has been so internalized in contemporary consciousness that experience can no longer be perceived as immediate without the electronic representation.

11. Huyssen rightly points out that Benjamin tends to fetishize "technique, science, and production in art, hoping that modern technologies could be used to build a socialist mass culture." Nevertheless, for Huyssen, Benjamin's essays of the 1930s represent the last articulation of a way to think about the relation "between avant-garde art and the utopian hope for an emancipatory mass culture" that does not simply reduce to high culture vs. low culture (14).

12. Of such moments Lentricchia wittily notes: "Jacques Lacan said the unconscious is structured like a language. He forgot to add the words 'of Madison Avenue'" ("Tales" 102).

13. Ferraro says of this scene that "Jack's urge to shop" is largely motivated by "a sense of disappointment in the supposed 'community' of the university" (22). Such a reading seems to psychologize Jack and shift the focus away from the productive forces that created Jack as a consumer.

14. DeLillo's Mid-Village Mall seems to come straight out of Baudrillard, who sees in such spaces "the *sublimation* of real life, of objective social life, where not only work and money are abolished, but all the seasons as well—the distant vestige of a cycle finally domesticated! Work, leisure, nature, culture, all previously dispersed, separate, and more or less irreducible activities that produced anxiety and complexity in our real life, and in our 'anarchic and archaic' cities, have finally become mixed, massaged, climate controlled, and domesticated into the simple activity of perpetual shopping" ("Consumer" 34).

Because Jack shops in the corporate space of the mail, it does not matter what he buys, only that he buys: "Consumers are mutually implicated, despite themselves, in a general system of exchange and in the production of coded values" ("Consumer" 46).

15. This catalogue of consumption does not find its completion until Jack, raking through the grotesque and equally detailed catalogue of garbage compressed by the family trash compactor, confronts "the dark underside of consumer consciousness" (259). This confrontation occurs because the immediacy of the nebulous mass in Jack's body, the result of his exposure to the toxic cloud, overwhelms the aestheticizing power of shopping and television to repress death; he seeks in the trash the stronger anti-depressant Dylar. Jack the ironist is ironized for he sees in the garbage only an "ironic modernist sculpture," noting with formalist pleasure "a complex relationship between the sizes of the loops, the degree of the knots (single or double) and the intervals between knots with loops and freestanding knots" (259). By this aestheticizing, Jack misses the more relevant loop of production, consumption, and pollution that have created the very chemical spill that may cause the death he seeks to block from his thoughts. As is so often the case, Jack's sense of life's mystery is actually a mystification.

16. Jack's assertion seems to serve as the basis for DeLillo's subsequent novel about the assassination of President Kennedy. In *Libra* a CIA plot to stage a simulated assassination—with a shot intended to miss—is transformed more by happenstance than design into what actually occurred in Dallas. Like the simulations of *White Noise*, the conspiracy to kill JFK functions in Baudrillard's hyperreal:

> If we are on the outside, we assume a conspiracy is the perfect working of a scheme. Silent nameless men with unadorned hearts. A conspiracy is everything ordinary life is not. It's the inside game, cold, sure, undistracted, forever closed off to us. We are the flawed ones, the innocents, trying to make some rough sense of the daily jostle. Conspirators have a logic and a daring beyond our reach. (*Libra* 440)

If we substitute mass murderers, including Hitler, or the nuns of Germantown from *White Noise*, we see the link between the auratic and the fascist urge; it is the collective belief that, even if we personally have no access to a transcendent realm, there are still those whose relation to the logos is special. DeLillo consistently portrays as foundationless the collective perception of seamless authority and intention.

17. In his reading of the barn, Lentricchia argues that "the real subject is the electronic medium of the image as the active context of contemporary existence in America" ("Tales" 88); the scene opens up the question "What strange new form of human collectivity is born in the postmodern moment of the aura, and at what price?" ("Tales" 92). For a parallel but differently articulated reading of the barn, see Lentricchia's discussion in "*Libra* as Postmodern Critique" (195–97).

18. Without I hope becoming like the members of DeLillo's Department of American Environments, each of whom "trafficks in his own childhood" (69), I recall from my youth a plastic model a friend of mine built, a caricature statue of Hitler, large-headed, jackboot on a grave, with the inscription "the world's worst" at the base. Had Germany won World War II, Hitler, our century's Transcendent Horror, never would have been imaged forth as such, and perhaps Hitler might now be lionized as a great leader, the world's most photographed benevolent dictator; in both the case of the barn and Hitler, the aura, which everyone assumes to be authentic, is revealed as media(ted) construct.

19. See Cantor (51–53) for a detailed comparison of the way Jack's Hitler and Murray's Elvis are paralleled.

20. My reading of Murray in part grows out of Tom LeClair's comments. LeClair registers the significance of Jack and Murray's final conversation, noting that "Siskind's advice promotes a profoundly immoral act" (221).

21. Since *White Noise* was published, the moment of the generic food product has passed, but not before it was thoroughly reified and commodified, the familiar white background with black letters used to sell everything from shirts to coffee mugs and even English basic courses (Robert Scholes, et al., *Textbook*).

22. For Lentricchia, "Willy [sic] Mink is a compacted image of the consumerism in the society of the electronic media, a figure of madness ..." ("Tales" 113).

23. The aftermath of the Los Angeles riots generated an eerie moment of the Baudrillardian hyperreal, the effacement of the real and the imaginary. The lead story on network news on April 20, 1992 was Vice-President Dan

Quayle's attack on the sit-com "Murphy Brown." Quayle's claim that Murphy Brown's decision to have a child outside of marriage "caused" the riots is an example of the specious television logic one might expect from DeLillo's Babette or Jack. (How, after all, does the representation of an affluent white woman's decision to become a single mother impact African-American culture?) More significant than the specific illogic of Quayle's argument was the resulting aestheticizing of the political. For an incredible moment, the leading issue in the presidential campaign became not the problems of the inner city, health care, education, the post-Cold War defense budget, or the recession but rather where one stood on the Murphy Brown question.

WORKS CITED

Baudrillard, Jean. "Consumer Society." *Jean Baudrillard: Selected Writings*. Ed. Mark Poster. Stanford: Stanford University Press, 1988. 29–56.

———. *Simulations*. Trans. Paul Foss, et al. New York: Semiotext(e), 1983.

Benjamin, Walter. "The Work of Art in the Age of Mechanical Reproduction." *Illuminations*. New York: Harcourt, 1955. 219–53

Cantor, Paul A. "'Adolph, We Hardly Knew You.'" *New Essays on* White Noise. Ed. Frank Lentricchia. New York: Cambridge University Press, 1990. 39–62

DeLillo, Don. *Libra*. New York: Viking, 1988.

———. *White Noise*. Harmondsworth, England: 1986. [1985]

Ferraro, Thomas J. "Whole Families Shopping at Night!" *New Essays on* White Noise. Ed. Frank Lentricchia. New York: Cambridge University Press, 1990. 15–38.

Frow, John. "Notes on *White Noise*." *Introducing Don DeLillo*. Ed. Frank Lentricchia. Durham, N.C.: Duke University Press, 1991. 175–91.

Goodheart, Eugene. "Don DeLillo and the Cinematic Real." *Introducing Don DeLillo*. Ed. Frank Lentricchia. Durham, N.C.: Duke University Press, 1991. 117–30.

Jameson, Fredric. *Postmodernism, or, The Cultural Logic of Late Capitalism*. Durham, N.C.: Duke University Press, 1991.

Hutcheon, Linda. *The Poetics of Postmodernism*. London: Routledge, 1988.

———. *The Politics of Postmodernism*. London: Routledge, 1989.

Huyssen, Andreas. *After the Great Divide: Modernism, Mass Culture, Postmodernism*. Bloomington: Indiana University Press, 1986.

LeClair, Tom. *In the Loop: Don DeLillo and the Systems Novel*. Urbana: University of Illinois Press, 1987.

Lentricchia, Frank, *"Libra* as Postmodern Critique." *Introducing Don DeLillo*. Durham, N.C.: Duke University Press, 1991. 193–215.

———. "Tales of the Electronic Tribe." *New Essays on* White Noise. Ed. Frank Lentricchia. New York: Cambridge University Press, 1990. 87–113.

Messmer, Michael W. "'Thinking It Through Completely': The Interpretation of Nuclear Culture." *The Centennial Review* 32 (1988): 397–413.

Moses, Michael Valdez. "Lust Removed from Nature." *New Essays on* White Noise. Ed. Frank Lentricchia. New York: Cambridge University Press, 1990. 63–85.

Neumann, Franz. Behemoth: *The Structure and Practice of National Socialism*. [1944] New York: Octagon, 1963.

ARTHUR M. SALTZMAN

The Figure in the Static: White Noise

In the course of naming contemporary novels he admires, Don DeLillo credits their importance to their common capacity to "absorb and incorporate the culture without catering to it" (Interview with Begley 290). In DeLillo's own fiction, the challenge has always been to find a way of simultaneously engaging and resisting "the ambient noise," and that challenge has been answered by means of novels whose cunning does not compose its materials into some decorous conclusion. The DeLillo protagonist must locate some reliable avenue of free agency, some outpost of personal dimension, in face of ambiguous threats disclosed (although never completely elucidated) by the same sensitivities that recognize the need for aesthetic refuge.

For DeLillo himself, the paradox lies at the heart of the writer's profession: he must break the grip of idiom while continuing to exploit its pressures artistically. "Word on a page, that's all it takes to help him separate himself from the forces around him," he declares (Interview with Begley 277). Nevertheless, even as the writer hammers privileged habitats and crafts vantages above the vague extratextual roll—"How liberating to work in the margins outside the central perception," claims archaeologist Owen Brademas in *The Names* (77)—his task is to assimilate, not to exclude.[1] Thus

From *Modern Fiction Studies* 40, no. 4 (Winter 1994): 807-825. © 1995 by the Purdue Research Foundation.

DeLillo goes on in this same interview to compromise the so-called ideal segregation of the novelist:

> You want to exercise your will, bend the language your way, bend the world your way. You want to control the flow of impulses, images, words, faces, ideas. But there's a higher place, a secret aspiration. You want to let go. You want to lose yourself in language, become a carrier or messenger. The best moments involve a loss of control. It's a kind of rapture, and it can happen with words and phrases fairly often—completely surprising combinations that make a higher kind of sense, that come to you out of nowhere. (interview with Begley 282)

Notice the trammeled quality of DeLillo's "rapture": he is describing a release saturated with words, which retain the effects of everyday use. Whatever transcendence he pretends to is derivative, obligated to the medium whose undertow he means to supervene.

As DeLillo redefines the terms of access and surrender to language, arbitrating his contradictory drives; he arrives at metaphor, which encapsulates the anxious status between planned exactitude and exhilaration, between decision and accident, out of which he prefers to constitute his projects. In *White Noise*, however, the task is further complicated by the way in which figures are disarmed by the flood of data, cultural debris, and otherwise indigestible stimuli that contribute to the condition that titles the novel. Whereas metaphor depends upon uniqueness and verbal defamiliarization to earn attention, white noise thwarts distinction, for the proliferation of language, typically through such vulgarized forms as advertisements, tabloid headlines, and bureaucratic euphemisms, submerges difference into the usual cultural murmur. There is always more, but always more of the same. The danger, as it is defined in *Great Jones Street*, is "sensory overload" (252): technological fallout in all its multifarious forms, including such linguistic manifestations as secret codes, arcana, and all the kabbala of conspiracy. "I realized the place was awash in noise," Jack Gladney notes as he moves through the burnished interiors of the supermarket. Here everything has an exclamatory glow about it, a euphemistic sheen to needs manufactured and met. But dread penetrates: "The toneless systems, the jangle and skid of carts, the loudspeaker and coffee-making machines, the cries of children. And over it all, or under it all, a dull and unlocatable roar, as of some form of swarming life just outside the range of human apprehension" (*White Noise* 36).[2]

Anxiety is awareness that remains on the far side of enlightenment. During an interaction with an automatic bank teller, Jack thinks, "The system was invisible, which made it all the more impressive, all the more disquieting to deal with." Hence, there is not much consolation in the sense that "we were in accord, at least for now. The networks, the circuits, the streams, the harmonies," if such congruities reduce their consumers (46).

Faced with that prospect, the DeLillo protagonist tends to respond with atavistic recoil, seeking out communes, caverns, and other enclaves of pristine, primitive behavior. Reacting to chemical disaster, Jack realizes that he and a fellow victim of the dispersal are speaking to one another from an "aboriginal crouch" (137), a posture of withdrawal that seems to suggest a kind of Ur-conspiracy on the most instinctive level of human exchange.[3] Ironically, then, efforts to escape depersonalization end up verifying its influence. For Gary Harkness in *End Zone*, the disease is "team spirit"; for rock star Buddy Wunderlick in *Great Jones Street*, it is the tide of adoration of his fans; for Bill Gray in *Mao II*, it is the phenomenon of the crowd, the reinforced huddle and animate pack in whose context, argues Elias Canetti in *Crowds and Power*, "liberation can be found from all stings" (327). Its mutuality and density are pitted against surrounding tensions as seen in the phenomenon of the arena:

> There is no break in the crowd which sits like this, exhibiting itself to itself. It forms a closed ring from which nothing can escape. The tiered ring of fascinated faces has something strangely homogenous about it. It embraces and contains everything which happens below; no-one relaxes his grip on this; no-one tries to get away. Any gap in the ring might remind him of disintegration and subsequent dispersal. But there is no gap; this crowd is doubly closed, to the world outside and in itself. (Canetti 28)

The crowd is an agreement whose main objective is to "form a shield against *their* own dying" at the cost of one's *own* dying (*White Noise* 73: italics mine).

"There's something about a crowd which suggests a sort of implicit panic," DeLillo contends. "There's something menacing and violent about a mass of people which makes us think of the end of individuality, whether they are gathered around a military leader or around a holy man" (interview with Nadotti 87). It is a theme to which he often returns in his fiction, perhaps most memorably in *Mao II*, which is a novel obsessed by the terrifying and the numbing impact of human surfeit:

> The rush of things, of shuffled sights, the mixed swagger of the avenue, noisy storefronts, jewelry spread across the sidewalk, the

deep stream of reflections, heads floating in windows, towers liquefied on taxi doors, bodies shivery and elongate, all of it interesting to Bill in the way it blocked comment, the way it simply rushed at him, massively, like your first day in Jalalabad, rushed and was. Nothing tells you what you're supposed to think of this. (94)

Crowds may confer magnitude, or at least the illusion of magnitude, but its price is clarity—a hemorrhage in the field of vision. Images and ideals are exaggerated, leaving the human equivalent of white noise.

In his novella, *Pafko at the Wall*, DeLillo explains, "Longing on a large scale is what makes history" (35), and crowds (here, the crowd gathered at the Polo Grounds for the Giants' pennant-clinching victory) are the collaborative embodiment of that longing. Once again, the crowd operates as a self-conscious entity in search of historical dimension of its own, not just the satisfaction of standing witness to history. Indeed, the baseball crowd has historical reach: it is temporally extended through retellings of the game down through the generations and spatially extended through radio broadcasts into remote, anonymous precincts, later to be reborn as mythic coherences ("I remember where I was when Bobby Thompson's shot was heard 'round the world' ...").[4] Once again, the media fortify this sensation of significant assembly, of "the kindred unit at the radio, old lines and ties and propinquities" on which the announcer bases his faith: "He pauses to let the crowd reaction build. Do not talk against the crowd. Let the drama come from them" (*Pafko* 55, 58). And once again, the expense of team spirit is a waste of self, as our announcer realizes when, in the wake of celebration, he has to "get down to the field and find a way to pass intact through all that mangle" (62). In DeLillo's fiction. one tries to defect from the failure of differentiation, but his defection threatens disappearance.

A denuded language deprived of texture and abiding context is both another example and a means of disseminating the disease of attrition. Whereas the language of *Ratner's Star* constituted a naked assault on the sensibilities of the uninitiated—Billy Twillig is occasionally frightened by the "intimation of compressed menace" contained in scientific jargon—the language of *White Noise* is more threatening for being so commonplace. It lulls us into its death. Circumambient infection seems to have no origin, when in fact, no meditation escapes linguistic mediation; and because commercials, official press releases, academic pedantries, and the like foster verbal regimentation, that mediation must be viewed as co-optation of private motives. Even transcendence is leveraged at this level; satori is scripted according the tawdriest common denominator, as Jack witnesses through his daughter Steffie's talking in her sleep: "I was convinced she was saying something, fitting together units of stable meaning. I watched her face, waited. Ten minutes passed. She uttered two clearly audible words, familiar and elusive at the same time, words that seemed to have a ritual meaning, part of a verbal spell or ecstatic chant. *Toyota Celica* ..." (155). The familiar is elusive on the one hand, inescapable on the other. Advertisers have pre-programmed the content and destination of our associations, so even when we imagine, we tend to imagine in the direction of media-induced debts, as evidenced by Jack's own relation of seeing his sleeping children to a "TV moment" or of cloud formations to brand-name mints and gums (Frow 183, 188). Although Steffie appears to be mumbling "a language not of this world," closer inspection reveals that it is utterly of this world, a carrier of the same grim stimulants, at once as synthetic and as deadly as Nyodene D.

Thus the novel is filled with disappointed verges—DeLillo builds to the point of revelation, only to resubmerge into the usual blather. Gladney's sentences exhibit "something like shock, a seeming inability to sort into contexts and hierarchies the information he receives and the thinking he does" (LeClair, *In the Loop* 211), which is to say that they repeat what they mean to address critically. For instance, here is Jack completing a frantic bout of dispossession of his personal ballast:

> I stalked the rooms, flinging things into cardboard boxes. Plastic electric fans, burnt-out toasters, *Star Trek* needlepoints. It took well over an hour to get everything down to the sidewalk. No one helped me, I didn't want help or company or human understanding. I just wanted to get the stuff out of the house. I sat on the front steps alone, waiting for a sense of ease and peace to settle in the air around me. A woman passing on the street said, "A decongestant, an antihistamine, a cough suppressant, a pain reliever." (262)

The prophets are sick with the same disease; promises of solace, words of cure, are contaminated by the same plague of enervation. The same congestion in the house is in the air. White noise becomes the societal equivalent of cliché, the uniform influx in which particularity dissolves into static, and the metamorphic potential of words may not be heard above the universal monotone toward which all utterances tend.[5]

If routine tethers ecstasy, it also reins in raw panic. The death fears that assault Jack and Babette Gladney are more invidious for the illusion of inviolability in which they grow. Here in the quiet college town of Blacksmith, "We're not smack in the path of history and its contaminations"

(85); television provides contact with trauma, of course, but it is a sublimely conditioned contact, filtered by the promise of distance. No wonder, then, that when the Airborne Toxic Event strikes, not only are the townspeople forced to rely on simulated behaviors, having had no other context to turn to, they are simultaneously threatened and mollified by the impenetrability of the experience. The cloud itself, an unpredictable, protean mass, is identified by inconsistent reports and linguistic evasions. Although it is designated by news reports as a "feathery plume," then recast as "a black billowing cloud," neither reliably approximates the threat whose malignancy is also a matter of its resistance to metaphorical compartmentalization: it is "Like a shapeless growing thing," Jack offers. "A dark black breathing thing of smoke. Why do they call it a plume?" (111). They do it to console the population with definition—to show that they have literally come to terms with the thing and to batten down our hunches with official rhetoric. So goes the romance of postulation. Uncircumscribable, nebulous in content, contour and consequence, the passage of the toxic event is assimilated with astonishing rapidity into the normative, where its ambiguities do not cease but rather function undetected among so many others. Consumers are returned to their polished matrices. Meaning restabilizes where the gravity of dailiness draws it out.

A similar irony infects the Gladneys' several strategies of psychic insulation against their death fears. With the urgency of addicts or patriots, they accumulate material possessions to defend their sense of presence, to lend them personal density and the illusion of spiritual "snugness" (20). Unfortunately, as Jack realizes, conspicuous consumption is self-defeating: "Things, boxes. Why do these possessions carry such sorrowful weight? There is a darkness attached to them, a foreboding" (6). Their daughter, a rapt collector of childhood memorabilia, seeks to protect her own history: "It is part of her strategy in a world of displacements to make every effort to restore and preserve, keep things together for their value as remembering objects, a way of fastening herself to a life" (103). But abundance numbs only so far, and stays against death seem deadly themselves.

From this perspective, Murray Siskind's rhapsodies on congestive kitsch contain warnings against the very swaddlings they celebrate and contribute to. Jack's colleague and confidant, Siskind has made a handsome career out of extracting "psychic data" from such concentrations of camp as cineplexes, malls, and ballparks.

> Supermarkets this large and clean and modern are a revelation to
> me. I spent my life in small steamy delicatessens with slanted

display cabinets full of trays that hold soft wet lumpy matter in pale colors. High enough cabinets so you had to stand on tiptoes to give your order. Shouts, accents, in cities no one notices specific dying. Dying is a quality of the air. It's everywhere and nowhere. (38)

The burden of this informal lecture is that we can ride the exponential increase of the supermarket out of oblivion and shape identities that belie analogy to "soft lumpy matter in pale colors." Malls and supermarkets are our epiphanic parlors, bastions of spiritual purchase. Murray Siskind delights and prospers in "the trance of matter," to use a phrase of poet Sharon Olds ("The Swimmer"). However, as this analysis of the glamour of groceries progresses, plenitude proves just as lethal to uniqueness and individuality. Infinity is only the far pole of confinement—the anonymity of endless shelves of generic items. Fewer citizens may crowd the scope in smaller towns, but their distinctive markings—the Tide above the Maytag, the Mazda ticking in the garage—hardly distinguish them from their urban counterparts, nor are they spared. The appetite for favored brands robs us of contact even with our own dying. Shopping suffocates us in the fortifications it supposedly effects; the hollow men are the stuffed men.

If death is capitulation to rutted beliefs and behaviors, life is refutation of predictability. When Jack enters a state of frenzied dispossession, trying to slough the personal sediment that fills his house, he finds "an immensity of things, an overburdening weight, a connection, a mortality" (262). Blessed excess reveals its lethal propensities. We may recall Daniel Isaacson's creed in E. L. Doctorow's *The Book of Daniel*: "The failure to make connections is complicity" (227). Here, the making of connections paradoxically complies with the Establishment because even meditation and desire are pre-channeled. So it seems that when Jack determines to avenge the adultery of Babette at the hands of Willie Mink, alias Mr. Gray, to whom she has traded sexual favors for a supply of Dylar, he is inspired less by moral outrage than by the "advance of consciousness" occasioned by his decision (in deference to Siskind's logic) to become a killer rather than a dier—the most heinous manifestation of Jack's assimilation of Hitler Studies. Ideally, shooting Gray would be like smashing through the television: reclaiming immediacy by reviving the visceral.[6]

The precision of plotting exhilarates him: "With each separate step, I became aware of processes, components, things relating to other things. Water fell to earth in drops. I saw things new" (304). Here is discreteness wrested from the general slur. Single-mindedness enables Jack to approach the psychic plateau that his sleeping daughter could not:

> I continued to advance in consciousness. Things glowed, a secret
> life rising out of them. Water struck the earth in elongated orbs,
> splashing drams. I knew for the first time what rain really was. I
> understood the neurochemistry of my brain, the meaning of
> dreams (the waste material of premonitions). Great stuff
> everywhere, racing through the room, racing slowly. A richness,
> a density. I believed everything. (310)

That this advance results from a murderous commitment makes us hesitate
to embrace it, and indeed, close reading reveals its insufficiency. For while
the world lays out so invitingly, expansive and elemental at the same time, the
effect—"I believed everything"—shows Jack to be overwhelmed by a wealth
of stimulants.

There is really no difference between this open admission policy to
every spectacle and a wholesale renunciation of the capacity for disbelief, as
is indicated by Jack and Babette's willingness to accept as true the craziest
headlines out of the supermarket tabloids. What more comfortable disease is
there than adoration? How secure the transfixion by such glossy fictions, the
dependable "grip of self-myth" (72)? The plausible quickly escalates into the
portentous, until no speck, no deception, is large enough to cause the
undifferentiating transparent eyeball to wince at all: "The extra dimensions,
the super perceptions, were reduced to visual clutter, a whirling miscellany,
meaningless" (313). In other words, Jack has not earned an uncoopted
vantage point above the conditioned atmosphere of television antennae. His
resolve is psychopathic, not poetical; he is as much a political zombie as he
ever had been meekly encysted in his Hitler Studies chair.

Earlier in the novel, Jack experienced a myclonic jerk that shattered his
sleep, and perhaps that is what he is hoping to accomplish by shooting Willie
Mink—a sudden, inarticulate decompression that breaks through the
unremitting dial tone that is contemporary American consciousness (and
which variously masquerades as theme parks, jingoism, or religious awe).
The point is, however, that the myclonic jerk is like *deja vu*, untrustworthy, a
synaptic glitch. It is likelier what preempts insight, not the insight itself.
Similarly, the novel's typical refrains—the sound of clothes twisting in the
dryer, a commercial announcement, the dance of taillights on the highway—
seem heavy with prescience when they may actually represent nothing more
than the sporadically detectable horizon of "brain fade."

As a random gathering of townspeople dispossessed by the toxic cloud
sift rumors, "We began to marvel at our own ability to manufacture awe"
(153); when Jack later smuggles one of his wife's Dylar pills to a colleague in
order to penetrate its chemistry, she explains, "We still lead the world in

stimuli" (189). In each case, technology manifests breakdowns in distinguishability. White noise is a uniform distraction, so that, as with the malfunctioning smoke alarm that is *always* buzzing, no one knows how, or whether, to react. At one point Wilder starts crying with unnatural persistence. It goes on for hours unabated, as though the youngest Gladney were an early warning system for the atmospheric danger to come. Eventually, though, the urgency of his wailing gives way to something Jack interprets as keening, a practiced, inbred lament. Jack not only begins to get used to it, he finds it strangely soothing, and he thinks of joining his son inside this "lost and suspended place" where "we might together perform some reckless wonder of intelligibility" (78).[7] But the sound does not enlighten as it enfolds. When the crying ceases after seven hours, as inexplicably as it began—we might remember Emily Dickinson's "certain Slant of light / Winter Afternoons," whose massive impact is due in part to its indeterminacy—Jack ascribes mystical properties to the episode: "It was as though he'd just returned from a period of wandering in some remote and holy place, in sand barrens or snowy ranges—a place where things are said, sights are seen, distances reached which we in our ordinary toil can only regard with the mingled reverence and wonder we hold in reserve for feats of the most sublime and difficult dimensions" (79). Again, the assumption of metaphysical import is entirely a matter of faith, not unlike the faith that leads the citizens of Blacksmith to trust in anonymous officials to handle the airborne toxic event (or, for that matter, the faith that leads us to believe that salvation lies in the right combination of brand-name products). And Jack remains distant from the sublimity he imagines there.

Saturation by awe renders us immune to alert, "In the psychic sense a forest fire on TV is on a lower plane than a ten-second spot for Automatic Dishwasher All," Murray Siskind argues (67), nodding to the principal avatar of that awe. Television's *om* is carefully pitched to keep us tuned in to the All in whose ultimate impenetrability we trust. "Watching television was for Lyle a discipline like mathematics or Zen," we read in *Players* (16), but its electrostatic bath soon becomes an end in itself. So too does the surface brilliance of the local mail, wedding mass and pall, keep us sleepy with its friendly bombardment of light and promise. We become commoditized buyers, consumers consumed by pre-regulated passions, melded into the same matrix. Excess "is a sort of electrocution.... [t]he individual burns its circuits and loses its defenses," writes Jean Baudrillard (qtd in Keesey 140). But the blissed-out buyer does not mind.[8]

The political implication of this is a sort of placidity of last resort, which during the airborne toxic event takes the form of the belief that the system responsible for engineering the crisis is also the best hope of assessing, digesting (with man-made poison-gobbling bacteria?), and rendering it harmless. The linguistic implication is the desolate voice of the novel, with its enormous clutter of gleaming cultural fragments and unborn insights that shimmer momentarily only to settle back into the collective hum. Metaphor implies a richer insistence, a greater command of hierarchy, resonance and relation, than we can marshal. Thus, white noise is literally an anaesthetic, paving the imagination for the transportation of sanctioned simulations. In this way, insulation is really infiltration, for the things we collect and consume in order to stave off mortality may be tainted by it:

> I walked up the driveway and got in the car. There were trash caddies fixed to the dashboard and seat-backs, dangling plastic bags full of gum wrappers, ticket stubs, lipstick-smeared tissues, crumpled soda cans, crumpled circulars and receipts, ashtray debris, popsicle sticks and french fries, crumpled coupons and paper napkins, pocket combs with missing teeth. Thus familiarized, I started up the engine, turned on the lights and drove off. (302)

Familiarity breeds content, a slew of duplication, our numbed slough. Everything is crumpled—DeLillo employs the same participle three times in the same sentence to emphasize the stultifying effect of modern fallout; there is nothing lyrical or empowering about familiarization in this mute, useless context. We recall Jack's being confronted by the electronic proof of his contamination by Nyodene D: graphically splayed on the computer screen, his fate seemed to him alien and beyond petitioning. "It makes you feel like a stranger in your own dying," he realizes. "I wanted my academic gown and dark glasses" (142).

Recoil is a conventional reaction to the brunt of understanding, which is to say that white noise is as likely to be treated by the characters in the novel as the cure as it is the curse. In addition to the ubiquitous bearings of personal property and media-shaped inducements, there are Jack's Hitler Studies and Babette's Dylar supply to personalize respective hiding places. By affiliating himself with Hitler, Jack pretends to guarantee himself a measure of mythical proportion; by taking Dylar, an experimental drug that presumably eliminates one's fear of death, Babette hopes to liberate her consciousness for life-affirming pursuits. However, neither tactic works. Because Hitler's posterity has to do with his perpetration of death, not with his transcendence of it—because in the end, killers and diers are tied to the same false criteria—Jack's absorption nearly destroys him. Only his humane reflex—he takes the man he has accidentally wounded to the hospital—saves him. As for Dylar, not only does Babette's secret commitment to it undermine instead of enable her loving herself and her family, the drug does not work. Indeed, its side effects, grotesquely inflated in the ravenousness of Willie Mink, include extreme paranoia and the inability to separate words from things, which means that Dylar actually exacerbates what it was designed to quell.

The latter consequence in particular, a kind of Saussurean nightmare, represents the equally paralyzing converse of white noise—a murderous convergence of words and things. For if in the slather of white noise signs lose their signifying function, in the Dylar-induced psychosis (in which Jack need merely say the words "hail of bullets" to strafe his crazed adversary) signs afford no contemplative distance. Either way, we yield utterly.[9]

The consolation for both Jack and Babette is that the ambiguous sky left in the wake of the Airborne Toxic Event encourages "an exalted narrative life," which seems to render preconditioned responses obsolete—"it transcends previous categories of awe"—but has the advantage of inspiring new attitudes, new stories (324–325). In the end, neither homicidal nor pharmaceutical failures, respectively, relegate them exclusively to false electronic relations. There remain "the old human muddles" (313), which, for all the anxieties and misgivings they occasion, sustain personality with challenges to routinized beliefs and behaviors. To put it another way, not all of the "unexpected themes and intensities" buzzing in the deep structure of the commonplace are necessarily inimical to human growth even if they appear to evade human understanding (184).

To return again to linguistic consequences, DeLillo is peculiarly conscious among contemporary American writers of predicating his fictions in environments hostile to the individual's capacity to use words that have not been irrevocably sworn to prior manipulations, whose forms include official communiques and press releases (*Libra*), conventional bigotry (*End Zone*), commercialism (*Americana*), pedantry and jargon (*Ratner's Star*). To combat wholesale manipulation of language into "lullabies processed by intricate systems" (*End Zone* 54), DeLillo proposes a creed of resistance. On the one hand, he intends to exploit the marginality of the serious writer as a posture of unassimilatability, as a means of avoiding becoming one more shelf item, which has to do not only with the thematic politicization of the novel but also with the tinge of dread that structural unresolvability instills. On the other hand, he hopes to create a sense of "radiance in dailiness" that restores the edge to everything we have accumulated (DeLillo, Interview with DeCurtis 63). In *White Noise* it is seen in the spell that seems to render the post-toxic event sky incandescent. "The sky takes on content, feeling, an exalted narrative life," but its effects oscillate between wonder and dread, between inspiration and angst (324–325). What is certain is that people linger, exchange, participate—instead of pressing heedlessly, habitually onward, they are moved to interpret and dwell upon the defamiliarized heavens.

"Symmetry is a powerful analgesic," postulated one of the crypticians housed in Field Experiment Number One in *Ratner's Star* (115). Dead metaphors deaden; clichés inspire clichéd reactions that keep ad executives, political spin doctors, and probability experts comfortable. Lyricism destabilizes the system of rutted assumptions, but because its radiance originates from dailiness, its departures actually restore the possibilities inherent in the ordinary by stoking its latencies—by extending, to use a favorite phrase of Stanley Elkin's, the range of the strange.[10] Tenor and vehicle—worldly origin and word-driven ambition—are interdependent components of successful metaphorical operations, which promise a livelier, more vivid transaction than what grocers of governments purvey. To be sure, if we accept the premise (borrowed from *The Princeton Encyclopedia of Poetry and Poetics*) that one of the defining roles of metaphor is to create "agreeable mystification" (Whalley 490), the "powerful and storied" sky that concludes *White Noise* is a most accommodating setting for it.[11]

Although DeLillo does fashion startling metaphors in his novels, his vision of the abiding, empowering mystery of language does not solely rely on traditional metaphorical constructions. In fact, he consistently suggests that individual words have a kind of lambency at the core that goes beyond their referential employment. Owen Brademas, in *The Names*, is particularly attuned to the "beautiful shapes" of the physical constituents of words, finding letters themselves "so strange and reawakening. It goes deeper than conversations, riddles.... It's an unreasoning passion" (36). Gary Harkness finds himself dismantling a slogan advocating rugged play to find a similar beauty beneath the meaning (*End Zone* 28), just as Pammy Wynant intuits a discontented essence underlying a street sign (*Players* 207), and Bucky Wunderlick turns to aleatory techniques that may discover novel, positive options outside "the mad weather of language" that society has contrived (*Great Jones Street* 265).

I choose these examples because they are also precisely the ones alluded to by Bruce Bawer in his dismissal of such preoccupations in DeLillo's fiction as mere epistemological flap, which is to say, more of the very sort of rhetoric that DeLillo means to expose (41–42). Bawer is disappointed that DeLillo's characters seem to be incapable of real conversations, that they are primarily generators of theory who tend to preside like commissioned discussants or convention delegates. Leaving aside for the moment the accuracy of this complaint—indeed, leaving aside the question of how many "real conversations" take place in, say, the drawing rooms of Henry James—let us consider just how exotic an office words are being asked to perform here. There is often an implicit dais beneath DeLillo's speakers; those who are not interpreters or social critics by trade are so by personal constitution. The fact is, we know how real people really talk, and I would maintain that DeLillo is actually exceptionally attuned to the rhythms and nuances of those conversations, not to mention the evidence of media fertilization they indicate.

As to the argument that these people do not so much talk as testify, perhaps their private verbal contrivances are efforts to extricate them from the contrivances they daily breathe and echo. Bawer's consternation that "when their mouths open, they produce clipped, ironic, self-consciously clever sentences full of offbeat metaphors and quaint descriptive details" comes from his failed expectations (37), but can DeLillo's assault on predictability rightly be faulted for not living up to standards of verisimilitude?[12] Perhaps no contemporary other than Thomas Pynchon is so assiduous as DeLillo when it comes to rooting-out the menace that inheres beneath the smooth surfaces of contemporary America like buried drums of radioactive waste. Nowhere is that menace so insidiously compressed as in the language we absorb and employ—a menace made all the more effective by the comforts afforded by "uttering the lush banalities" (*End Zone* 54). When speculation could be a carrier of the linguistic abuse that prompts speculation in the first place, a certain artificiality is likely to creep into one's diction. When people sense that the room is bugged, that their very vocabularies are tainted, that every utterance could itself become an airborne toxic event, a self-conscious weight accompanies even casual encounters. "What writing means to me is trying to make interesting, clear, beautiful language.... Over the years it's possible for a writer to shape himself as a human being through the language he uses," DeLillo argues (Interview with LeClair 82), and a similar priority—deliberately shaping the self in the course and through the act of vocalizing the self—seems to have been bequeathed to his characters.

The question remains as to how we can counteract the haze when the haze is so inviting. "In societies reduced to bloat and glut, terror is the only meaningful act," confides a character in *Mao II*. Only the "lethal believer" has the force to resist absorption into the inertia of super-saturated cities, airwaves, consciousnesses (157). This is the source of DeLillo's reputation among detractors for reducing the spectrum of human options to either capitulation to enigma or murderous outrage (a la Lee Harvey Oswald in *Libra*). It is born out of the notion that, in the words of the chairman of the Department of American Environments at the College-on-the-Hill, "We need an occasional catastrophe to break up the incessant bombardment of information" (66), a sentiment that reiterates the suspicion voiced in *The Names* that "[t]he forces were different, the orders of response eluded us. Tenses and inflections. Truth was different, the spoken universe, and men with guns were everywhere" (94). Fortunately, DeLillo also manages detonations more optimistic than bombings, yet more historically palpable than a myclonic jerk. There are the products of the writer's imagination, which "increase the flow of meaning. This is how we reply to power and beat back our fear, by extending the pitch of consciousness and human possibility" (*Mao II* 200). The way the athlete can suddenly invest his efforts with eloquence, "doing some gaudy thing that whistles up out of nowhere" (*Pafko* 37), the writer can disarm the mundane, name-branded mentality and penetrate the collectivized comforts of customized buying, reading, and belief By delivering the inexhaustible, incalculable facts of us, he has the knack of breaking through "the death that exists in routine things" (*White Noise* 248) to restore us to wonder. Or to borrow again from *The Names*, the "hovering sum of things" remains tantalizingly aloft (123),[13] "So much remained. Every word and thing a beadwork of bright creation.... A cosmology against the void" (*White Noise* 243).[14]

Not a wordless remove but a studied wonder is what may finally preserve by enlarging us. We may recall in this regard Robert Frost's idealization of the person who is educated by metaphor: while he is unafraid of enthusiasm, he specifically embraces enthusiasm that inspires the intellect and "the discreet use" of metaphor. Cruder enthusiasms—"it is oh's and ah's with you and no more"—are the stuff of "sunset raving" (Frost 36), and are finally infertile, ineloquent (a pointed admonition, as it happens, to the rapt gazers upon the unprecedented sunsets that conclude *White Noise*). On the other hand, while Frost champions quality of expression, he recognizes that metaphor, as well as the "figurative values" it heralds, is not a permanent argument but a momentary stay. You need to know "how far you may expect to ride it and when it may break down with you" (Frost 39). The poignancy, the beauty of metaphor is kept alive by the way that "we stop just short" of conclusiveness, as seen in the churning sky over Blacksmith and in the unsettled ending of the novel.

"Reality is not a matter of fact, it is an achievement," writes William Gass in "The Artist and Society" (282), and art is no less profound for its subtlety than other revolutionary activities. The irony is that while we admire works of art less for the theses they profess than for "the absolute way in which they exist" (282), that absolute existence is not as simple as a political rally or an explosion. As DeLillo assesses them, the recurring themes in his novels are "Perhaps a sense of secret patterns in our lives. A sense of ambiguity" (Interview with DeCurtis 57). Patterns attended by ambiguities—art posits the former while respecting the latter.

Throughout his canon, DeLillo discredits the "subdue and codify" mentality on two grounds: its sheer inadequacy and its imitation of absolutist behaviors (which also include the bright-packaging-to-blissful-purchase reflex). On the contrary, the artist "is concerned with consciousness, and he makes his changes there. His inaction is only a blind, for his books and buildings go off under everything—not once but a thousand times" (Gass 288). Or as Richard Poirier puts it, skepticism is the lesson and the legacy of our greatest poets, artists, and intellectuals: it inhabits the words they use to interrogate the words we use, and it results in "a liberating and creative suspicion as to the dependability of words and syntax, especially as it relates to matters of belief in the drift of one's feelings and impressions" (5). When the revolution goes well, the sentences the writer hands down do not consign us to locked rooms but refute them, And so it is in *White Noise*, where DeLillo whistles in an undissipating but most precipitous dark.

Notes

1. By contrast, the same novel relates through James Axton the risk analyst's lament: "We have our self-importance. We also have our inadequacy. The former is a desperate invention of the latter" (5). The liberated artist may be the marooned artist.

2. In the following exchange, the possibility is advanced that this subterranean buzz is not just death's harbinger but the thing itself:

"What if death is nothing but sound?"
"Electrical noise."
"You hear it forever. Sound all around. How awful."
"Uniform, white." (*White Noise* 198)

3. "At the edge of every disaster," we learn in *Great Jones Street*, "people collect in affable groups to whisper away the newsless moment and wait for a messenger from the front" (254). In this novel as well, people come to rely on tranquilizers to short-circuit input and to help "run the lucky hum through our blood" (138).

4. In an example of a simulacrum readily relatable to *White Noise* and meriting the attention of Jean Baudrillard, these were also the days of "ghost game" broadcasts, in which nimble announcers had to recreate on radio the illusion of games wholly on the basis of inning-by-inning statistics received

over the wire. "In this half-hell of desperate invention he did four years of Senators baseball without ever seeing them play" (*Pafko* 45).

5. Consider in this regard the paradoxical tourist trap of the most photographed barn in the world. The collective perception confers an aura of importance upon its object, but because its uniqueness is based on extraordinary familiarity, uniqueness is actually overwhelmed by the cumulative effect of a "maintained" image. We no longer see the barn so many see the same way (*White Noise* 12–13).

6. Mr. Gray serves as a nominal and psychological precursor to Bill Gray, the shadow-dwelling author who is rudely thrust into the spotlight of world events in *Mao II*.

7. Compare the novel-in-progress being authored by Tap in *The Names*, whose dynamic, untotalizable progress of "White words ... Pure as the drivelin' snow" (336) offers an optimistic spin to DeLillo's consistent sense that language proliferates enigmas it cannot dissolve. Art is not the antidote to the environment it derives from.

8. Arguably, he does not have the ability to mind. In "The Ecstasy of Communication," Baudrillard describes his pathology as "this state of terror proper to the schizophrenic: too great a proximity of everything, the unclean promiscuity of everything which touches, invests and penetrates without resistance, with no halo of private protection..." (132).

9. A related malady afflicts James, the mathematician's assistant in DeLillo's play *The Engineer of Moonlight*: instead of grunting, he says "grunt," or, panicked, says "Loud and prolonged cries for help" (44).

10. Similarly, DeLillo's refusal to tie up the numerous loose ends of his narrative (the result of Jack's diagnosis, whether Murray gets approval for his Elvis Studies center, and so on) actually helps to keep *White Noise* from the inevitable deathward progress to which, so it is rumored in the novel, all plots tend (Zinman 77).

11. John Frow suggests that we might speak of an "airborne aesthetic event" in the wake of the toxic scare. He quickly notes, however, that this does not replace the poisonous cloud but joins with it (176). In other words, the beautiful, protracted sunsets that conclude *White Noise* are, like good metaphors, mysterious incorporations, open-ended messages.

12. "I do sort of emit a certain feudal menace," concedes a character in *Players* (171), and this is the manner of expression Bawer indicts. In fact, this quality goes beyond the conversational arcane. At the end of that novel, for example, the sight of a naked woman asleep in bed prompts the following considerations: how women "seem at such times to embody a mode of wholeness, an immanence and unit truth ..."; how motels tend "to turn things inward" and serve as repositories of private fears; how bucolic street names

constitute "a liturgical prayer, a set of moral consolations"; and how sunlight through the window reveals "the animal glue of physical properties and functions," thereby "absolving us of our secret knowledge" (209–212). Evidently, nothing is off-hand in DeLillo; every moment is richly textured and tilled, charged with scholarship and suspicion.

13. The trick, of course, is to distinguish this presumably enabling "hovering sum" from the tactical deceptions of the power elite, as David Ferrie puts it in *Libra*: "There's something they aren't telling us. Something we don't know about. There's more to it. There's always more to it. This is what history consists of. It's the sum total of all the things they aren't telling us" (321).

14. Capitulation to the void takes several forms in the novel, including Steffie's eager acceptance of the role of disaster victim during simulation exercises and competitions among Jack's colleagues as to who can drive longest on the highway with his eyes shut. This is the Zen of self-erasure without transcendent end.

WORKS CITED

Baudrillard, Jean. "The Ecstasy of Communication." Trans. John Johnston. *The Anti-Aesthetic: Essays on Postmodern Culture.* Ed. Hal Foster. Port Townsend, WA: Bay P. 1983. 126–134.

Bawer, Bruce. "Don DeLillo's America." *New Criterion* 3 (April 1985): 34–42.

Canetti, Elias. *Crowds and Power.* Trans. Carol Stewart. New York: Viking, 1963.

DeLillo, Don. *Americana.* Boston: Houghton Mifflin, 1971.

———. "The Art of Fiction CXXXV." Interview with Adam Begley, *Paris Review* 128 (Fall 1993): 275–306.

———. *End Zone,* Boston: Houghton Mifflin, 1972.

———. *The Engineer of Moonlight. Cornell Review* 5 (Winter 1979): 21–47.

———. *Great Jones Street.* Boston: Houghton Mifflin, 1973.

———. "An Interview with Don DeLillo." With Toni LeClair. *Anything Can Happen: Interviews with Contemporary American Novelists.* Ed. Tom LeClair and Larry McCaffery. Urbana: U of Illinois P 1981. 79–90.

———. "An Interview with Don DeLillo." With Maria Nadotti. Trans. Peggy Boyers. *Salmagundi* 100 (Fall 1993): 86–97.

———. *Libra.* New York: Viking, 1988.

———. *Mao II.* New York: Viking, 1991.

————. *The Names*. New York: Alfred A, Knopf, 1982.

————. "'An Outsider in This Society': An Interview with Don DeLillo." With Anthony DeCurtis. Lentricchia 43–66.

————. *Pafko at the Wall. Harpers* October 1992: 35–70.

————. *Players*. New York: Alfred A. Knopf, 1977.

————. *Ratner's Star*. New York; Alfred A. Knopf, 1976.

————. *White Noise*. New York: Viking, 1985.

Dickinson, Emily. "There's a certain Slant of light." *The Poems of Emily Dickinson*. Vol. 1. Ed. Thomas H. Johnson. Cambridge: Harvard UP 1963. 185.

Doctorow, E. L. *The Book of Daniel*. New York: Random, 1971.

Frost, Robert. "Education by Poetry." *Selected Prose of Robert Frost*. Ed. Hyde Cox and Edward Connery Lathem. New York: Holt, Rinehart and Winston, 1966. 33–46.

Frow, John. "The Last Things Before the Last: Notes on *White Noise*." Lentricchia 175–191.

Gass, William. "The Artist and Society." *Fiction and the Figures of Life*. Boston: Godine, 1971. 276–88.

Keesey, Douglas. *Don DeLillo*. Twayne's United States Authors Series 629. New York: Macmillan/Twayne, 1993.

LeClair, Tom. *In the Loop: Don DeLillo and the Systems Novel*. Urbana: U of Illinois P 1988.

Lentricchia, Frank, ed. *Introducing Don DeLillo*. Durham and London: Duke UP 1991.

Olds, Sharon. "The Swimmer." *The Father*. New York: Alfred A. Knopf, 1992. 56.

Poirier, Richard. *Poetry and Pragmatism*. Cambridge; Harvard UP 1992.

Whalley, George, "Metaphor," *Princeton Encyclopedia of Poetry and Poetics*. Enlarged edition. Ed. Alex Preminger. Princeton: Princeton UP 1974. 490–495.

Zinman, Toby Silverman. "Gone Fission: The Holocaustic Wit of Don DeLillo." *Modern Drama* 34 (March 1991): 74–87.

PAUL MALTBY

The Romantic Metaphysics of Don DeLillo

W hat is the postmodern response to the truth claims traditionally made
on behalf of visionary moments? By "visionary moment," I mean that flash
of insight or sudden revelation which critically raises the level of spiritual or
self-awareness of a fictional character. It is a mode of cognition typically
represented as bypassing rational thought processes and attaining a "higher"
or redemptive order of knowledge (gnosis). There are, conceivably, three
types of postmodern response which merit attention here.

First, in recognition of the special role literature itself has played in
establishing the credibility of visionary moments, postmodern writers might
draw on the resources of metafiction to parodically "lay bare" the essentially
literary nature of such moments. Baldly stated, the visionary moment could
be exposed as a literary convention, that is, a concept that owes more to the
practice of organizing narratives around a sudden illumination (as in, say, the
narratives of Wordsworth's *Prelude* or Joyce's *Dubliners*) than to real-life
experience. Thomas Pynchon's *The Crying of Lot 49* is premised on this
assumption. Pynchon's sleuthlike protagonist, Oedipa Maas, finds herself in
a situation in which clues—contrary to the resolution of the standard
detective story—proliferate uncontrollably, thereby impeding the emergence
of a final enlightenment or "stelliferous Meaning" (82). It is a situation that
not only frustrates Oedipa, who is continually tantalized by the sense that "a

From *Contemporary Literature* 37, 2 © 1996 by the Board of Regents of the University of
Wisconsin System

revelation ... trembled just past the threshold of her understanding" (24), but which also mocks the reader's expectation of a revelation that will close the narrative.

A second postmodern response might be to assess the credibility of the visionary moment in the light of poststructuralist theory. Hence the representation of a visionary moment as if it embodied a final, fast-frozen truth, one forever beyond the perpetually unstable relationship of signifier to signified, would be open to the charge of "logocentrism" (where the transient "meaning effects" generated by the endless disseminations of language are mistaken for immutable meanings). Moreover, implied here is the subject's transcendent vantage point in relation to the visionary moment. For the knowledge that the "moment" conveys is always apprehended in its totality; there is no current of its meaning that escapes or exceeds this implicitly omnipotent consciousness. As if beyond the instabilities and surplus significations of language, the subject is assumed to be the sole legislator of meaning. (All of which is to say nothing of any *unconscious* investment in the meaning of the visionary moment.)

A third postmodern response might deny the very conditions of possibility for a visionary moment in contemporary culture. The communication revolution, seen by sociologists like Baudrillard to be the key constitutive feature of our age, has aggrandized the media to the point where signs have displaced their referents, where images of the Real have usurped the authority of the Real, whence the subject is engulfed by simulacra. In the space of simulation, the difference between "true" and "false," "actual" and "imaginary," has imploded. Hence Romantic and modernist conceptions of visionary moments—typically premised on metaphysical assumptions of supernal truth—are rendered obsolete in a culture suffused with simulacra; for under these "hyperreal" conditions, the visionary moment can only reproduce the packaged messages of the mass media.

What these three responses to the truth claims of the visionary moment share is a radically antimetaphysical stance. We see the visionary moment, with all its pretensions to truth and transcendence, exposed as (1) a literary convention, (2) a logocentric illusion, and (3) a hyperreal construct. In short, the metaphysical foundations of traditional conceptions of the visionary moment cannot survive the deconstructive thrust of postmodern thinking.

This essay will examine the status of the visionary moment in particular, and of visionary experience in general, in three of Don DeLillo's novels, namely, *White Noise* (1985), *The Names* (1982), and *Libra* (1988). DeLillo has been widely hailed as an exemplar of postmodernist writing. Typically, this assessment rests on readings that focus on his accounts of the postmodern experience of living in a hyperreality.[1] But to postmodernize DeLillo is to risk losing sight of the (conspicuously unpostmodern) metaphysical impulse that animates his work. Indeed, the terms in which he identifies visionary experience in his fiction will be seen to align him so closely with a Romantic sensibility that they must radically qualify any reading of him as a postmodern writer.

In part 2 of *White Noise*, the Gladney family shelters at a local barracks from the toxic cloud of a chemical spill. As Jack Gladney observes his children sleeping, he recounts a visionary moment. It begins as follows:

> Steffie ... muttered something in her sleep. It seemed important that I know what it was. In my current state, bearing the death impression of the Nyodene cloud, I was ready to search anywhere for signs and hints, intimations of odd comfort.... Moments later she spoke again.... but a language not quite of this world. I struggled to understand. I was convinced she was saying something, fitting together units of stable meaning. I watched her face, waited.... She uttered two clearly audible words, familiar and elusive at the same time, words that seemed to have a ritual meaning, part of a verbal spell or ecstatic chant.
> *Toyota Celica*. (154–55)

Before I continue the quotation, consider the following issues. Up to this point, DeLillo has manipulated his readers' expectations; what we expect from Gladney's daughter, Steffie, is a profound, revelatory utterance. Instead, we are surprised by (what appears to be) a banality: "Toyota Celica." Here it looks as if DeLillo is mocking the traditional faith in visionary moments or, more precisely, ironically questioning the very possibility of such moments in a postmodern culture. After all, a prominent feature of that culture is the prodigious, media-powered expansion of marketing and public relations campaigns to the point where their catchwords and sound bites colonize not just the public sphere but also, it seems, the individual unconscious. Henceforth, even the most personal visionary experience appears to be constituted by the promotional discourses of a consumer society. However, the irony of this apparently postmodern account of a visionary moment proves to be short-lived as Gladney immediately recounts his response to Steffie's words:

> A long moment passed before I realized this was the name of an automobile. The truth only amazed me more. The utterance was beautiful and mysterious, gold-shot with looming wonder. It was

like the name of an ancient power in the sky, tablet-carved in
cuneiform. It made me feel that something hovered. But how
could this be? A simple brand name, an ordinary car. How could
these near-nonsense words, murmured in a child's restless sleep,
make me sense a meaning, a presence? She was only repeating
some TV voice.... Whatever its source, the utterance struck me
with the impact of a moment of splendid transcendence. (155)

The tenor of this passage is not parodic; the reader is prompted by the
analytical cast and searching tone of Gladney's narration to listen in earnest,
Gladney's words are not to be dismissed as delusional, nor are they to be
depreciated as those of "a modernist displaced in a postmodern world"
(Wilcox 348). The passage is typical of DeLillo's tendency to seek out
transcendent moments in our postmodern lives that hint at possibilities for
cultural regeneration. Clearly, the principal point of the passage is not that
"Toyota Celica" is the signifier of a commodity (and as such has only illusory
significance as a visionary utterance), but that *as a name* it has a mystical
resonance and potency: "It was like the name of an ancient power in the sky,"
a name that is felt to be "part of a verbal spell or ecstatic chant." For what is
revealed to Gladney in this visionary moment is that names embody a
formidable power. And this idea is itself the expansive theme, explored in its
metaphysical implications, of *The Names*, the novel that immediately
preceded *White Noise*. Indeed, when read in conjunction with *The Names*, the
metaphysical issues of *White Noise* can be brought into sharper relief.

 The Names addresses the question of the mystical power of names:
secret names (210, 294), place names (102–3, 239–40), divine names (92,
272).[2] For DeLillo wants to remind us that names are often invested with a
significance that exceeds their immediate, practical function. Names are
enchanted; they enable insight and revelation. As one character explains:
"We approach nameforms warily. Such secret power. When the name is itself
secret, the power and influence are magnified. A secret name is a way of
escaping the world. It is an opening into the self" (210).

 Consider the remarkable ending of *The Names*—an extract from the
manuscript of a novel by Tap, the narrator's (James Axton's) nine-year-old
son, replete with misspellings. In Tap's novel, a boy, unable to participate in
the speaking in tongues at a Pentecostal service, panics and flees the church:
"Tongue tied! His fait was signed. He ran into the rainy distance, smaller and
smaller. This was worse than a retched nightmare. It was the nightmare of
real things, the fallen wonder of the world" (339). These lines conclude both
Tap's novel and *The Names* itself. "The *fallen* wonder of the world" connotes
the failure of language, in its (assumed) post-lapsarian state, to invest the

world with some order of deep and abiding meaning, to *illuminate* existence. More specifically, the language that has "fallen" is the language of name, the kind of pure nomenclature implied in Genesis where words stand in a necessary, rather than arbitrary, relationship to their referents.[3] The novel follows the lives of characters who seek to recover this utopian condition of language. For example, people calling themselves "abecedarians" (210) form a murder cult whose strategy is to match the initials of their victims' names to those of the place names where the murders occur—all in a (misguided) effort to restore a sense of the intrinsic or self-revealing significance of names. And note Axton's response to the misspellings in his son's manuscript:

> I found these mangled words exhilarating. He'd made them new again, made me see how they worked, what they really were. They were ancient things, secret, reshapable.
> ... The spoken poetry in those words.... His ... misrenderings ... seemed to contain curious perceptions about the words themselves, second and deeper meanings, original meanings. (313)

The novel suggests that the visionary power of language will only be restored when we "tap" into its primal or pristine forms, the forms that can regenerate perception, that can *reveal* human existence in significant ways. Hence the novel's inquiry into "original meanings," the concern with remembering "the prototype" (112–13), whence "[i]t was necessary to remember, to dream the pristine earth" (307). The "gift of tongues" is also understood as a primal, and hence visionary, language—"talk as from the womb, as from the sweet soul before birth" (306)—and, as such, it is revered as "the whole language of the spirit" (338), the language by which "[n]ormal understanding is surpassed" (307). (And far from DeLillo keeping an ironic distance from such mystical views of glossolalia, he has endorsed them in interviews.)[4] Moreover, one can hardly miss the novel's overall insistence on the spoken word—especially on talk at the familiar, everyday, pre-abstract level of communication—as the purest expression of primal, visionary language:

> We talked awhile about her nephews and nieces, other family matters, commonplaces, a cousin taking trumpet lessons, a death in Winnipeg.... The subject of family makes conversation almost tactile. I think of hands, food, hoisted children. There's a close-up contact warmth in the names and images. Everydayness....

> This talk we were having about familiar things was itself
> ordinary and familiar. It seemed to yield up the mystery that is
> part of such things, the nameless way in which we sometimes feel
> our connections to the physical world. *Being here*.... Our senses
> are collecting at the primal edge.... I felt I was in an early stage of
> teenage drunkenness, lightheaded, brilliantly happy and stupid,
> knowing the real meaning of every word.[5] (31–32)

The affirmation of a primal, visionary level of language which, moreover, finds its purest expression in "talk" (glossolalia, conversation) is vulnerable to postmodern critique on the grounds that it is premised on a belief in original and pure meanings. Suffice it to say here, such meanings are assumed to exist (as in some transcendent realm) outside the space of intertextuality, or beyond the "logic of supplementarity" whereby, according to Derrida, "the origin ... was never constituted except reciprocally by a nonorigin" (*Of Grammatology* 61).

The idea that language has "fallen" or grown remote from some pure and semantically rich primal state is characteristically (though not exclusively) Romantic, and most reminiscent of views held by, among others, Rousseau and Wordsworth. In his "Essay on the Origins of Languages" and *Confessions*, Rousseau identified speech, as opposed to writing, as the natural condition of language because it "owes its form to natural causes alone" ("Essay" 5). In the face of a culture that conferred greater authority on writing than on speech, he affirmed the priority of the latter on the grounds that "Languages are made to be spoken, writing serves only as a supplement to speech" (qtd. in Derrida 144). While writing "substitut[es] exactitude for expressiveness" ("Essay" 21), the bias of speech is toward passionate and figurative expression which can "penetrate to the very depths of the heart" (9). Indeed, "As man's first motives for speaking were of the passions, his first expressions were tropes.... [Hence] [a]t first only poetry was spoken; there was no hint of reasoning until much later" (12). Moreover, it was "primitive," face-to-face speech—as opposed to the sophistications of writing, and especially the tyranny made possible by the codification of laws—that, according to Rousseau's anthropology, once bound humans together naturally in an organic, egalitarian community. And recall that in his "Preface" to the *Lyrical Ballads*, Wordsworth deplored the "arbitrary and capricious habits of expression" of poets who, following urbane conventions of writing, had lost touch with the elemental language of rustics. The latter, by virtue of their "rural occupations" (that is, their regular intercourse with nature) are "such men [who] hourly communicate with the best objects from which the best part of language is *originally* derived" (emphasis added).

Furthermore, this is "a far more philosophical language" than that used by poets (735). Of course, all this is not to suggest that DeLillo would necessarily endorse Rousseau's or Wordsworth's specific claims. But what all three share in is that familiar Romantic myth of some primal, pre-abstract level of language which is naturally endowed with greater insight, a pristine order of meaning that enables unmediated understanding, community, and spiritual communion with the world around.

If we return to Jack Gladney's visionary moment, we should note that while "Toyota Celica" may be a brand name, Gladney perceives it as having an elemental, incantatory power that conveys, at a deeper level, another order of meaning. He invokes a range of terms in an effort to communicate this alternative meaning: "ritual," "spell," "ecstatic," "mysterious," "wonder," "ancient" (155). Similarly, for Murray Siskind, Gladney's friend and media theorist, the recurring jingle "*Coke is it, Coke is it*" evokes comparisons with "mantras." Siskind elaborates: "The medium [that is, television] practically overflows with sacred formulas if we can remember how to respond innocently" (51). DeLillo highlights the paradox that while so much language, in the media society, has degenerated into mere prattle and clichés, brand names not only flourish but convey a magic and mystical significance. Hence they are often chanted like incantations: "Toyota Corolla, Toyota Celica, Toyota Cressida" (155); "Tegrin, Denorex, Selsun Blue" (289); "Dacron, Orlon, Lycra Spandex" (52).

Earlier passages in *White Noise* derive their meaning from the same Romantic metaphysics of language as Gladney's "moment of splendid transcendence." First, consider Gladney's response to the crying of his baby, Wilder (and note, by the way, the typically Romantic impression of the mystique of desolate spaces, and the appeal to "the mingled reverence and wonder" of the Romantic sublime):

> He was crying out, saying nameless things in a way that touched me with its depth and richness. This was an ancient dirge.... I began to think he had disappeared inside this wailing noise and if I could join him in his lost and suspended place we might together perform some reckless wonder of intelligibility....
>
> ... Nearly seven straight hours of serious crying. It was as though he'd just returned from a period of wandering in some remote and holy place, in sand barrens or snowy ranges—a place where things are said, sights are seen, distances reached which we in our ordinary toil can only regard with the mingled reverence and wonder we hold in reserve for feats of the most sublime and difficult dimensions. (78–79)

And, for Siskind, "Supermarkets this large and clean and modern are a revelation to me"; after all, "Everything is concealed in symbolism, hidden by veils of mystery and layers of cultural material. But it is psychic data, absolutely.... All the letters and numbers are here, ... all the code words and ceremonial phrases" (38, 37–38). Evidently, for DeLillo, language operates on two levels: a practical, denotative level, that is, a mode of language oriented toward business, information, and technology, and a "deeper," primal level which is the ground of visionary experience—the "second, deeper meanings, original meanings" that Axton finds in Tap's childishly misspelled words; the "ancient dirge" that Gladney hears in Wilder's wailing; the "language not quite of this world" that he hears in Steffie's sleep-talk; the "psychic data" that Siskind finds beneath white noise.

In communications theory, "white noise" describes a random mix of frequencies over a wide spectrum that renders signals unintelligible. DeLillo applies the metaphor of a circumambient white noise to suggest, on the one hand, the entropic state of postmodern culture where in general communications are degraded by triviality and irrelevance—the culture of "infotainment," factoids, and junk mail, where the commodity logic of late capitalism has extended to the point that cognition is mediated by its profane and quotidian forms. Yet, on the other hand, DeLillo suggests that within that incoherent mix of frequencies there is, as it were, a low wavelength that carries a flow of spiritually charged meaning. This flow of meaning is barely discernible, but, in the novel, it is figured in the recurring phrase "waves and radiation" (1, 38, 51, 104, 326)—an undercurrent of invisible forces or "nameless energies" (12) that have regenerative powers. And how do we "tune in" to this wavelength? Siskind says of his students, who feel alienated from the dreck of popular television, "they have to learn to look as children again" (50), that is to say, to perceive like Gladney's daughter, Steffie, or Axton's son, Tap, are said to perceive. In an interview, DeLillo has observed, "I think we feel, perhaps superstitiously, that children have a direct route to, have direct contact to the kind of natural truth that eludes us as adults" ("Outsider" 302). The boy protagonist of *Ratner's Star* (1976) is considered, by virtue of his minority, more likely than adults to access the "primal dream" experience of "racial history," of "pure fable, myth, archetype"; as one character tells him, "you haven't had time to drift away from your psychic origins" (264–65). And here it must be remarked that this faith in the insightfulness of childhood perception is a defining feature of (but, of course, not exclusive to) that current of Romantic writing which runs from Rousseau's *Emile* (1762), through the writings of Blake and Wordsworth, to De Quincey's *Suspiria de Profundis* (1845). For Coleridge, "To carry on the feelings of childhood into the powers of manhood; to combine the child's sense of wonder and novelty with the appearances which every day for perhaps forty years had rendered familiar ... this is the character and privilege of genius" (49). And recall, especially, the familiar lines from Wordsworth's "Intimations of Immortality" which lament the (adult's) loss of the child's "visionary gleam," that "master-light of all our seeing"; which celebrate the child as a "Seer blest! / On whom those truths do rest, / Which we [adults] are toiling all our lives to find, / In darkness lost" (460–61). In *The Prelude*, Wordsworth also argued that adult visionary experience is derived from childhood consciousness, the "seed-time [of] my soul," a consciousness that persists into adulthood as a source of "creative sensibility," illuminating the world with its "auxiliar light" (498, 507).

The Romantic notion of infant insight, of the child as gifted with an intuitive perception of truth, sets DeLillo's writing apart from postmodern trends. For, of all modes of fiction, it is postmodernism that is least hospitable to concepts like insight and intuition. Its metafictional and antimetaphysical polemic has collapsed the "depth model" of the subject (implied by the concept of *inner* seeing) and, audaciously, substituted a model of subjectivity as the construct of chains of signifiers. In such fiction as Robert Coover's *Pricksongs and Descants*, Walter Abish's *In the Future Perfect*, and Donald Barthelme's *Snow White*, for example, we find subjectivity reconceived as the conflux of fragments of texts—mythical narratives, dictionaries and catalogues, media clichés and stereotypes.

In an interview, DeLillo has said of *White Noise* that "Perhaps the supermarket tabloids are ... closest to the spirit of the book" ("I Never Set Out" 31). What one might expect from any critique of postmodern culture is a satirical assault on the tabloids as a debased and commodified form of communication. Yet the frequency with which DeLillo cites tabloid news stories—their accounts of UFOs, reincarnation, and supernatural occurrences (see, for example, *White Noise* 142–46)—suggests that there is more at issue than simply mocking their absurd, fabricated claims. For he recognizes our need for a "weekly dose of cult mysteries" (5), and that, by means of tabloid discourse, "Out of some persistent sense of large-scale ruin, we kept inventing hope" (146–47). In *White Noise*, the tabloids are seen to function as a concealed form of religious expression, where extraterrestrials are substituted for messiahs and freakish happenings for miracles. In short, on a wavelength of which we are virtually unconscious, the tabloids gratify our impulses toward the transcendental; "They ask profoundly important questions about death, the afterlife, God, worlds and space, yet they exist in an almost Pop Art atmosphere" ("I Never Set Out" 31).

White Noise abounds with extensive discussions about death and the afterlife (38, 99, 196–200, 282–92, and elsewhere), a concern of the book that is surely symptomatic of a nostalgia for a mode of experience that lies *beyond* the stereotyping and banalizing powers of the media, a mode of experience not subject to simulation. In a culture marked by an implosive de-differentiation of the image and its referent, where "Once you've seen the signs about the barn, it becomes impossible to see the barn" (12), the nonfigurability of death seems like a guarantee of a domain of human experience that can transcend hyperreality.

In another visionary experience, Gladney has mystical insight into the force—a huge, floating cloud of toxic chemicals—that threatens his life:

> It was a terrible thing to see, so close, so low ... But it was also spectacular, part of the grandness of a sweeping event.... Our fear was accompanied by a sense of awe that bordered on the religious. It is surely possible to be awed by the thing that threatens your life, to see it as a cosmic force, so much larger than yourself, more powerful, created by elemental and willful rhythms. (127)

This "awed," "religious" perception of a powerful force, which seems in its immensity capable of overwhelming the onlooker, is characteristic of that order of experience explored by the Romantics under the name of "the Sublime." The concept of the sublime has had a long and complex evolution since Longinus's famous treatise on the subject, and here it must suffice to note just one key statement that has served as a foundation for the notion of the Romantic sublime. In his *Philosophical Enquiry into the Origin of Our Ideas of the Sublime and the Beautiful* (1757), Edmund Burke advanced the following definition: "Whatever is fitted in any sort to excite the ideas of pain, and danger, that is to say, whatever is in any sort terrible, or is conversant about terrible objects, or operates in a manner analogous to terror, is a source of the *sublime*; that is, it is productive of the strongest emotion which the mind is capable of feeling" (39). Burke identified the *sources* of "terrifying" sublimity in such attributes as "power," "vastness," "infinity," and "magnificence," and among the effects of the *experience* of the sublime, he identified "terror," "awe," "reverence," and "admiration." It is remarkable that Gladney's experience of the sublime yields almost identical terms: "terrible," "grandness," "awed," "religious," "cosmic," "powerful." Moreover, such terms are familiar to us from descriptions of sublime experience in Romantic literature. For example, in *The Prelude*, in such accounts as his epiphany at the Simplon Pass and the ascent of Mount Snowdon (535–36, 583–85), Wordsworth frequently invokes impressions of the "awful," the "majestic," "infinity," and "transcendent power" to convey his sense of the terrifying grandeur of nature. In the violent, turbulent landscape of the Alps, he perceived "Characters of the great Apocalypse, / The types and symbols of Eternity, / Of first, and last, and midst, and without end" (536). Wordsworth's invocation of "Apocalypse," like the sense, in *White Noise*, of a life-threatening "cosmic force," reveals a defining property of the experience of the sublime: the subject's anxious intimation of a dissolution of the self, of extinction, in the face of such overwhelming power, "[T]he emotion you feel," says Burke of such "prodigious" power, is that it might "be employed to the purposes of ... destruction. That power derives all its sublimity from the terror with which it is generally accompanied" (65). And here it should be added that the experience is all the more disturbing because such immense power defies representation or rational comprehension (hence the recourse of Wordsworth, DeLillo, and others to hyperbole—"cosmic," "infinite," "eternal," and so on).[6]

The Romantic-metaphysical character of DeLillo's rendering of sublime experience is evident in the pivotal place he gives to the feeling of "awe." Not only is the term repeated in Gladney's description of his feelings toward the toxic cloud, but it is used three times, along with the kindred terms "dread" and "wonder," in a later account of that characteristically Romantic experience of the sublime, namely, gazing at a sunset:[7]

> The sky takes on content, feeling, an exalted narrative life....
> There are turreted skies, light storms.... Certainly there is awe, it
> is all awe, it transcends previous categories of awe, but we don't
> know whether we are watching in wonder or dread.... (324)

Given the Romantics' valorization of "I-centered" experience (in respect of which, *The Prelude* stands as a preeminent example), the feeling of awe has received special attention in their literature. After all, that overwhelming feeling of spellbound reverence would seem like cogent testimony to the innermost life of the psyche, an expression of what Wordsworth, in "Tintern Abbey" and *The Prelude*, called the "purer mind" (164, 506). However, that deep-rooted, plenitudinous I-centered subject of awe is a far cry from postmodern conceptions of the self as, typically, the tenuous construct of intersecting cultural codes. As noted earlier, this is the model of the self we find in the quintessentially postmodern fiction of Abish, Barthelme, and Coover, among others. It is a model which accords with Roland Barthes's view of the "I" that "is already itself a plurality of other texts, of codes which are infinite.... [Whence] subjectivity has ultimately the generality of stereotypes" (10). Evidently, DeLillo's awestruck subjects contradict the postmodern norm.[8] Finally, why create such subjects at all? Perhaps they may be regarded as an instance of DeLillo's endeavor to affirm the integrity and spiritual energy of the psyche in the face of (what the novel suggests is) late capitalism's disposition to disperse or thin out the self into so many consumer subject positions (48, 50, 83–84). In short, we might say that sublimity is invoked to recuperate psychic wholeness.

Studies of *Libra*, which identify it as a postmodernist text, typically stress its rendering of Lee Harvey Oswald as the construct of media discourses and its focus on the loss of the (historical) referent and the constraints of textuality.[9] And yet for all its evident postmodern concerns, there is a current of thinking in the novel that is highly resistant to any postmodernizing account of it. Consider, for example, this observation by David Ferrie, one of the book's anti-Castro militants:

> Think of two parallel lines.... One is the life of Lee H. Oswald. One is the conspiracy to kill the President. What bridges the space between them? What makes a connection inevitable? There is a third line. It comes out of dreams, visions, intuitions, prayers, out of the deepest levels of the self. It's not generated by cause and effect like the other two lines. It's a line that cuts across causality, cuts across time. It has no history that we can recognize or understand. But it forces a connection. It puts a man on the path of his destiny. (339)

Observations of this type abound in *Libra*: elsewhere we read of "patterns [that] emerge outside the bounds of cause and effect" (44); "secret symmetries" (78); "a world inside the world" (13, 47, 277); "A pattern outside experience. Something that *jerks* you out of the spin of history" (384). Clearly, repeated invocations of invisible, transhistorical forces which shape human affairs do not amount to a *postmodern* rejection of empiricist historiography. Rather, this is the stuff of metaphysics, not to say the occult. Indeed, in a discussion of *Libra*, published in *South Atlantic Quarterly*, DeLillo seriously speculates on supernatural interventions in human history:

> But Oswald's attempt on Kennedy was more complicated. I think it was based on elements outside politics and, *as someone in the novel says, outside history*—things like dreams and coincidences and even the movement or the configuration of the stars, which is one reason the book is called *Libra*....
>
> ... When I hit upon this notion of coincidence and dream and intuition and the possible impact of astrology on the way men act, I thought that Libra, being Oswald's sign, would be the one title that summarized what's inside the book.
>
> ("Outsider" 289, 293-94; emphasis added)

I also cite this interview as evidence that DeLillo is more likely to endorse his characters' beliefs in transcendent realities than to dismiss them as, in the words of one commentator, a "fantasy of secret knowledge, of a world beyond marginalization that would provide a center that would be immune to the play of signification" (Carmichael 209).

Libra appeals to the truth and sovereignty of "the deepest levels of the self," that is, the levels of "dreams, visions, intuitions" (339). Indeed, alongside those readings of the novel that point to its postmodern rendering of the subject without psychic density—"an effect of the codes out of which he is articulated" (Carmichael 206); "a contemporary *production*" (Lentricchia, "*Libra*" 441)—we must reckon with the book's insistent focus on "another level, ... a deeper kind of truth" (260), on that which "[w]e know ... on some deeper plane" (330), on that which "speaks to something deep inside [one] ... the life-insight" (28). Such appeals to insight or intuition are common in Romantic literature and conform with Romanticism's depth model of subjectivity. That model is premised on the belief that truth lies "furthest in," that is, in the domain of the "heart" or "purer mind"; the belief that truth can only be accessed by the "inner faculties" (Wordsworth), by "inward sight" (Shelley), or, recalling the American Romantics, by "intuition." "[W]here," Emerson rhetorically inquired, "but in the intuitions which are vouchsafed us from within, shall we learn the Truth?" (182).[10] The comparisons may be schematic but, still, are close enough to indicate that the mindset of *Libra* is neither consistently nor unequivocally postmodern. No less emphatic than the book's evidence for a model of mind as an unstable "effect" of media codes is the evidence for a model of it as self-sufficient and self-authenticating, as an interior source of insight or vision.

What are the ideological implications of DeLillo's Romantic metaphysics? A common reading of Romanticism understands its introspective orientation in terms of a "politics of vision."[11] This is to say that, first, Romantic introspection may be seen as an attempt to claim the "inner faculties" as an inviolable, sacrosanct space beyond the domain of industrialization and the expanding marketplace. Second, the persistent appeal to the visionary "faculty" of "insight" or "intuition" or "Imagination" supplied Wordsworth, Blake, and others with a vantage point from which to critique the utilitarian and positivist ethos of capitalist development. But the crucial component of the "politics of vision" is the concept of what M. H. Abrams has called "the redemptive imagination" (117–22). Abrams notes how Blake repeatedly asserts that the "Imagination ... is the Divine Body of the Lord Jesus" (qtd. in Abrams 121) and quotes from *The Prelude* to emphasize that Wordsworth also substituted Imagination for the Redeemer:

Here must thou be, O Man!
Strength to thyself; no Helper hast thou here;
. . . .
The prime and vital principle is thine
In the recesses of thy nature, far
From any reach of outward fellowship[.]
(qtd. in Abrams 120)

What needs to be added here is that this faith in the "redemptive imagination" is premised on an idealist assumption that personal salvation can be achieved primarily, if not exclusively, at the level of the individual psyche. Indeed, this focus on salvation as chiefly a private, spiritual affair tends to obscure or diminish the role of change at the institutional level of economic and political practice as a *precondition* for the regeneration of the subject.[12] And it is a similar "politics of vision" that informs DeLillo's writing and that invites the same conclusion. DeLillo's appeals to the visionary serve to affirm an autonomous realm of experience and to provide a standard by which to judge the spiritually atrophied culture of late capitalism. Thus against the impoverishments and distortions of communication in a culture colonized by factoids, sound bites, PR hype, and propaganda, DeLillo endeavors to preserve the credibility of visionary experience and, in particular, to validate the visionary moment as the sign of a redemptive order of meaning. He has remarked, "The novelist can try to leap across the barrier of fact, and the reader is willing to take that leap with him as long as there's a kind of redemptive truth waiting on the other side" ("Outsider" 294). Yet, as we have already seen, that "leap" is into the realm of the transhistorical, where "redemptive truth" is chiefly a spiritual, visionary matter. And it is in this respect that his fiction betrays a conservative tendency; his response to the adverse cultural effects of late capitalism reproduces a Romantic politics of vision, that is, it is a response that obscures, if not undervalues, the need for radical change at the level of the material infrastructure.

The fact that DeLillo writes so incisively of the textures of postmodern experience, of daily life in the midst of images, commodities, and conspiracies, does not make him a postmodern writer. His Romantic appeals to a primal language of vision, to the child's psyche as a medium of precious insight, to the sublime contravene the antimetaphysical norms of postmodern theory. Moreover, while there is, to be sure, a significant strain of irony that runs through his fiction, it does not finally undercut his metaphysics. As Tom LeClair has noted in a discussion of *White Noise*, "DeLillo presses beyond the ironic, extracting from his initially satiric materials a sense of wonderment or mystery" (214). "Wonder" and "mystery," to say nothing of "extrasensory flashes" (*White Noise* 34), are frequently invoked in DeLillo's writing as signifiers of a mystical order of cognition, an affirmation that the near-global culture of late capitalism cannot exhaust the possibilities of human experience. But it is precisely this metaphysical cast of thinking that separates DeLillo's fiction from the thoroughgoing postmodernism of, say, Walter Abish or Robert Coover, and that should prompt us to qualify radically our tendency to read him as an exemplary postmodern writer.

NOTES

1. See, for example, Lentricchia, "Tales" and "Libra"; Frow; Messmer; and Wilcox.

2. Perhaps the choice of title for the novel is, among other things, calculated to evoke that long tradition of Neo-Platonist and medieval mysticism which meditated on divine names. One might cite the writings of Pseudo-Dionysius, author of *The Divine Names*, or the Merkabah mystics, early Kabbalists who speculated on the secret names of God and the angels. For such mystics, the way to revelation is through the knowledge of secret names.

3. This is precisely the theme of an early essay by Walter Benjamin, who, reflecting on the degeneration of language into "mere signs," observed: "In the Fall, since the eternal purity of names was violated, ... man abandoned immediacy in the communication of the concrete, name, and fell into the abyss of the mediateness of all communication, of the word as means, of the empty word, into the abyss of prattle" (120).

4. "I do wonder if there is something we haven't come across. Is there another, clearer language? Will we speak it and hear it when we die? Did we know it before we were born? ... Maybe this is why there's so much babbling in my books. Babbling can be ... a purer form, an alternate speech. I wrote a short story that ends with two babies babbling at each other in a car. This was something I'd seen and heard, and it was a dazzling and unforgettable scene. I felt these babies *knew* something. They were talking, they were listening, they were *commenting*.... Glossolalia is interesting because it suggests there's another way to speak, there's a very different language lurking somewhere in the brain" ("Interview" 83–84). And "Glossolalia or speaking in tongues ... could be viewed as a higher form of infantile babbling. It's babbling which seems to mean something" ("Outsider" 302). (Such comments help explain the significance of the crying of Baby Wilder in *White Noise* [78–79], an episode I shall discuss later.)

5. A little later we read: "People everywhere are absorbed in conversation.... Conversation is life, language is the deepest being" (52).

6. Kant formulated the following succinct definition: "We can describe the sublime in this way: it is an object (of nature) the representation of which determines the mind to think the unattainability of nature as a presentation of [reason's] ideas" (qtd. in Weiskel 22).

7. Recall these lines from Wordsworth's "Tintern Abbey": "a sense sublime / Of something far more deeply interfused, / Whose dwelling is the light of setting suns" (164). I am indebted to Lou Caton, of the University of Oregon, for drawing my attention to a possible Romantic context for the sunsets in *White Noise*.

8. Here, I anticipate two likely objections, First, the "airborne toxic event" may seem like an ironic postmodern version of the sublime object insofar as DeLillo substitutes a man-made source of power for a natural one. Yet Gladney's words emphasize that that power is experienced as a natural phenomenon: "This was a death made in the laboratory, defined and measurable, but we thought of it at the time in a simple and primitive way, as some seasonal perversity of the earth like a flood or tornado" (127). Second, I disagree with Arthur Saltzman (118–19) and others who see postmodern irony in the account of the sunset insofar as (to be sure) (1) the sunset has been artificially enhanced by pollution and (2) most observers of the spectacle "don't know ... what it means." After all, the passage in question clearly insists on the sense of awe irrespective of these factors.

9. See, for example, Lentricchia, "Libra"; Carmichael; and Cain.

10. In his lecture "The Transcendentalist," Emerson asserted, "Although ... there is no pure transcendentalist, yet the tendency to respect the intuitions, and to give them, at least in our creed, all authority over our experience, has deeply colored the conversation and poetry of the present day" (207).

11. Jon Klancher notes that it was M. H. Abrams who tagged Romanticism as a "politics of vision." However, he argues that insofar as Romanticism is an uncircumscribable, historically variable category, one whose construction alters in response to "institutional crises and consolidations," its "politics of vision" can be, and has been, read as not only radical but also conservative (77–88).

12. It is often argued that social history gets repressed in Wordsworth's "extravagant lyricizing of the recovered self" and in his "'sense sublime'" (Klancher 80).

WORKS CITED

Abish, Walter. *In the Future Perfect*. New York: New Directions, 1975.

Abrams, M. H. *Natural Supernaturalism: Tradition and Revolution in Romantic Literature*. New York: Norton, 1971.

Barthelme, Donald. *Snow White*. New York: Atheneum, 1967.

Barthes, Roland. *S/Z*. Trans. Richard Miller. New York: Hill and Wang, 1974.

Benjamin, Walter. "On Language as Such and on the Language of Man." 1916. *One-Way Street and Other Writings*. Trans. E. Jephcott and Kingsley Shorter. London: Verso, 1985. 107–23.

Burke, Edmund. *A Philosophical Enquiry into the Origin of Our Ideas of the Sublime and the Beautiful*. 1737. Ed. J. T. Boulton. U of Notre Dame P, 1958.

Cain, William E. "Making Meaningful Worlds: Self and History in *Libra*." *Michigan Quarterly Review* 29 (1990): 275–87.

Carmichael, Thomas. "Lee Harvey Oswald and the Postmodern Subject: History and Intertextuality in Don DeLillo's *Libra*, *The Names*, and *Mao II*." *Contemporary Literature* 34 (1993): 204–18.

Caton, Lou. "Setting Suns and Imaginative Failure in Don DeLillo's *White Noise*." Twentieth-Century Literature Conference. University of Louisville, Louisville, KY. 1995.

Coleridge, Samuel Taylor. *Biographia Literaria*. 1817. Ed. George Watson. London: Dent, 1975.

Coover, Robert. *Pricksongs and Descants*. New York: Plume, 1969.

DeLillo, Don. "I Never Set Out to Write an Apocalyptic Novel." Interview with Caryn James. *New York Times Book Review* 13 Jan. 1985: 31.

———. "An Interview with Don DeLillo." With Tom LeClair. *Anything Can Happen: Interviews with Contemporary American Novelists*. Ed. Tom LeClair and Larry McCaffery. Urbana: U of Illinois P, 1983. 79–90.

———. *Libra*. 1988. Harmondsworth, Eng.: Penguin, 1989.

———. *The Names*. 1982. New York: Vintage, 1989.

———. "An Outsider in This Society: An Interview with Don DeLillo." With Anthony DeCurtis. *The Fiction of Don DeLillo*. Ed. Frank Lentricchia. Spec. issue of *South Atlantic Quarterly* 89 (1990): 281–304.

———. *Ratner's Star*. 1976. New York: Vintage, 1989.

———. *White Noise*. 1985. Harmondsworth, Eng.: Penguin, 1986.

Derrida, Jacques. *Of Grammatology*. Trans. Gayatri Chakravorty Spivak. Baltimore: Johns Hopkins UP, 1976.

Emerson, Ralph Waldo. *Nature, Addresses, and Lectures*. Cambridge, MA: Belknap-Harvard UP, 1971. Vol. 1 of *The Collected Works of Ralph Waldo Emerson*. 4 vols. 1971–1987.

Frow, John. "The Last Things Before the Last: Notes on *White Noise*." *The Fiction of Don DeLillo*. Ed. Frank Lentricchia. Spec. issue of *South Atlantic Quarterly* 89 (1990): 413–29.

Klancher, Jon. "English Romanticism and Cultural Production." *The New Historicism*. Ed. H. Aram Veeser. New York: Routledge, 1989. 77–88.

LeClair, Tom. *In the Loop: Don DeLillo and the Systems Novel*. Urbana: U of Illinois P, 1987.

Lentricchia, Frank. "*Libra* as Postmodern Critique." *The Fiction of Don DeLillo*. Ed. Frank Lentricchia. Spec. issue of *South Atlantic Quarterly* 89 (1990): 431–53.

———. "Tales of the Electronic Tribe." *New Essays on "White Noise."* Ed. Frank Lentricchia. The American Novel. New York; Cambridge UP, 1991. 87–113.

Messmer, Michael W. "'Thinking It Through Completely': The Interpretation of Nuclear Culture," *Centennial Review* 32 (1988): 397–413.

Pynchon, Thomas. *The Crying of Lot 49*, 1966. New York: Perennial-Harper, 1990.

Rousseau, Jean-Jacques. "Essay on the Origin of Languages." Trans. John H. Moran. *On the Origin of Language*. Ed. John H. Moran and Alexander Gode. Milestones of Thought. New York: Ungar, 1966. 5–74.

Saltzman, Arthur M. *Designs of Darkness in Contemporary American Fiction*. Penn Studies in Contemporary American Fiction. Philadelphia: U of Pennsylvania P, 1990.

Weiskel, Thomas. *The Romantic Sublime: Studies in the Structure and Psychology of Transcendence*. Baltimore: Johns Hopkins UP, 1976.

Wilcox, Leonard, "Baudrillard, DeLillo's *White Noise*, and the End of Heroic Narrative." *Contemporary Literature* 32 (1991): 346–65.

Wordsworth, William. *Poetical Works*. Ed. Thomas Hutchinson. Rev. Ernest de Selincourt. Oxford: Oxford UP, 1978.

Chronology

1936	Born Donald Richard DeLillo on November 20 in the Bronx, New York. After a stint in Pottsville, Pennsylvania, the family returns to the Bronx, where DeLillo is raised by his parents, both Italian immigrants, in a house near the intersection of 182 Street and Adams Place.
1954	Graduates Cardinal Hayes High School.
1958	Graduates Fordham University with a degree in Communications.
1959	Works as a copywriter for Ogilvy & Mather advertising agency while living in an apartment in Murray Hill, New York City.
1960	First story, "The River Jordan," published in *Epoch* magazine.
1964	Quits Ogilvy & Mather. Works as a freelance writer.
1966	Starts work on *Americana*, his first novel.
1971	Publishes *Americana* with Houghton Mifflin and decides to devote himself, full-time, to writing. Begins *Endzone*, his second novel.
1972	Publishes *Endzone*. *Sports Illustrated* features "Total Loss Weekend," an essay on sports gambling.
1973	Publishes *Great Jones Street*.
1975	Marries Barbara Bennet and moves to Toronto, Canada, but resides there for only a year.

1976   Publishes *Ratner's Star*.

1977   Publishes *Players*.

1978   Publishes *Running Dog*.

1979   Travels to Greece while on a Guggenheim Fellowship and
            begins work on *The Names*. Publishes *The Engineer of
            Moonlight*, a play, in the *Cornell Review*.

1982   Publishes *The Names* and begins work on *White Noise*.
            Moves to New York City suburbs with his wife.

1984   Honored with the Award in Literature from the American
            Academy of Arts and Letters.

1985   Publishes *White Noise*.

1986   Wins the National Book Award for *White Noise*. *The Day
            Room* opens at the American Repertory Theater in
            Cambridge, Massachusetts.

1987   Publishes *The Day Room*, which runs at the Manhattan
            Theater Club in December.

1988   Publishes *Libra*, which garners the *Irish Times*-Aer Lingus
            International Ficton Prize and becomes a *New York Times*
            best-seller. Publishes essay on Nazism in *Dimensions* and
            stories in *Harper's* and *Granta*.

1991   Publishes *Mao II*.

1992   Earns PEN/Faulkner Award for Fiction for *Mao II*.

1994   Co-authors (with novelist Paul Auster) a pamphlet in
            defense of novelist Salman Rushdie, who was forced into
            hiding when Ayatollah Khomeini issued a *fawta* calling for
            Rushdie's death.

1997   Publishes *Underworld*, which makes the *New York Times*
            best-seller list, is nominated for a National Book Award,
            and is chosen as a main selection by the Book-of –the-
            Month Club. Later the novel wins the Howells Medal of
            the American Academy of Arts and Letters for the best
            work of fiction of the past half-decade.

1999   Becomes the first American to win the Jerusalem Prize.

2001   Publishes *The Body Artist*.

2002   Publishes the prologue to *Underworld* as *Pafko at the Wall*,
            a novella.

Contributors

HAROLD BLOOM is Sterling Professor of the Humanities at Yale University and Henry W. and Albert A. Berg Professor of English at the New York University Graduate School. He is the author of over 20 books, including *Shelly's Mythmaking* (1959), *The Visionary Company* (1961), *Blake's Apocalypse* (1963), *Yeats* (1970), *A Map of Misreading* (1975), *Kabbalah and Criticism* (1975), *Agon: Toward a Theory of Revisionism* (1982), *The American Religion* (1992), *The Western Canon* (1994), and *Omens of Millennium: The Gnosis of Angels, Dreams, and Resurrection* (1996). *The Anxiety of Influence* (1973) sets forth Professor Bloom's provocative theory of the literary relationships between the great writers and their predecessors. His most recent books include *Shakespeare: The Invention of the Human*, a 1998 National Book Award finalist, and *How to Read and Why*, which was published in 2000. In 1999, Professor Bloom received the prestigious American Academy of Arts and Letters Gold Medal for Criticism.

TOM LECLAIR teaches English at the University of Cincinnati and has published a pair of novels—*Passing Off* and *Well-Founded Fear*—in addition to *Anything Can Happen: Interviews with Contemporary American Novelists* and *The Art of Excess*.

JOHN FROW is a Professor of English at the University of Queensland. He is the author of *Marxism and Literary History*, *Cultural Studies and Cultural Value*, and *Time and Commodity Culture*.

PAUL CANTOR is a professor of English at the University of Virginia. He is the author of *Shakespeare's Rome: Republic and Empire* and *Creature and Creator: Myth-Making* and *English Romanticism* as well as numerous articles on contemporary fiction, Shakespeare, and Romanticism.

FRANK LENTRICCHIA, Katherine Everett Gilbert Professor of Literature at Duke University, is the author of *After the New Criticism* and *Criticism and Social Change*.

LEONARD WILCOX, a specialist in 20th century literature and culture, is Head of the American Studies Department at the University of Canterbury in New Zealand.

ARNOLD WEINSTEIN is Edna and Richard Saloman Distinguished Professor of Comparative Literature at Brown University. His publications include *Vision and Response in Modern Fiction*, *Fictions of the Self: 1550-1800*, and *The Fiction of Relationship*.

MARK CONROY is Associate Professor of English at Ohio State University. A specialist in 19th and 20th century literature, he is the author of *Modernism and Authority: Strategies of Legitimation in Flaubert and Conrad*.

JOHN N. DUVALL is Professor of English at Purdue University. He has written *Faulkner's Marginal Couple: Invisible, Outlaw, and Unspeakable Communities* and has published many articles on contemporary fiction.

ARTHUR M. SALTZMAN is Professor of English at Missouri Southern State College and is the author of *The Novel in the Balance* and *This Mad "Instead": Governing Metaphor in Contemporary American Fiction*.

PAUL MALTBY is Associate Professor of English at West Chester University and the author of *Dissident Postmodernists: Barthelme, Coover, and Pynchon*.

Bibliography

Begley, Adam. "Don DeLillo: The Art of Fiction." *Paris Review* 35, no. 128 (Fall 1993): 274-306.

Bawer, Bruce. "Don DeLillo's America." *New Criterion* 3, no. 8 (April 1985): 34-42.

Bonca, Cornel. "Don DeLillo's *White Noise*: The Natural Language of the Species." *College Literature* 23, no. 2 (June 1996): 25-44.

Caton, Lou F. "Romanticism and the Postmodern Novel: Three Scenes from Don DeLillo's *White Noise*." *English Language Notes* 35 (September 1997): 38-48.

Conroy, Mark. "From Tombstone to Tabloid: Authority Figured in *White Noise*." *Critique* 35, no. 2 (Winter 1994): 97-110.

Dewey, Joseph. *In a Dark Time: The Apocalyptic Temper in the American Novel of the Nuclear Age.* W. Lafayette, IN: Purdue University Press, 1990.

Duvall, John N. "The (Super)marketplace of Images: Television as Unmediated Mediation in DeLillo's *White Noise*." *Arizona Quarterly* 50, no. 3 (Autumn 1994): 127-153.

Edmunson, Mark. "Not Flat, Not Round, Not There: Don DeLillo's Novel Characters." Yale Review 83, no. 2 (April 1995): 107-24.

Frow, John. "The Last Things Before the Last: Notes on *White Noise*." *South Atlantic Quarterly* 89 (Spring 1990): 414-429.

Hantke, Steffen. Conspiracy and Paranoia in Contemporary American Fiction: *The Works of Don DeLillo and Joseph McElroy*. Frankfurt: Peter Lang, 1994.

Harris, Robert R. "A Talk With Don DeLillo." *New York Times Book Review* (10 Oct. 1982): 26.

Hayles, N. Katherine. "Postmodern Parataxis: Embodied Texts, Weightless Information." *American Literary History* 2 (1990): 394-421.

Heffernan, Teresa. "Can Apocalypse Be Post?" in *Postmodern Apocalypse: Theory and Cultural Practise at the End*. Ed. Richard Dellamora. Philadelphia: University of Pennsylvania Press, 1995.

Howard, Gerald. "The American Strangeness: An Interview with Don DeLillo." *Hungry Mind Review* 43 (Fall 1997): 13-16.

Johnston, John. "Generic Difficulties in the Novels of Don DeLillo." *Critique* 30 (1989): 261-75.

Keesey, Douglas. *Don DeLillo*. New York: Twayne, 1993.

King, Noel. "Reading *White Noise*: Floating Remarks." *Critical Quarterly* 33, no. 3 (Autumn 1991): 66-83.

LeClair, Tom. *In the Loop: Don DeLillo and the Systems* Novel. Chicago: University of Illinois Press, 1987.

Lentricchia, Frank. "Don DeLillo." *Raritan* 8, no. 4 (1989): 1-29.

———.ed. *Introducing Don DeLillo*. Durham, NC: Duke University Press, 1991.

———.ed. *New Essays on* White Noise. New York: Cambridge University Press, 1991.

Leps, Marie-Christine. "Empowerment Through Information: A Discursive Critique." *Cultural Critique* 31 (1995): 179-96.

Maltby, Paul. "The Romantic Metaphysics of Don DeLillo." *Contemporary Literature* 37 (1996): 258-77.

McClure, John. A. *Late Imperial Romance*. New York: Verso, 1994.

———. "Postmodern/Post-Secular: Contemporary Fiction and Spirituality." *Modern Fiction Studies* 41 (1995): 141-63.

Messmer Michael W. "'Thinking It Through Completely': The Interpretation of Nuclear Culture." *Centennial Review* 23, no. 4 (Fall 1988): 397-413.

Moraru, Christian. "Consuming Narratives: Don DeLillo and the 'Lethal' Reading." *Journal of Narrative Technique* 27 (1997): 190-206.

Nodatti, Maria. "An Interview with Don DeLillo." *Salmagundi* 100 (Fall 1993): 83-97.

Parks, John G. "The Noise of Magic Kingdoms: Reflections on Theodicy in Two Recent American Novels." *Cithara* (May 1990): 56-61.

Pastor, Judith Lawrence. "Palomar and Gladney: Calvino and DeLillo Play with the Dialectics of Subject/Object Relationships." *Italian Culture* 9 (1991): 331-42.

Peyser, Thomas. "Globalization and America: The Case of Don DeLillo's *White Noise*." *Clio* 25 (1996): 255-71.

Reeve, N.H., and Richard Kerridge. "Toxic Events: Postmodernism and DeLillo's *White Noise*." *Cambridge Quarterly* 23 (1994): 303-23.

Remnick, David. "Exile on Main Street." *New Yorker* (15 Sept. 1997); 42-48.

Saltzman, Arthur M. "The Figure in the Static: *White Noise*." *Modern Fiction Studies* 40 (1994): 807-26.

Simmons, Phillip E. *Deep Surfaces: Mass Culture and History in Contemporary American Fiction*. Athens, GA: University of Georgia Press, 1997.

Weinstein, Arnold. *Nobody's Home: Speech, Self and Place in American Fiction* from Hawthorne to DeLillo. New York: Oxford University Press, 1993.

White, Patti. *Gatsby's Party: The System and the List in Contemporary Narrative*. W. Lafayette, IN: Purdue University Press, 1992.

Wilcox, Leonard. "Baudrillard, DeLillo's *White Noise*, and the End of the Heroic Narrative." *Contemporary Literature* 32 (1991): 346-65.

Acknowledgments

"Closing the Loop: *White Noise*," by Tom LeClair. From *In the Loop: Don DeLillo and the Systems Novel*. © 1987 by the Board of Trustees of the University of Illinois. Reprinted by permission.

"The Last Things Before the Last: Notes on *White Noise*," by John Frow. From *The South Atlantic Quarterly* 89, no. 2 (Spring 1990): 413-429. © 1990 by Duke University Press. Reprinted by permission.

"Adolf, We Hardly Knew You," by Paul A. Cantor. From *New Essays on White Noise*. © 1991 by Cambridge University Press. Reprinted by permission.

"Tales of the Electronic Tribe," by Frank Lentricchia. From *New Essays on White Noise*, edited by Frank Lentricchia. © 1991 by Cambridge University Press. Reprinted by permission.

"Baudrillard, DeLillo's *White Noise*, and the End of Heroic Narrative," by Leonard Wilcox. From *Contemporary Literature* 32, no. 3 (Fall 1991): 346-365. © 1991 by the Board of Regents of the University of Wisconsin System. Reprinted by permission.

"Don DeLillo: Rendering the Words of the Tribe," by Arnold Weinstein. From *Nobody's Home: Speech, Self, and Place in American Fiction from Hawthorne to DeLillo*. © 1993 by Oxford University Press, Inc. Reprinted by permission.

"From Tombstone to Tabloid: Authority Figured in *White Noise*," by Mark Conroy. From *Critique* 35, no. 2 (Winter 1994): 96-110. Reprinted with permission of the Helen Dwight Reid Educational Foundation.

Published by Iteldref Publications, 1319 Eighteenth St, NW Washington, DC 20036-1802.Copyright © 1994

"The (Super)Marketplace of Images: Television as Unmediated Mediation in DeLillo's *White Noise*," by John DuVall. From *Arizona Quarterly* 50, no. 3 (Autumn 1994): 127-153. © 1994 by the Arizona Board of Regents. Reprinted by permission.

"The Figure in the Static: *White Noise*," by Arthur M. Saltzman. From *Modern Fiction Studies* 40, no. 4 (Winter 1994): 807-825. © 1995 by the Purdue Research Foundation. Reprinted by permission.

"The Romantic Metaphysics of Don DeLillo," by Paul Maltby. From *Contemporary Literature* 37, no. 2 (Summer 1996): 258-277. © 1996 by the Board of Regents of the University of Wisconsin System. Reprinted by permission.

Index

Aldridge, John
  review of *White Noise*, 31-32
Alley, Keith
  quote of, 51
Amazons
  and *White Noise*, 18
Americana
  the 'he' or 'she' in, 74
  and *The Mayflower*, 74
  methodological fiction in, 29,
    74-75
  simplistic threat in, 15
  and *White Noise*, 15, 29-30
Anatomy of Criticism, (Frye)
  theme of aesthetic humanism,
    87-88
"Artist and Society, The", (Gass),
  208-209
Axton, James in *White Noise*, 8

Barthes, Roland
  and DeLillo's concern with
    language, 119-120
Bateson, Gregory, 24
  on non-rational commitment to
    truth and methodology, 25-26
  system approaches to mortality, 12
Baudrillard, Jean
  and similarities with DeLillo,
    97-115

Bawer, Bruce
  dismissal of preoccupations in
    DeLillo's novels, 206-207
  on Hitler as an issue in *White
    Noise*, 52-53, 58-59
Becker, Ernest
  existential and Rankian
    positions, 11-12
Bell, David, in *White Noise*, 8
Benjamin, Walter
  aesthetic tendency in America,
    171
  on phenomenology of the Aura,
    77-78
"Berlin to Memphis", (1988 Album)
  and DeLillo, 63
Beryle in *Libra*
  her clippings and concerns with
    language, 119-120
Birdwell, Cleo
  pseudonym for DeLillo, 18
Book of Daniel, The, (Doctorow)
  creed in, 201-202
Brademas, Owen in *The Names*
  assimilated, not excluded,
    195-196
  as chief quester, 122-123
  profound linguistic project, 123
  his tale-within-a-tale, 125-128
  and *White Noise*, 6